AIRCRAFT ARCHIVE

VOLUME 1

FIGHTERS OF WORLD WAR TWO

Contents

Introduction 2
Gloster Gladiator Mk I 4
Supermarine Spitfire Mk I 7
Messerschmitt Bf 109E-4 10
Mitsubishi A6M5 Zero-Sen 14
Boulton Paul Defiant Mks I and II 17
Curtiss Kittyhawk Mks I, III and IV 23
Messerschmitt Bf 110C-4, C-5, F and G 27
Hawker Typhoon Mk I 33
Republic P-47B and D Thunderbolt 42
Supermarine Spitfire Mks IX and XVI 49
De Havilland Mosquito Mks II, IV and VI 53
Grumman F6F-3, -5 and -5P Hellcat 58
Bristol Beaufighter Mks I, II, VI and X 64
Lavochkin La-5FN and La-7 71
Supermarine Spitfire Mks XII, XIV, XVIII and XIX 75
Dornier Do 335 83

A DETAILED COLLECTION OF ORIGINAL SCALE AIRCRAFT DRAWINGS

Introduction

Since the earliest days of the Wright Brothers and the pioneers of European aviation, the ever-changing shape of the aeroplane has always held a special fascination. At first, the basic distinction of canard, tractor, pusher monoplane or biplane conveyed an adequate identity of the design. However, sketches soon began to appear in the magazines which reported aerial races and the latest developments were eagerly sought by enthusiasts, among them model makers and even competitive designers.

So began a practice which became a major feature among aeronautical publications and one which this series of *Aircraft Archive* sets out to preserve in collective form. What follows is a selection from the files of 'Aeromodeller' and 'Scale Models', two of the many monthly magazines from the original Model Aeronautical Press, now part of Argus Specialist Publications.

The books in this series form a representative group of subjects. Each is a typical example of skill and dedication applied by an amateur researcher over countless hours of translating measurements and photographic interpretation into a multiple-view scale drawing which, in fact, no manufacturer could ever provide! For it may come as a surprise, but the reality is that manufacturers' general arrangement drawings have little value in the factories, are rarely accurate in shape or scale and, without exception, illustrate the aeroplane in a stage long since superseded by production variants. It is the sub-assembly, or component detail drawing, which offers priceless data for the researcher to complete the jigsaw puzzle of any aeroplane. That is, of course, if such drawings become available as many of the records are now destroyed.

Access to the real thing is the ideal but how can one measure each panel, check every angle and record all the shapes? It takes a special sort of dedication to undertake such a mammoth task. A museum visit will confirm the enormity of the undertaking. Aeroplanes are almost always bigger than imagined. The tape measure becomes inadequate when required to confirm distances between extremities that are intercepted by protrusions, and the draughtsman resorts to that original method of projecting chalk marks on the floor. In this way, the preparation of a drawing reverses early procedures when designs were actually created out of chalked plans on the factory concrete!

Similarly, half a century of progress later, the three-view draughtsman can reflect with pride on the compliment that some of the museum restorations could only be completed to such fine standards through the part his work had played in the re-build.

◄ Arthur Bentley is one of the renowned draughtsmen whose work is featured in this book. His Hellcat drawings appear on pages 58–63.

▲ Doug Carrick's speciality is the aircraft of the Luftwaffe. Here he is seen checking out a Heinkel He 111 for a new project.

Flattery comes in oblique forms. A priority requisite for film and documentary makers has been reference to the only general arrangement available, perpetuated for modellers and aero enthusiasts through plan services. The engineering director of a major airport has used these drawings to plan a new maintenance hangar. A restorer, on his acquisition of a foreign airframe, was able to complete his job and satisfy inspectorates through the research documentation borrowed from a three-view draughtsman, and that world famous *Magnificent Men in their Flying Machines* film depended to a considerable extent on those early sketches.

The modelling world owes another debt to the three-view draughtsman. True scale models, whether in moulded plastic or from such sophisticated composites as large radio controlled flying replicas, have emerged in vast numbers from kit boxes or individual designs, all based upon the initial researchers who produced a frozen view of the whole aeroplane.

Demand for accuracy and authenticity originated through the work of James Hay Stevens in 'Aeromodeller'. He was among the first to adopt 1/72nd scale, based on the Imperial measure of one sixth of an inch representing one foot. Opening standards, as set by James Stevens, were taken up through the series of *Aircraft of the Fighting Powers* volumes published by Harborough, an associated company. Wartime urgency quickly generated a new breed of detail draughtsman, typified by Harry Cooper and Owen Thetford. After seven volumes and the creation of an *Aircraft Described* series, centred on civil aircraft by Eddie Riding, 1/72nd scale was firmly established, and the fine detail in the drawings reached levels of intricacy to satisfy the most demanding enthusiast – though not for long!

From the immediate postwar years to the present day, the levels of minutiae have soared far beyond the first conceptions. Out of *Aircraft Described* came *Aeroplanes in Outline* and *Famous Biplanes* and, through forty years of publication in 'Aeromodeller' magazine, a band of skilled contributors built up a series which now comes in book form.

The drawings reflect the individual character of the originator. Each was in its time a labour of love, the fruits of which have been the immense pleasure given to students, collectors and aeromodellers. If, by reproduction in this form we commemorate their work permanently, rather than in a transient monthly magazine, then we will have rewarded both the draughtsmen and the reader with a treasure store.

Gloster Gladiator Mk I

Country of origin: Great Britain.
Type: Single-seat, land-based fighter.
Dimensions: Wing span 32ft 3in *9.83m*; length 27ft 5in *8.36m*; height 10ft 4in *3.15m*; wing area 323 sq ft *30.00m²*.
Weights: Loaded 4750lb *2155kg*.
Powerplant: One Bristol Mercury IX nine-cylinder radial engine rated at 840hp.
Performance: Maximum speed 250mph *402kph* at 15,500ft *4720m*; initial climb rate 2350ft/min *720m/min*; service ceiling 32,800ft *10,000m*; range 410 miles *660km*.
Armament: Four fixed 0.303in Browning machine guns.
Service: First flight (prototype) September 1934; service entry January 1937.

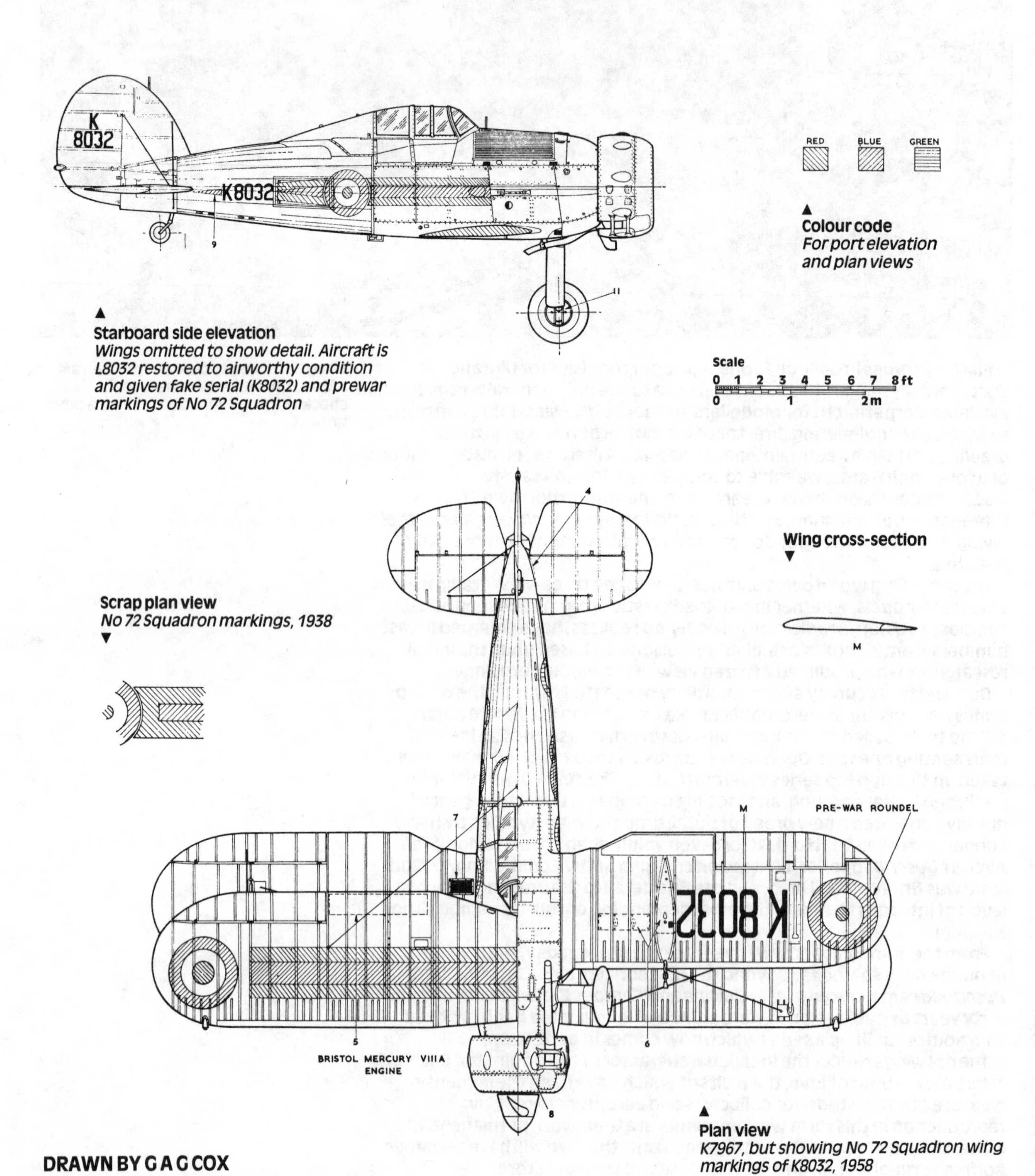

Starboard side elevation
Wings omitted to show detail. Aircraft is L8032 restored to airworthy condition and given fake serial (K8032) and prewar markings of No 72 Squadron

Colour code
For port elevation and plan views

Wing cross-section

Scrap plan view
No 72 Squadron markings, 1938

Plan view
K7967, but showing No 72 Squadron wing markings of K8032, 1958

DRAWN BY G A G COX

Gladiators K7967 (nearest camera), '8927 and '7972 of No 87 Squadron performing 'tied-together' aerobatics in a prewar display. ►

▲
Colour code
For starboard elevation

Port side elevation
No 87 Squadron markings
▼

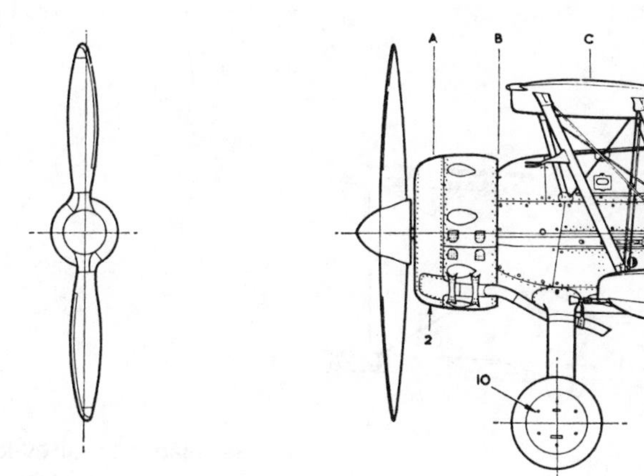

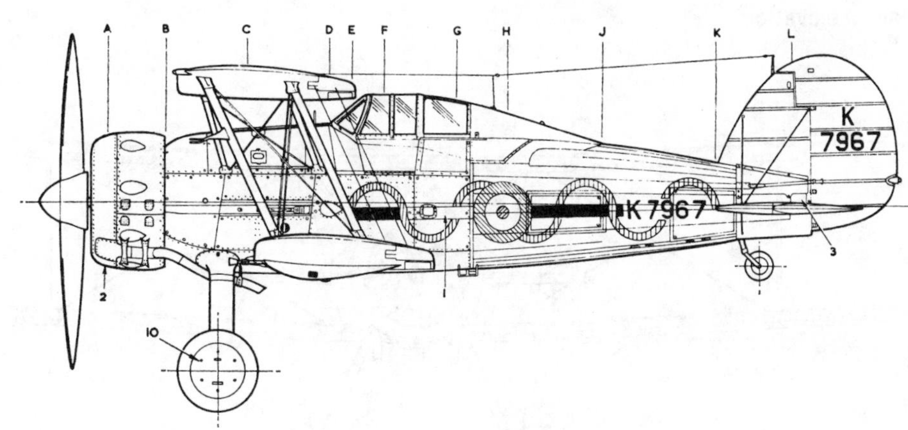

Fuselage cross-sections
▼

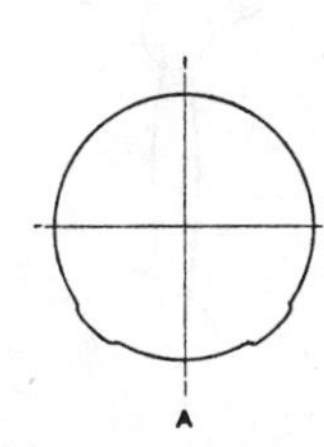

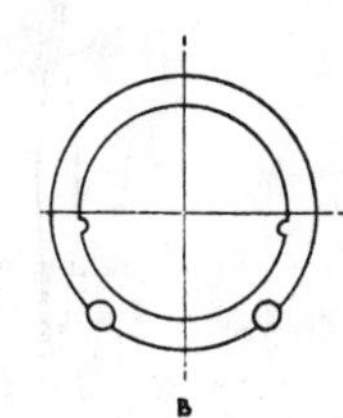

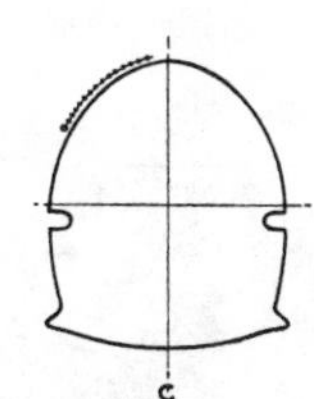

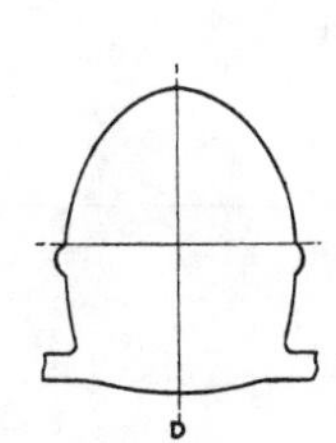

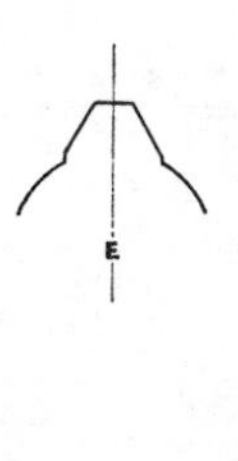

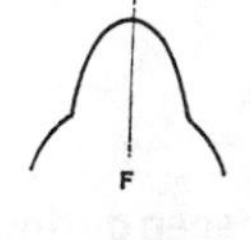

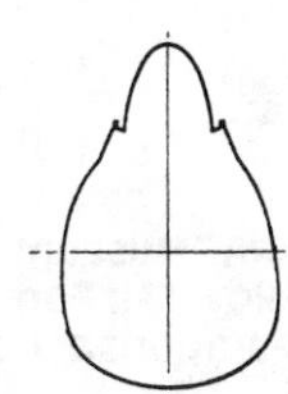

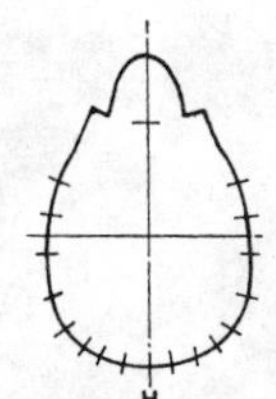

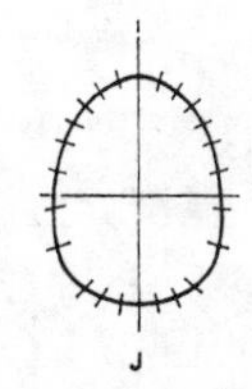

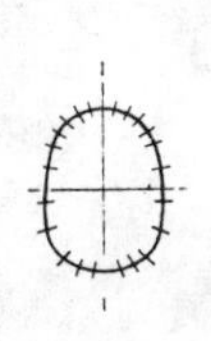

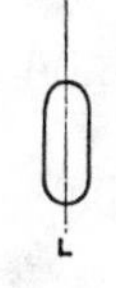

◄ Cockpit detail, showing standard blind flying panel, and gun button on control column hand grip.

CP DH Hamilton Standard propeller
Malta Sea Gladiators only
▼

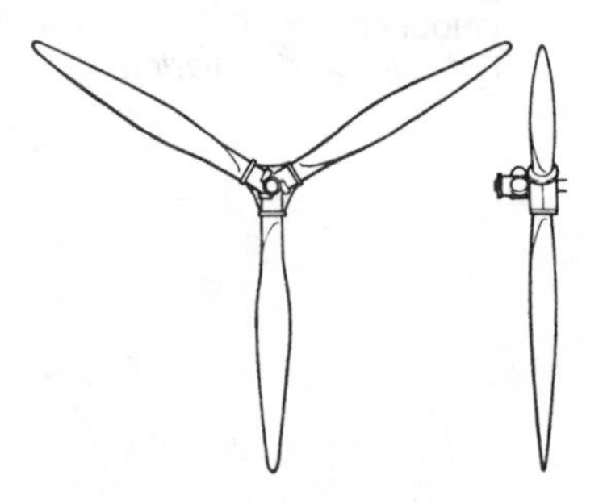

Front elevation
▼

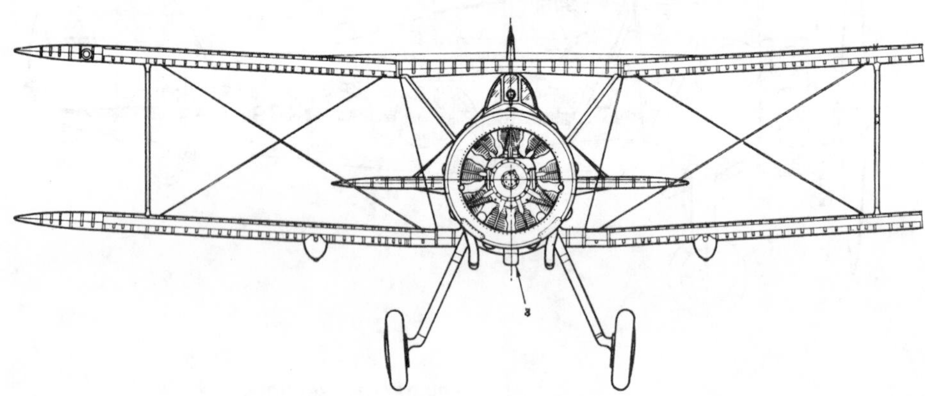

Sea Gladiator Fairey-Reed
▼ FP propeller

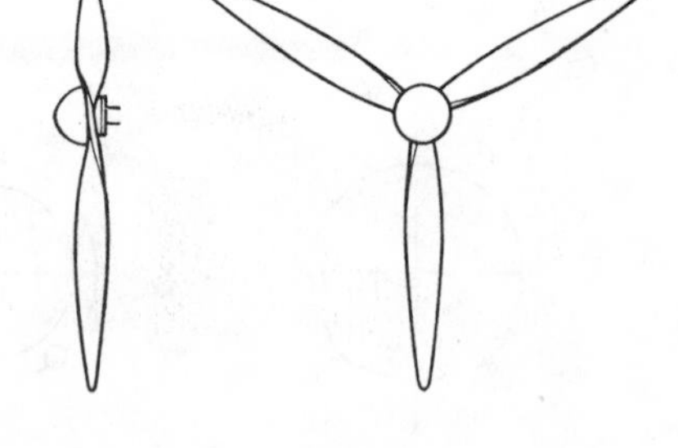

◄ The RAF Museum's Gladiator seen during the Royal Air Force's 50th anniversary celebrations at Abingdon in 1968.

Supermarine Spitfire Mk I

Country of origin: Great Britain.
Type: Single-seat, land-based fighter.
Dimensions: Wing span 36ft 10in *11.23m*; length 29ft 11in *9.12m*; height (maximum) 11ft 5in *3.48m*; wing area 242 sq ft *22.48m²*.
Weights: Empty 4332lb *1965kg*; loaded 5750lb *2609kg*.
Powerplant: One Rolls-Royce Merlin II V12, liquid-cooled piston engine rated at 1030hp, (Mk IB) Merlin III rated at 1030hp.
Performance: Maximum speed 387mph *623kph* at 18,400ft *5610m*; initial climb rate 2300ft/min *700m/min*; service ceiling 36,000ft *10,950m*; range 575 miles *925km*.
Armament: Eight fixed 0.303in Browning machine guns.
Service: First flight (prototype) 5 March 1936; service entry 4 August 1938.

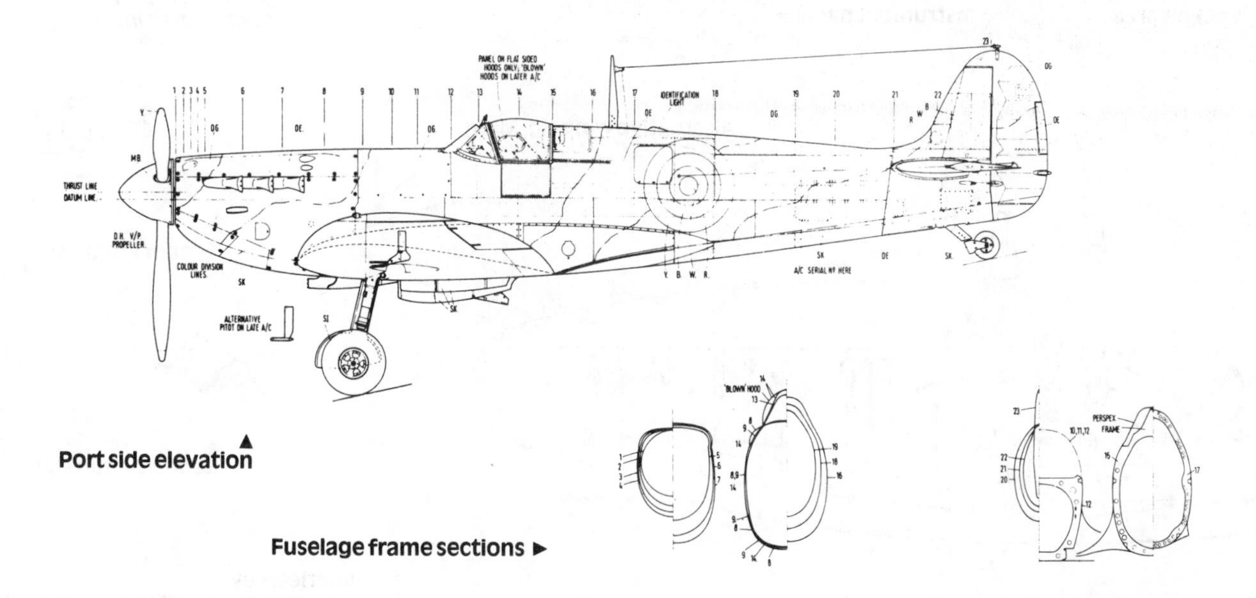

Port side elevation ▲

Fuselage frame sections ►

Scale

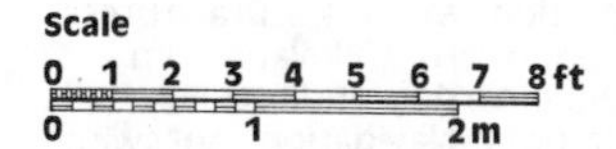

Immaculate line-up of Spitfire Is at RAF Duxford in May 1939. Aircraft belong to No 19 Squadron. ▼

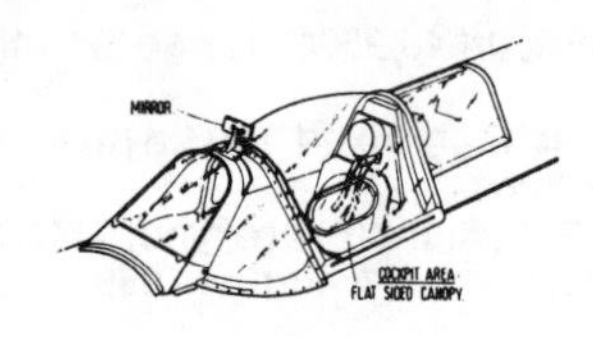

Cockpit area

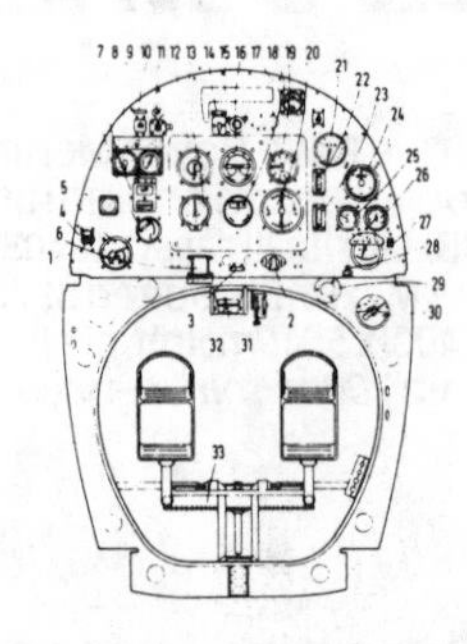

Instrument panel

Scrap elevation
Cockpit area interior

Alternative wing tip, Mk VI

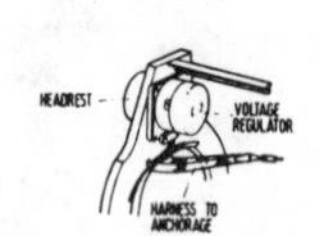

Rear of Frame 15

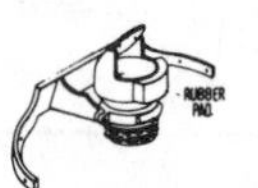

Reflector gun sight

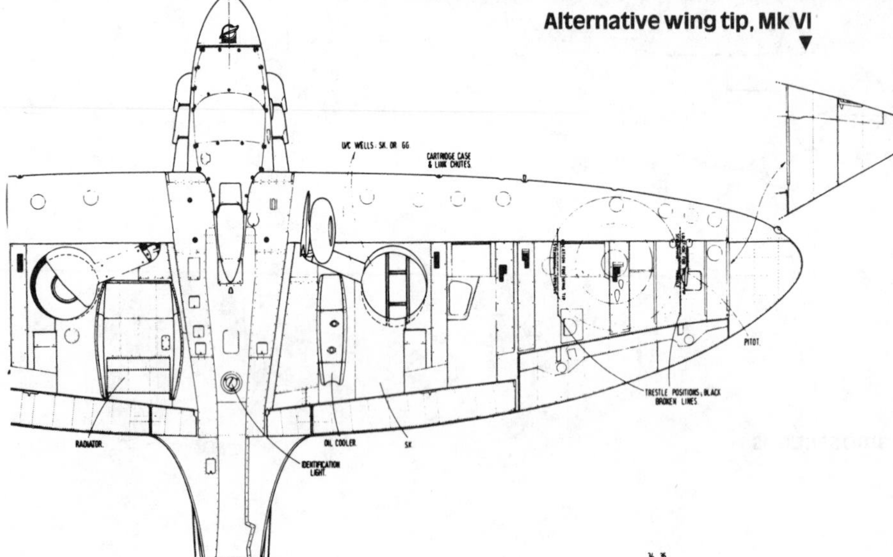

Numerical key
1. Instrument panel. **2.** Starter. **3.** Cabin light switches. **4.** Ignition switches. **5.** Brake press gauge. **6.** Deviation card. **7.** Elevator trim indicator. **8.** Undercarriage indicator. **9.** Oxygen regulator. **10.** Navigation light switch. **11.** Flaps. **12.** ASI. **13.** Altimeter. **14.** Reflector sight switch. **15.** Sun screen stowage. **16.** Artificial horizon. **17.** Voltmeter. **18.** Direction indicator. **19.** Rate of climb. **20.** Turn and bank. **21.** RPM. **22.** Oil pressure. **23.** Fuel pressure. **24.** Boost pressure. **25.** Oil temperature. **26.** Radiator temperature. **27.** Fuel pressure warning light. **28.** Fuel gauge and push-button. **29.** Priming pump. **30.** Fuel tank cock. **31.** Fuel cock control. **32.** Compass. **33.** Rudder bar. **34.** Brake level. **35.** Gun button. **36.** Camera button. **37.** VHF control box. **38.** Gun sight. **39.** Headrest. **40.** Voltage regulator. **41.** Very cartridge rack. **42.** Rudder trim wheel. **43.** Elevator trim wheel. **44.** Aileron cable drum. **45.** Two-level rudder pedal. **46.** Engine controls.

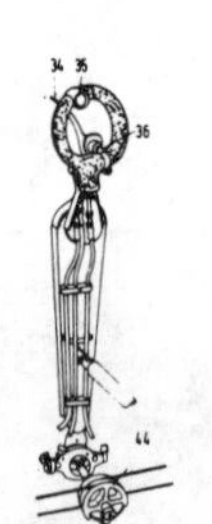

Control column

Rudder pedal

Underplan
Starboard outer wing panel omitted

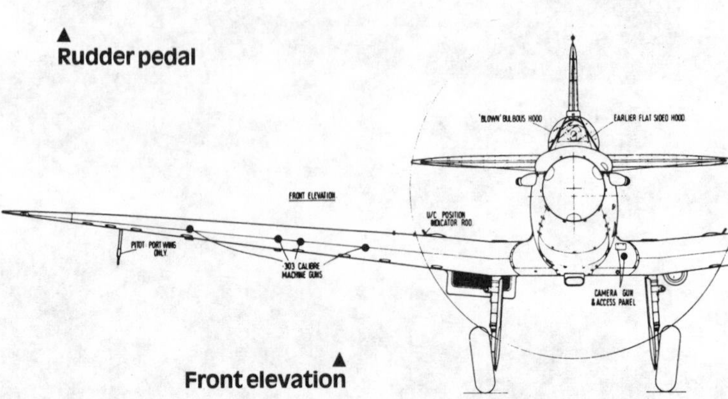

Front elevation

Colour notes
DE – Dark Earth; **DG** – Dark Green; **SK** – Sky; **MB** – Matt Black; **R** – Dull Red; **W** – White; **B** – Dark Blue; **Y** – Yellow; **SI** – Silver; **GG** – Grey-Green primer. Squadron letters – Sky or Light Grey; serial numbers – black. Camouflage pattern shown was standard and would not vary much on individual aircraft. Aircraft built before August 1940 had alternating left- and right-hand patterns, schemes 'A' and 'B'; drawing shows scheme 'A' (scheme 'B' would be mirror image of 'A').

▲
The Mks I and II were rapidly developed during World War II, and it was not long before the much improved Mk V was available.

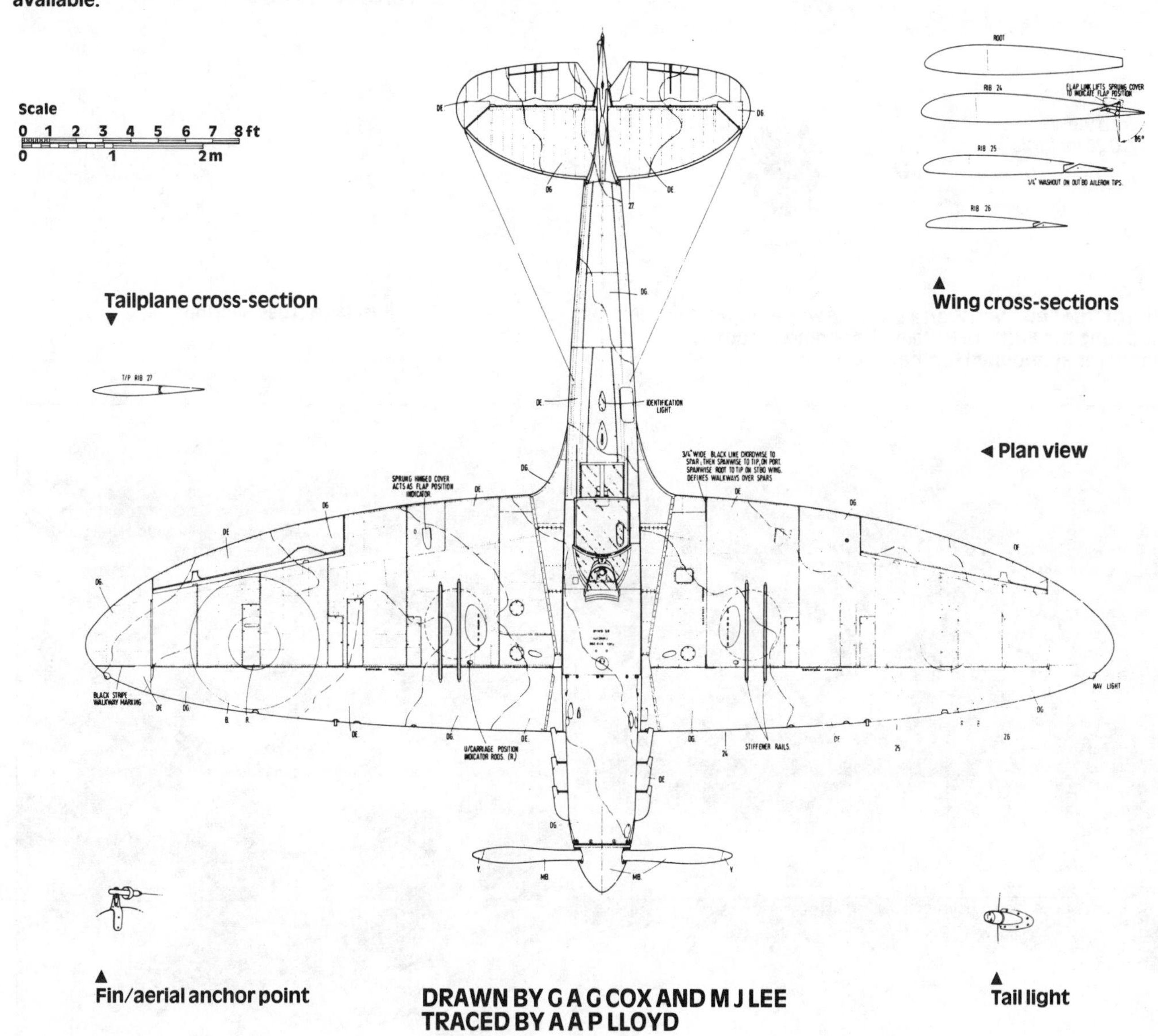

▲
Wing cross-sections

Tailplane cross-section
▼

◄ Plan view

▲
Fin/aerial anchor point

▲
Tail light

DRAWN BY G A G COX AND M J LEE
TRACED BY A A P LLOYD

Messerschmitt Bf 109E-4

Country of origin: Germany
Type: Single-seat, land-based fighter.
Dimensions: Wing span 32ft 4½in *9.87m*; length 28ft 4¼in *8.66m*; height 8ft 2½in *2.50m*; wing area 176.53 sq ft *16.40m²*.
Weights: Empty 4856lb *1840kg*; empty equipped 4431lb *2010kg*; loaded 5523lb *2506kg*.

Powerplant: One Daimler-Benz DB 601A twelve-cylinder, liquid-cooled piston engine rated at 1050hp.
Performance: Maximum speed 348mph *560kph* at 14,500ft *4420m*; initial climb rate 3280ft/min *1000m/min*; service ceiling 34,500ft *10,515m*; range 410 miles *660km*.

Armament: Two fixed 7.9mm MG 17 machine guns plus two fixed 20mm MG FF cannon.
Service: First flight (Bf 109V-1) summer 1935; service entry summer 1940.

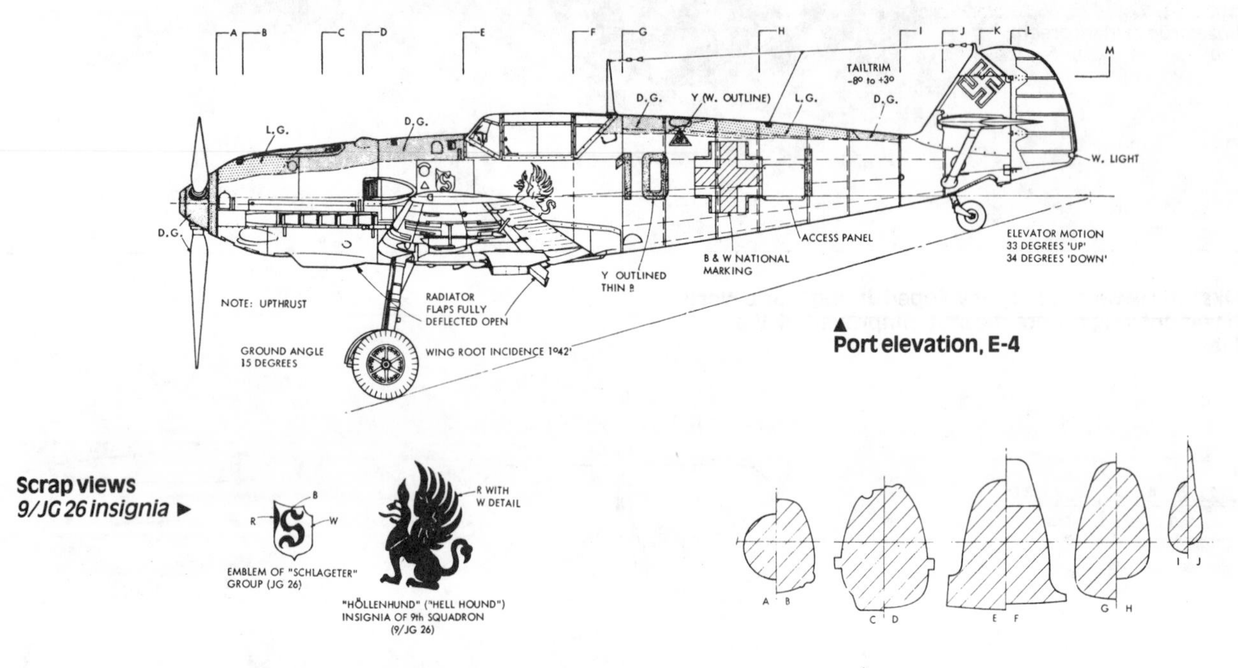

▲ **Port elevation, E-4**

Scrap views
9/JG 26 insignia ►

▲ **Fuselage cross-sections**

Victim of 'The Few', von Werra's Bf 109E was brought down in Kent during the Battle of Britain. The engine-mounted cannon was abandoned for the E-4 variant.
▼

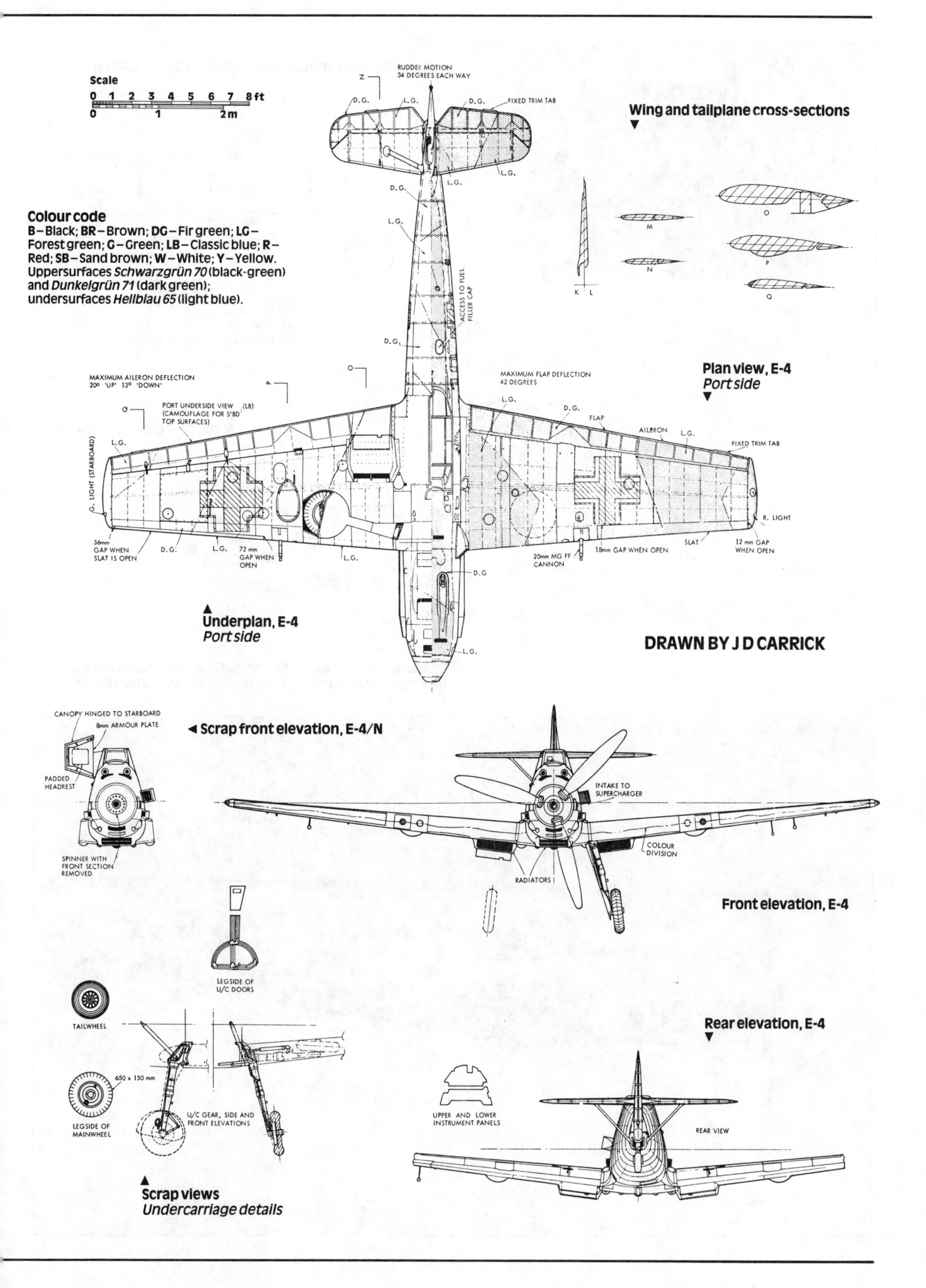

Scale
0 1 2 3 4 5 6 7 8ft
0 1 2m
Colour code
B–Black; BR–Brown; DG–Fir green; LG–Forest green; G–Green; LB–Classic blue; R–Red; SB–Sand brown; W–White; Y–Yellow. Uppersurfaces Schwarzgrün 70 (black-green) and Dunkelgrün 71 (dark green); undersurfaces Hellblau 65 (light blue).
RUDDER MOTION 34 DEGREES EACH WAY
FIXED TRIM TAB
Wing and tailplane cross-sections
ACCESS TO FUEL FILLER CAP
MAXIMUM AILERON DEFLECTION 20° 'UP' 13° 'DOWN'
PORT UNDERSIDE VIEW (LB) (CAMOUFLAGE FOR S'BD TOP SURFACES)
MAXIMUM FLAP DEFLECTION 42 DEGREES
FLAP
AILERON
Plan view, E-4
Port side
G. LIGHT (STARBOARD)
R. LIGHT
56mm GAP WHEN SLAT IS OPEN
72 mm GAP WHEN OPEN
20mm MG FF CANNON
18mm GAP WHEN OPEN
SLAT
12 mm GAP WHEN OPEN
Underplan, E-4
Port side
DRAWN BY J D CARRICK
CANOPY HINGED TO STARBOARD
8mm ARMOUR PLATE
PADDED HEADREST
SPINNER WITH FRONT SECTION REMOVED
Scrap front elevation, E-4/N
INTAKE TO SUPERCHARGER
COLOUR DIVISION
RADIATORS
Front elevation, E-4
LEGSIDE OF U/C DOORS
TAILWHEEL
650 x 150 mm
LEGSIDE OF MAINWHEEL
U/C GEAR, SIDE AND FRONT ELEVATIONS
Rear elevation, E-4
UPPER AND LOWER INSTRUMENT PANELS
REAR VIEW
Scrap views
Undercarriage details

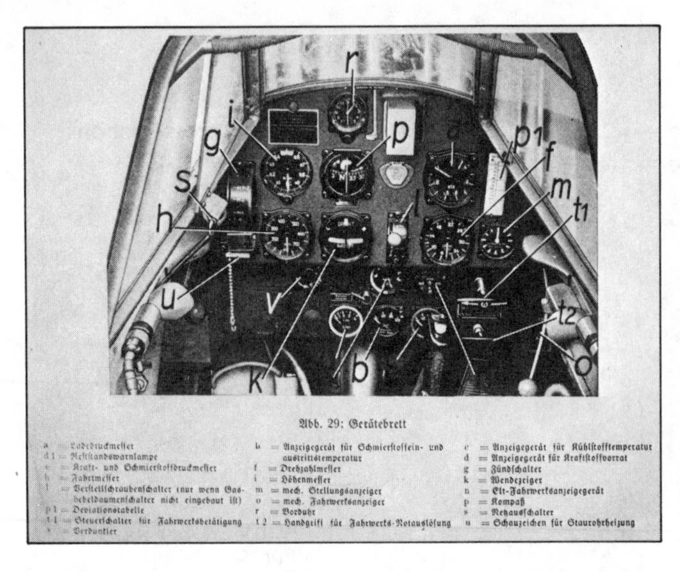

◄ **Official German photo shows Bf 109 instrumentation.**

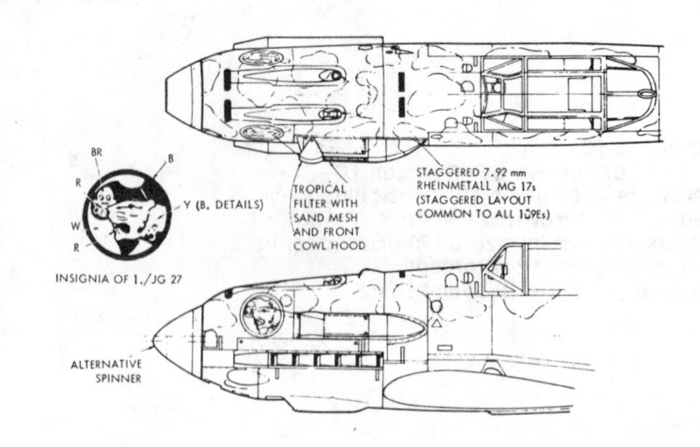

▲ **Scrap port elevation, E-4/N**

Starboard elevation, E-4/N ▼

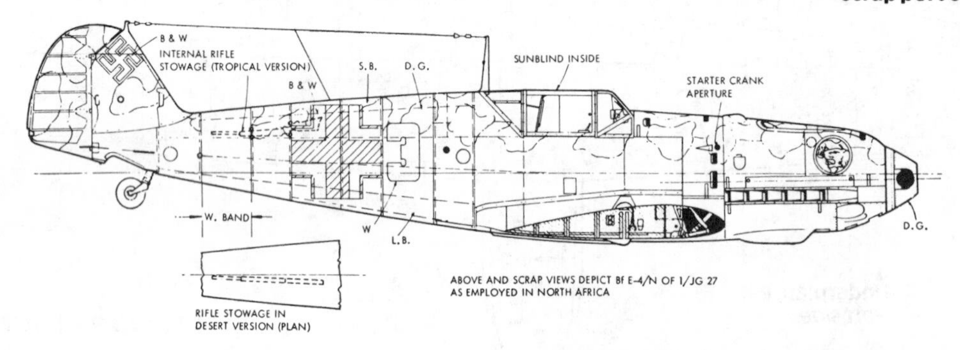

Captured Bf 109E with RAF camouflage and markings, but lacking cockpit canopy, seen during an evaluation flight. ▼

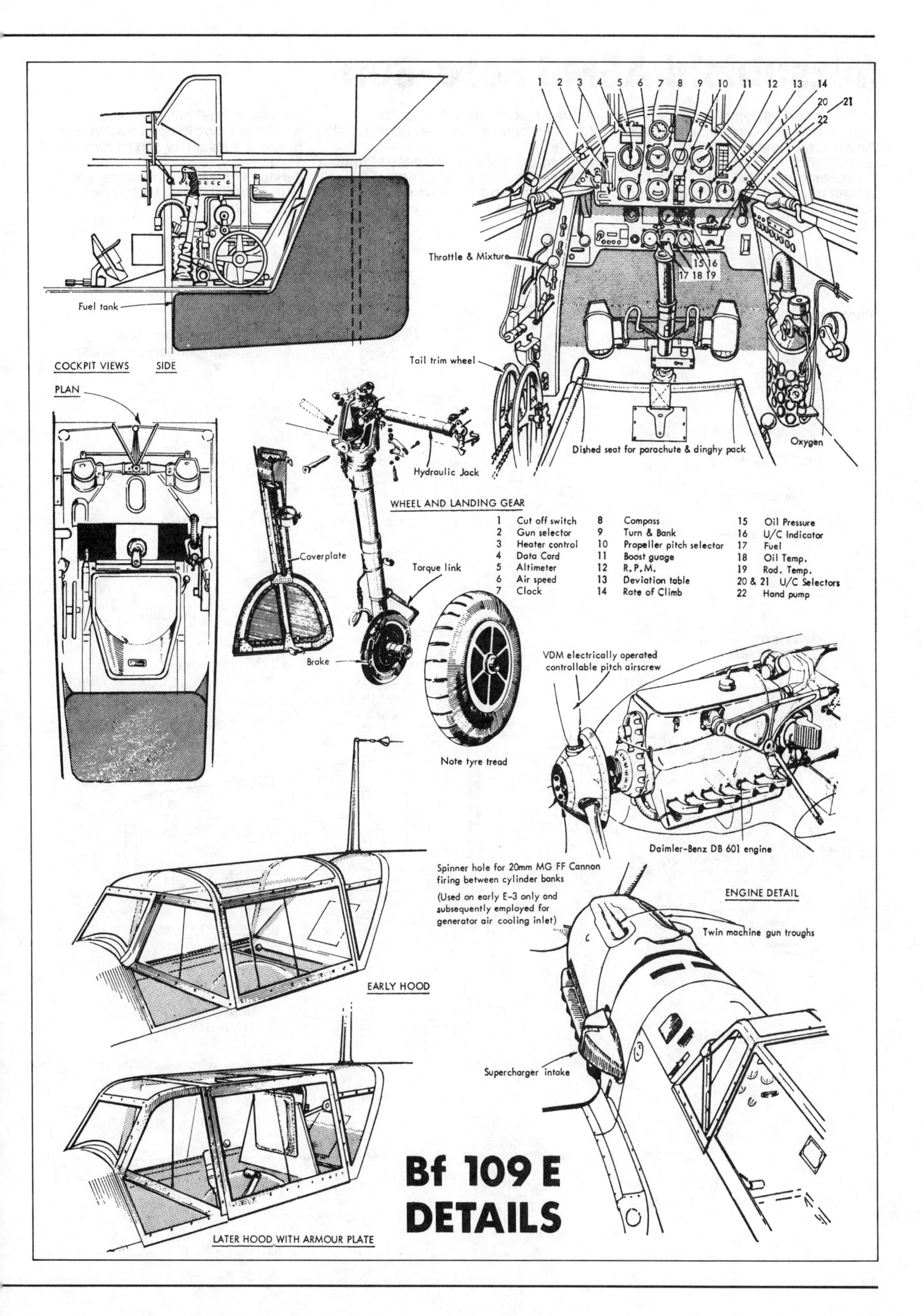

Bf 109 E DETAILS

Mitsubishi A6M5 Zero-Sen

Country of origin: Japan.
Type: Single-seat, carrier-based fighter.
Dimensions: Wing span 36ft 1in *11.00m*; length 29ft 11in *9.12m*; height 11ft 6in *3.51m*; wing area 229.3 sq ft *21.30m²*.
Weights: Empty 4135lb *1876kg*; loaded 6024lb *2733kg*.
Powerplant: One Nakajima Sakae 21 fourteen-cylinder radial engine rated at 1130hp.
Performance: Maximum speed 351mph *565kph* at 19,700ft *6000m*; initial climb rate 3150ft/min *960m/min*; service ceiling 38,500ft *11,740m*; range (maximum) 1195 miles *1925km*.
Armament: Two fixed 7.7mm Type 97 machine guns and two fixed 20mm Type 99 cannon.
Service: First flight (prototype) 1 April 1939, (A6M5) summer 1943; service entry (A6M5) autumn 1943.

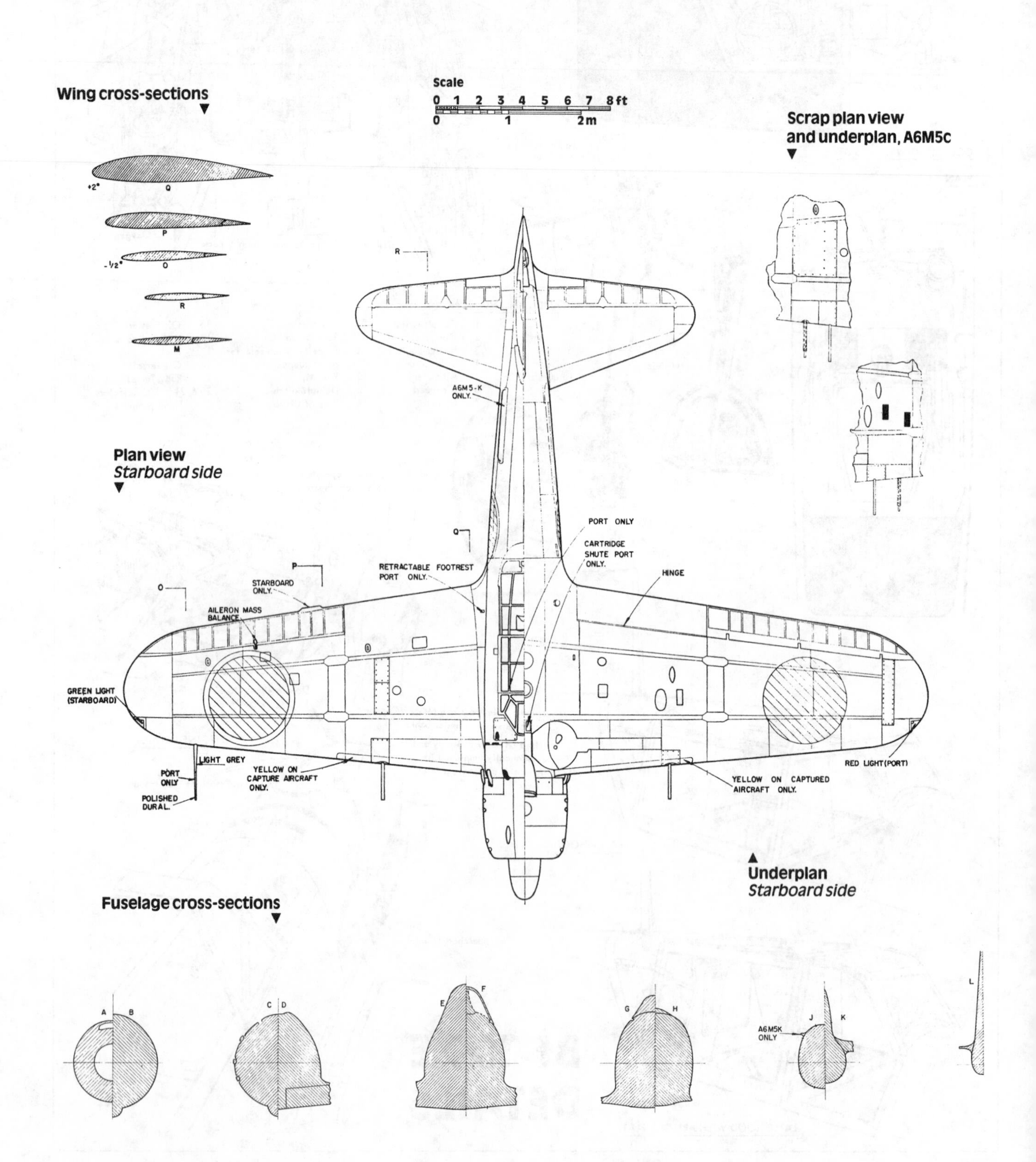

▲ **The compact, aggressive lines of the immortal Zero are well shown in this photo of a captured Type 52 aircraft.**

Scrap starboard elevation, A6M5-K trainer version
No wing cannon fitted ▼

Starboard elevation
Captured aircraft
▼

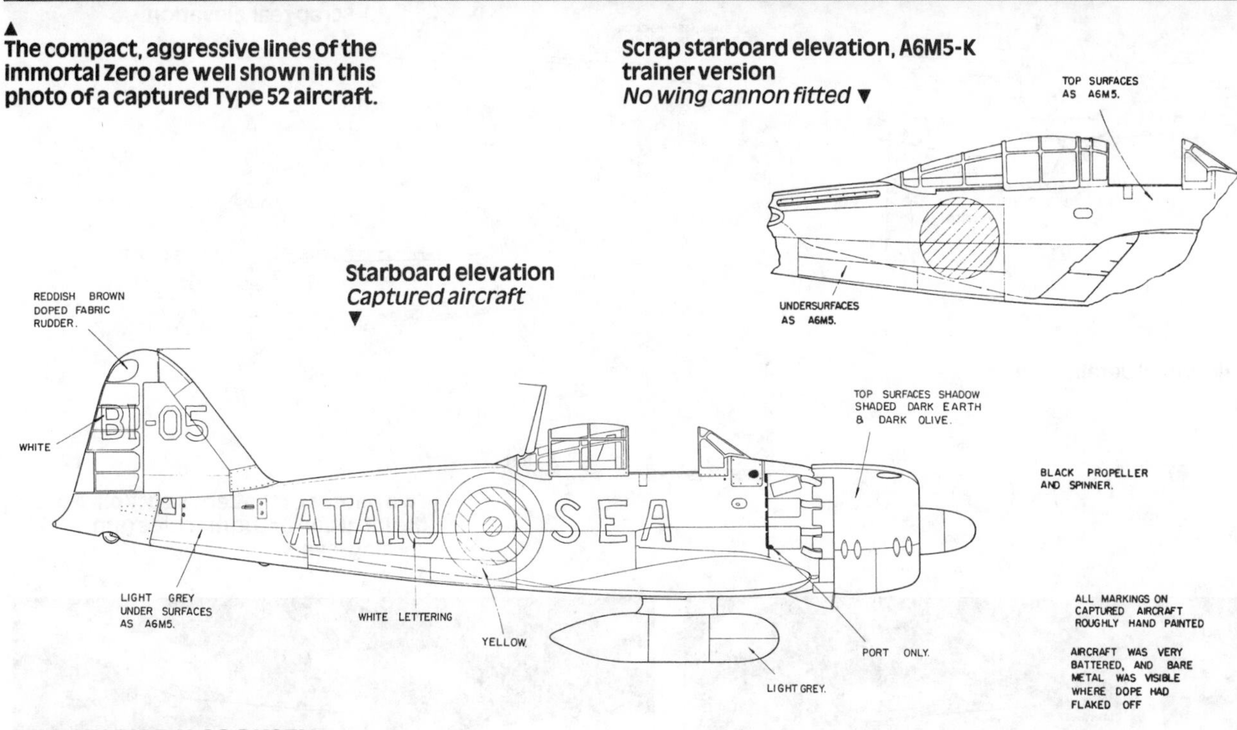

DRAWN BY D H COOKSEY

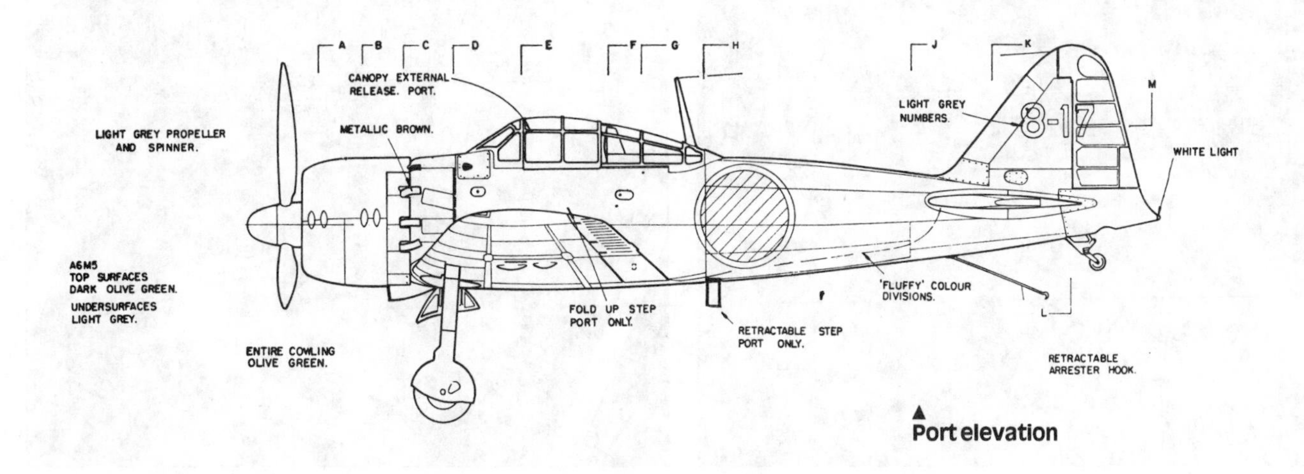

▲ **Port elevation**

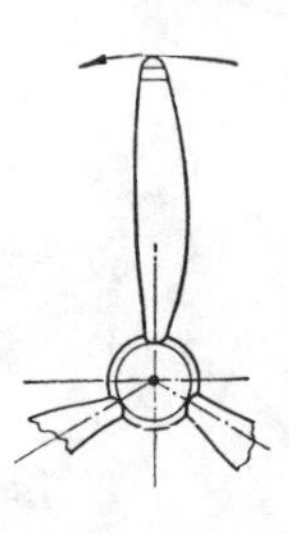

Scrap front elevation
Propeller

Captured A6M5 on test, companion aircraft to BI-05 shown in the main drawings.

Front elevation

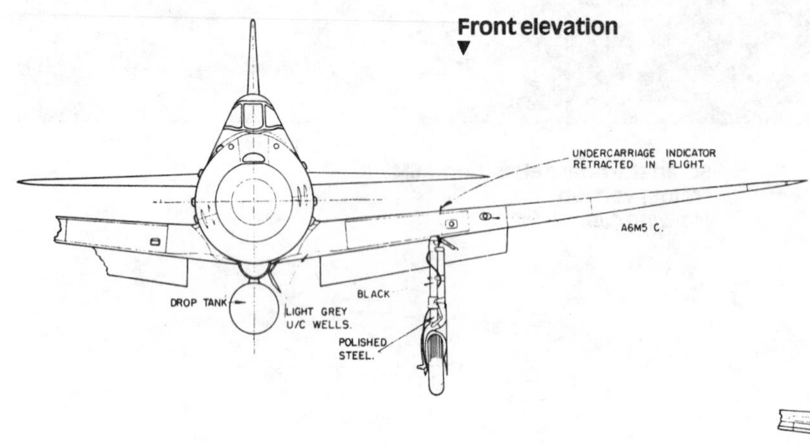

Scrap rear elevation

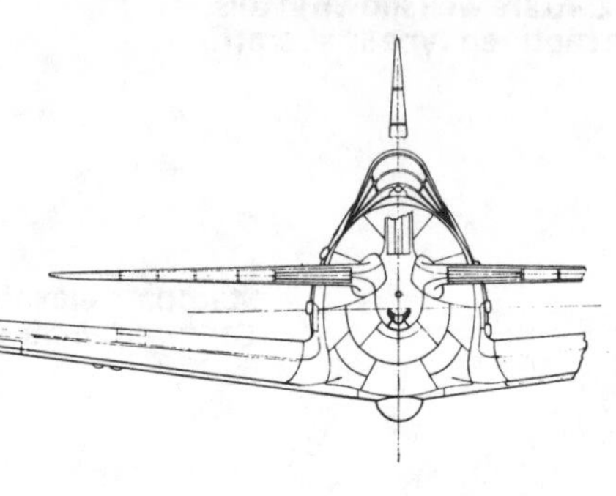

Main wheel details

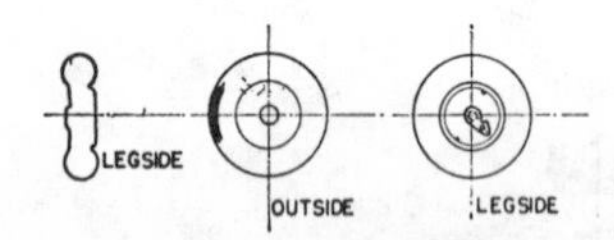

Scale
0 1 2 3 4 5 6 7 8ft
0 1 2m

Two photos of the Zero's cockpit. Note the intrusion of the machine gun cocking levers.

Boulton Paul Defiant Mks I and II

Country of origin: Great Britain.
Type: Two-seat, land-based fighter or night fighter and (TT Mk I) target tug.
Dimensions: Wing span 39ft 4in *11.99m*; length 35ft 4in *10.77m*; height 11ft 4in *3.45m*; wing area 250 sq ft *23.22m²*.
Weights: Empty 6078lb *2758kg*, (Mk II) 6282lb *2850kg*; normal 8318lb *3774kg*, (Mk II) 8424lb *3822kg*; maximum 8350lb *3789kg*, (Mk II) 8600lb *3902kg*.
Powerplant: One Rolls-Royce Merlin III V12, liquid-cooled piston engine rated at 1030hp at 16,250ft *4955m*, (Mk II) Merlin XX rated at 1260hp at 12,250ft *3735m*.
Performance: Maximum speed 304mph *490kph* at 17,000ft *5180m*, (Mk II) 313mph *505kph* at 19,000ft *5790m*.
Armament: Four turret-mounted 0.303in Browning machine guns.
Service: First flight (prototype) 11 August 1937, (Mk I) 30 July 1939, (Mk II) 20 July 1940; service entry (Mk I) May 1940.

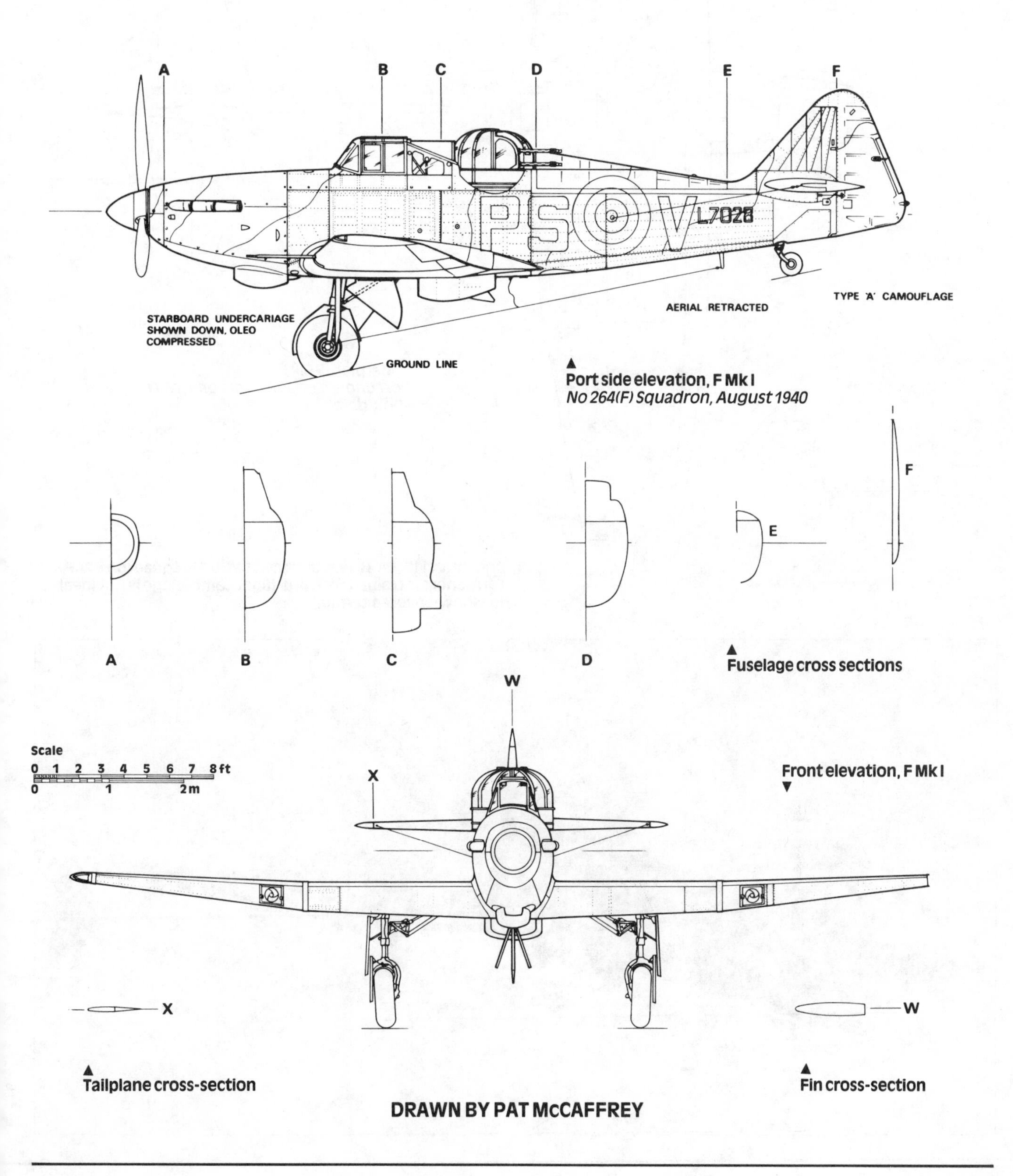

▲ **Port side elevation, F Mk I**
No 264(F) Squadron, August 1940

▲ **Fuselage cross sections**

Front elevation, F Mk I ▼

▲ **Tailplane cross-section**

▲ **Fin cross-section**

DRAWN BY PAT McCAFFREY

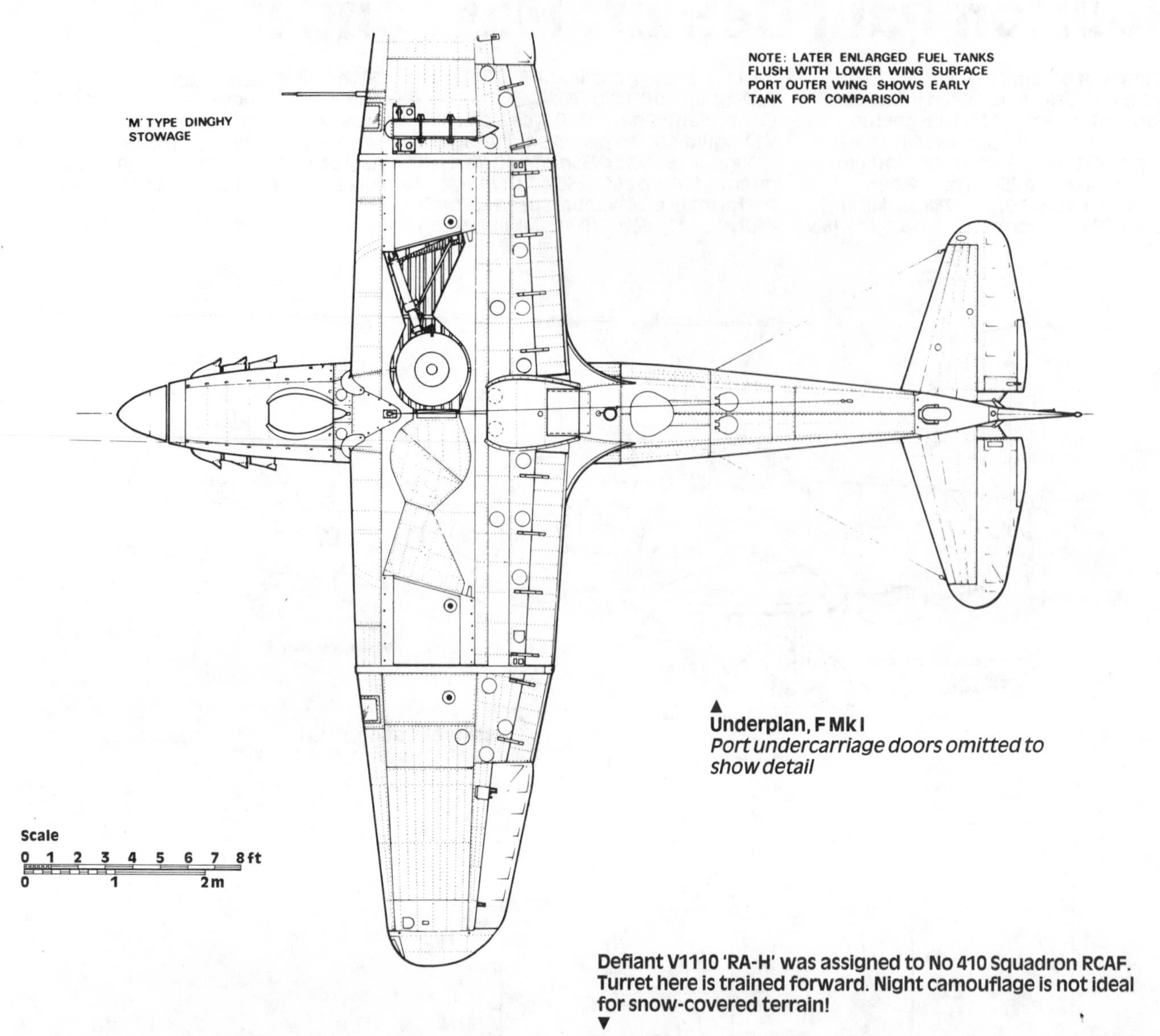

▲
Underplan, F Mk I
Port undercarriage doors omitted to show detail

Defiant V1110 'RA-H' was assigned to No 410 Squadron RCAF. Turret here is trained forward. Night camouflage is not ideal for snow-covered terrain!
▼

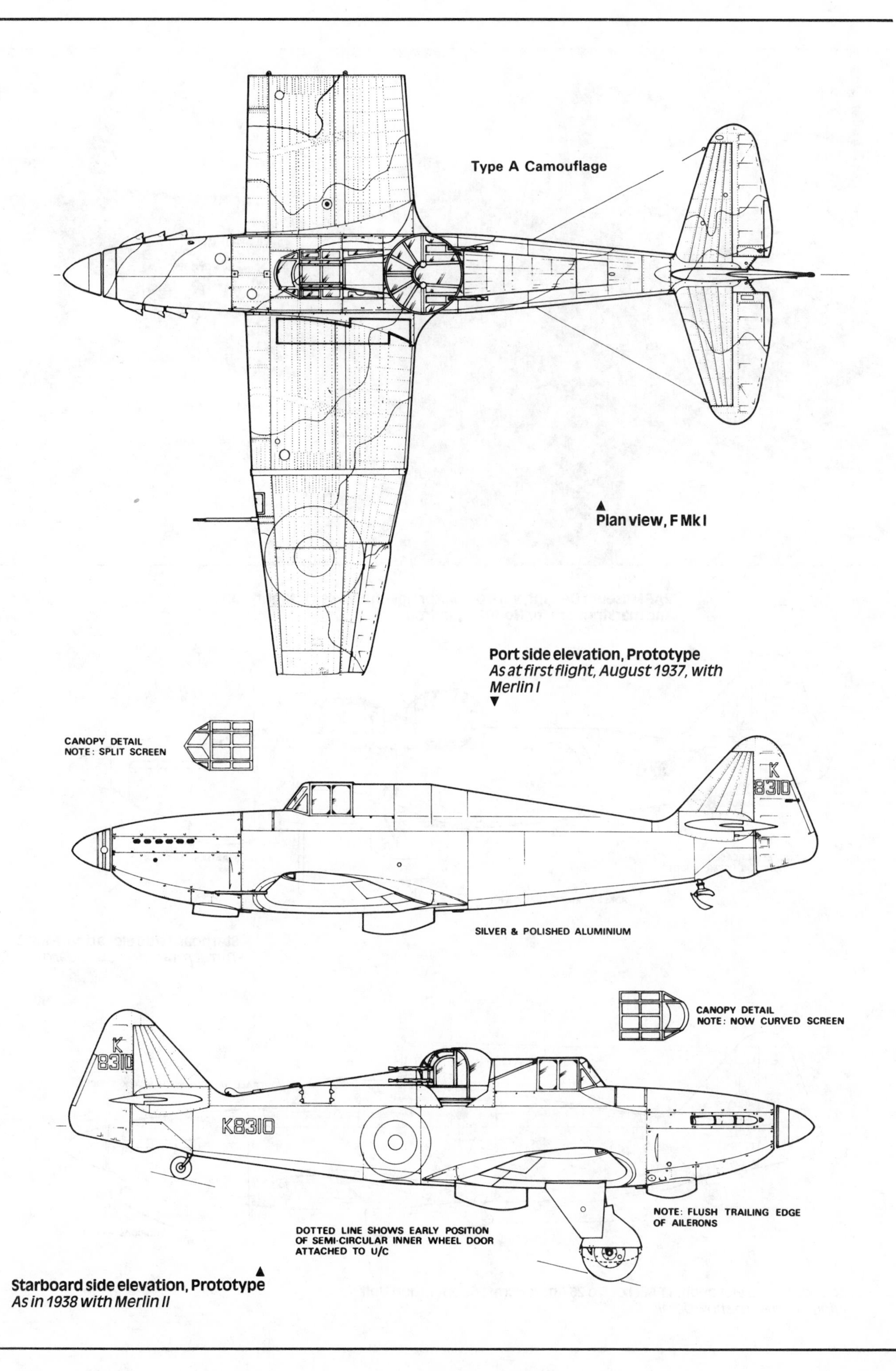

Plan view, F Mk I

Port side elevation, Prototype
As at first flight, August 1937, with Merlin I

Starboard side elevation, Prototype
As in 1938 with Merlin II

RAF Museum Defiant, with Gladiator beyond. Finish is Night, and markings are for No 307 Squadron.

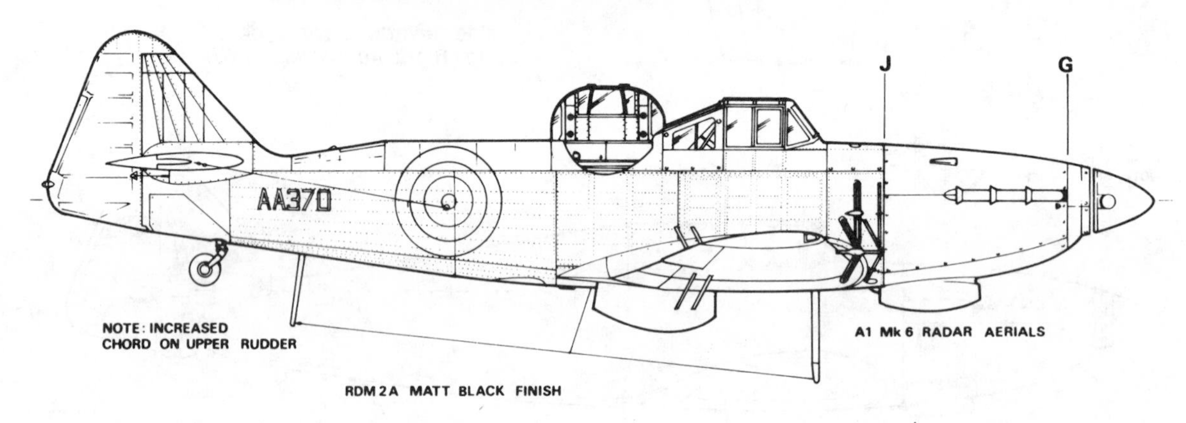

Starboard side elevation, F Mk 2
Turret rotated 90° starboard

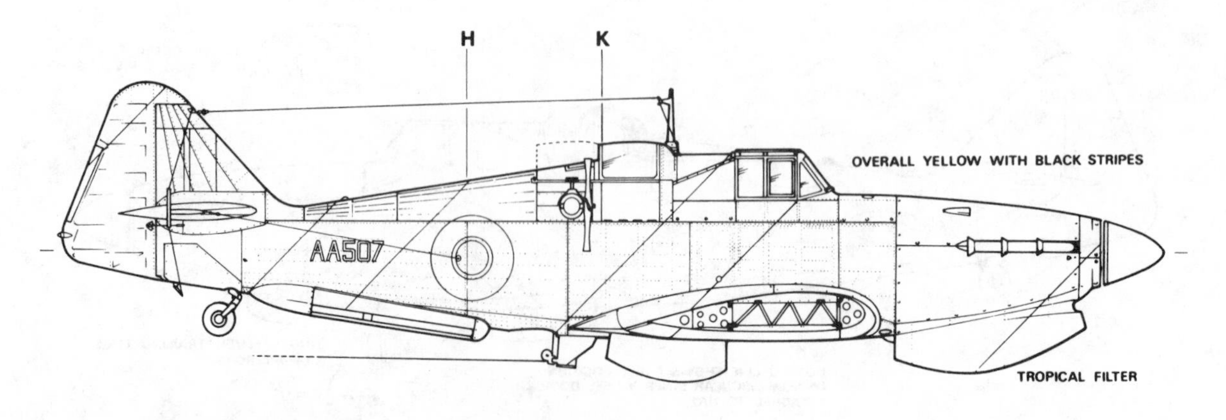

Starboard side elevation, TT Mk I of No 26 Anti-aircraft Cooperation Unit
Wing omitted to show detail

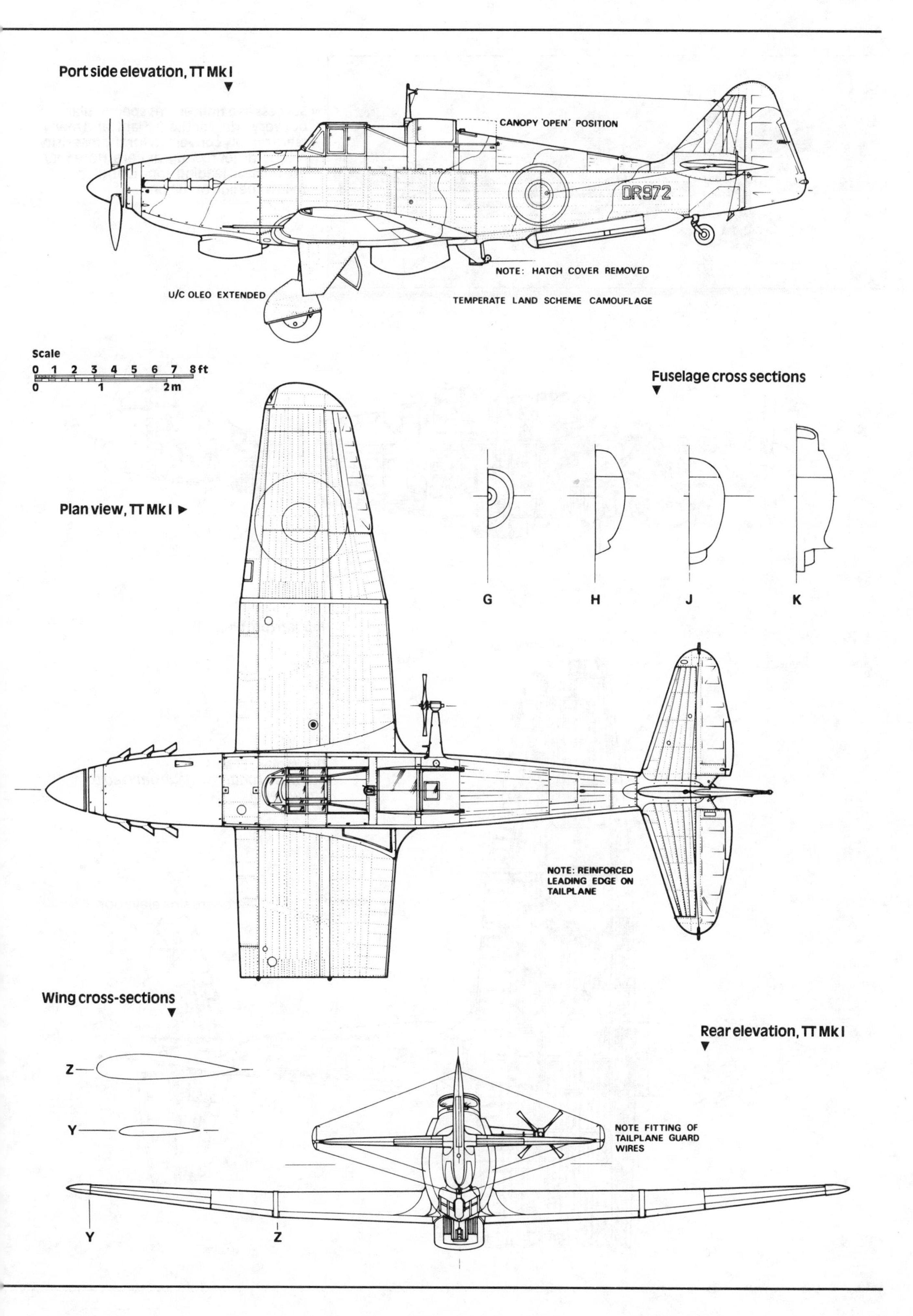
Port side elevation, TT Mk I
CANOPY 'OPEN' POSITION
DR972
NOTE: HATCH COVER REMOVED
U/C OLEO EXTENDED
TEMPERATE LAND SCHEME CAMOUFLAGE
Scale
0 1 2 3 4 5 6 7 8 ft
0 1 2 m
Fuselage cross sections
G
H
J
K
Plan view, TT Mk I
NOTE: REINFORCED LEADING EDGE ON TAILPLANE
Wing cross-sections
Z
Y
Rear elevation, TT Mk I
NOTE FITTING OF TAILPLANE GUARD WIRES
Y
Z

◄ Success as a fighter was spectacular but very brief for the Defiant, and many were rapidly converted for the less risky role of target towing, as here. Note that the fin flash leading edge is angled to follow the line of the fin.

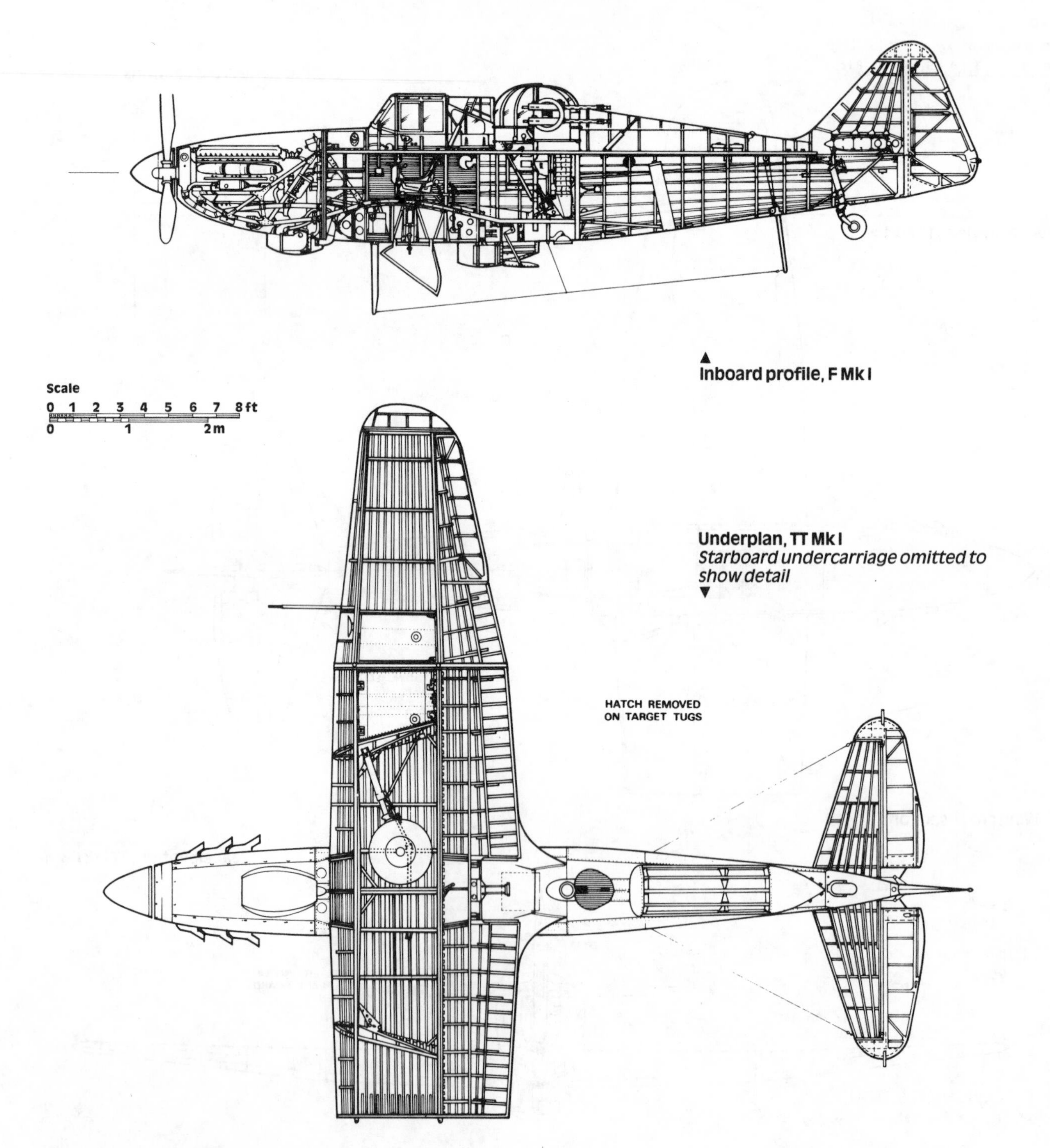

▲
Inboard profile, F Mk I

Underplan, TT Mk I
Starboard undercarriage omitted to show detail
▼

Curtiss Kittyhawk Mks I, III and IV

Country of origin: USA.
Type: Single-seat, land-based fighter and ground attack aircraft.
Dimensions: Wing span 37ft 3½in *11.36m*; length 31ft 2in *9.50m*, (Mks III, IV) 33ft 4in *10.16m*; height 12ft 4in *3.75m*; wing area 236 sq ft *21.92m²*.
Weights: Empty 6350lb *2880kg*, (Mk III) 6400lb *2903kg*, (Mk IV) 6200lb *2813kg*; maximum 9200lb *4173kg*, (Mk III) 10,000lb *4536kg*, (Mk IV) 11,500lb *5216kg*.
Powerplant: One Allison V-1710-39 V12, liquid cooled piston engine rated at 1150hp, (Mk III) V-1710-73 rated at 1325hp, (Mk IV) V-1710-81, -99 or -105 rated at 1200hp.
Performance: Maximum speed 362mph *583kph*, (Mk III) 363mph *584kph*, (Mk IV) 379mph *610kph*; climb rate 2100ft/min *640m/min* at 5000ft *1525m*, (Mk III) 2160ft/min *660m/min* at 5000ft, (Mk IV) 2120ft/min *645m/min* at 5000ft; service ceiling 29,000ft *8840m*, (Mk III) 28,000ft *8535m*, (Mk IV) 31,000ft *9450m*; range (clean) 650 miles *1045km* at 10,000ft *3050m*, (Mk III) 700 miles *1125km* at 10,000ft, (Mk IV) 750 miles *1205km* at 10,000ft.
Armament: Six fixed 0.5in Browning machine guns; (optional) one 500lb *227kg* plus two 100lb *45kg* bombs, (Mk IV) three 500lb bombs.
Service: First flight (XP-40) October 1938; service entry (Mk III) 1942.

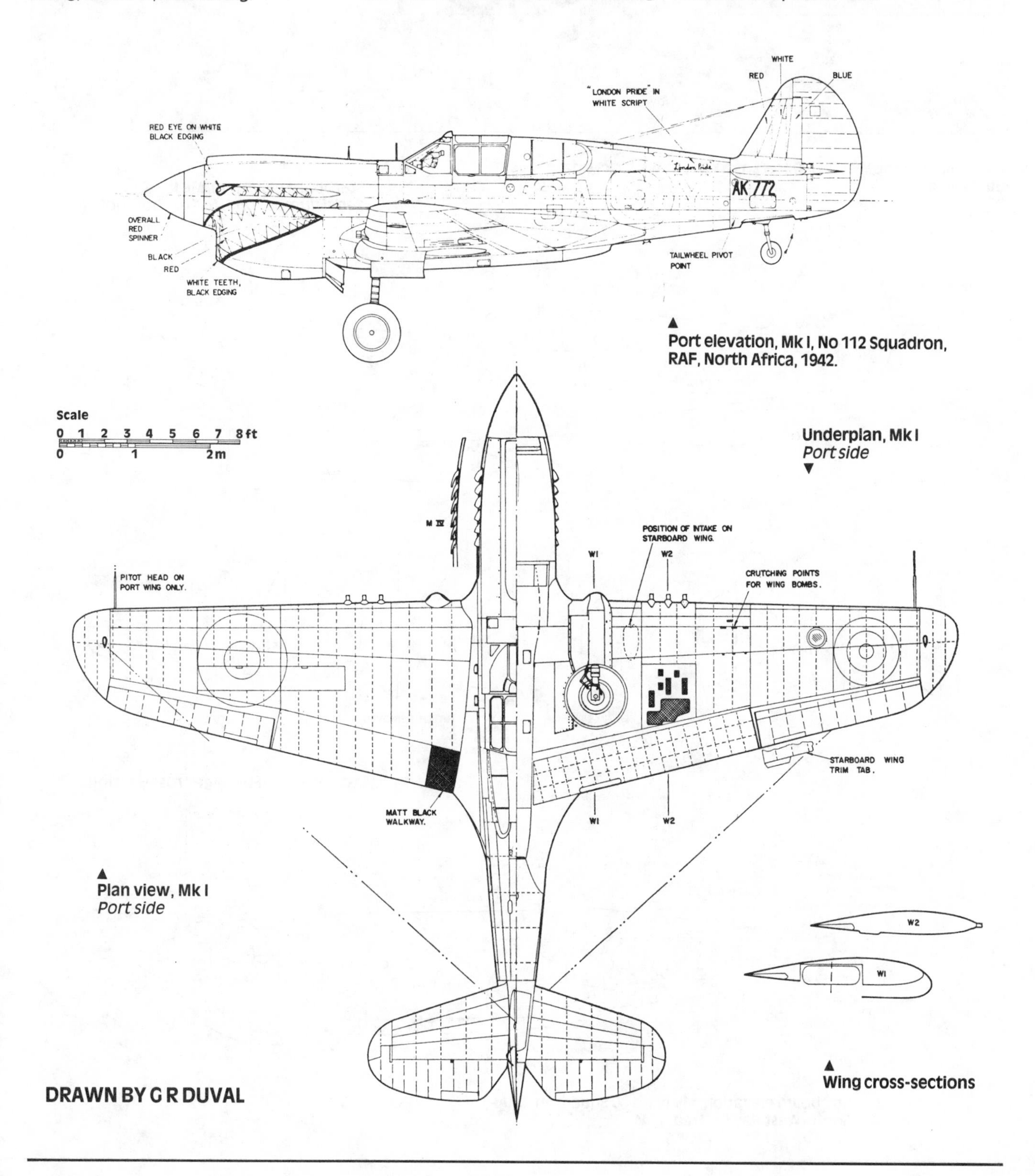

▲
Port elevation, Mk I, No 112 Squadron, RAF, North Africa, 1942.

Underplan, Mk I
Port side
▼

▲
Plan view, Mk I
Port side

▲
Wing cross-sections

DRAWN BY G R DUVAL

▲
High spirits in the Western Desert as a Kittyhawk kicks up a dust storm.

Starboard elevation, Mk I
Serial number omitted to show detail
▼

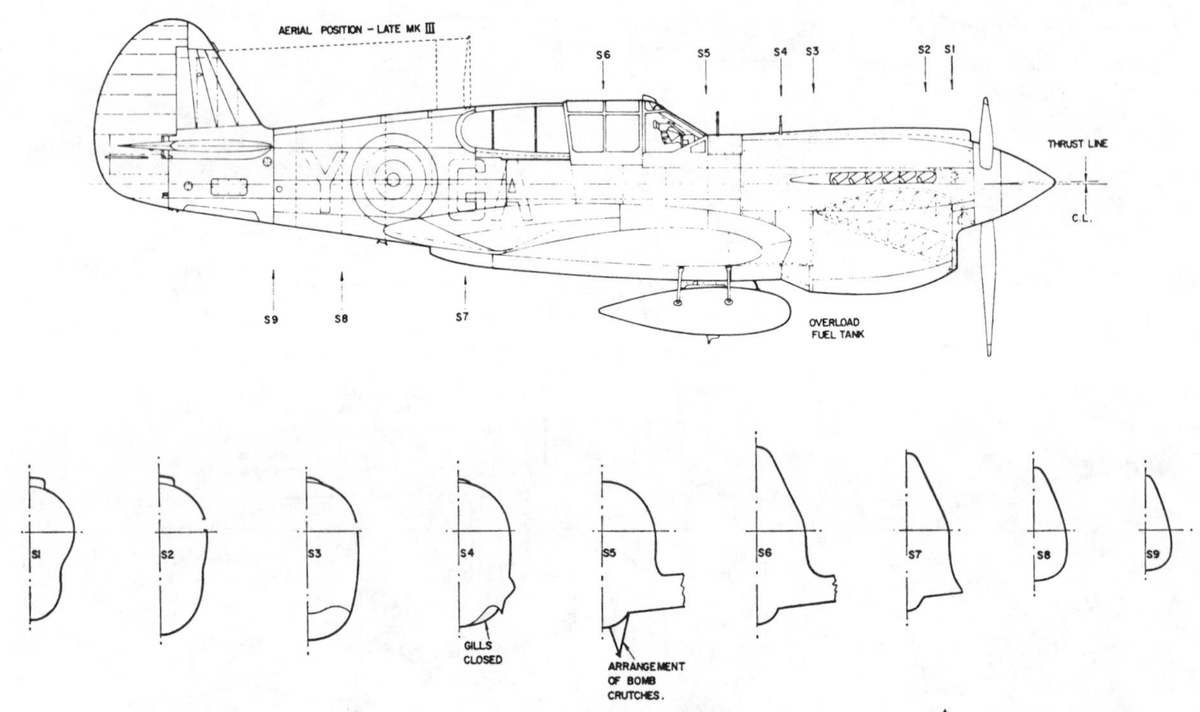

▲
Fuselage cross-sections

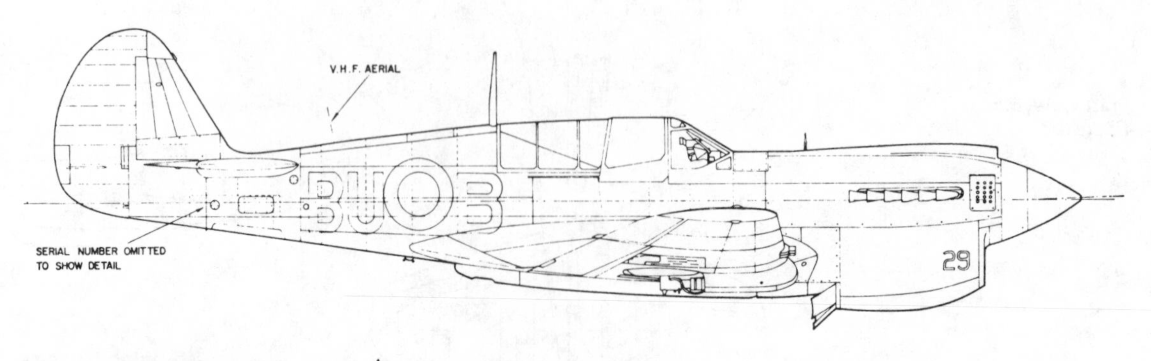

▲
Starboard elevation, Mk IV No 80 Squadron, RAAF, South-West Pacific Area, 1944.

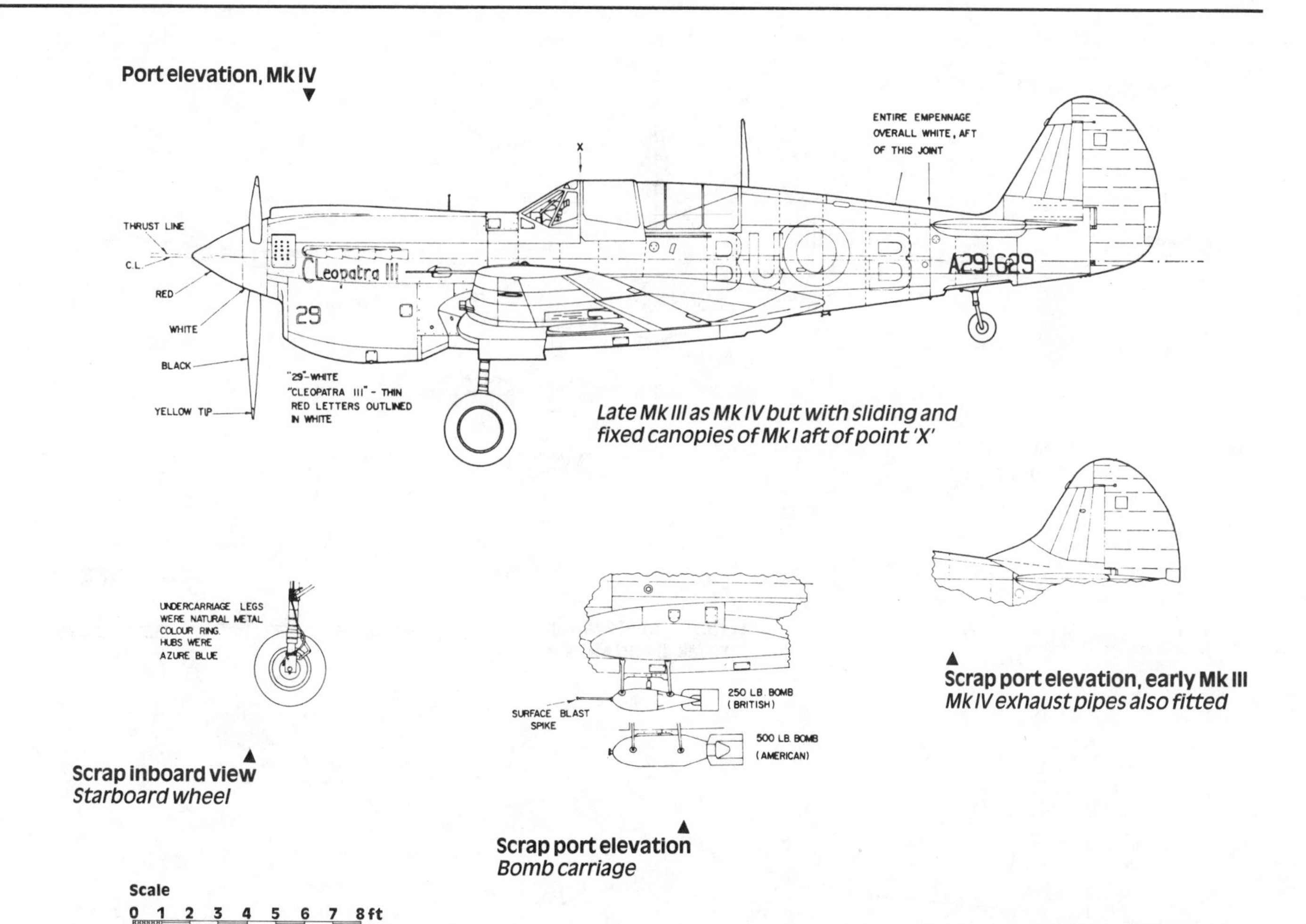

Port elevation, Mk IV ▼

Late Mk III as Mk IV but with sliding and fixed canopies of Mk I aft of point 'X'

▲ **Scrap port elevation, early Mk III**
Mk IV exhaust pipes also fitted

▲ **Scrap inboard view**
Starboard wheel

▲ **Scrap port elevation**
Bomb carriage

Preserved airworthy Kittyhawk N94466 seen in 1984. Note 'paired' exhaust pipes. ▼

Front elevation, Mk I

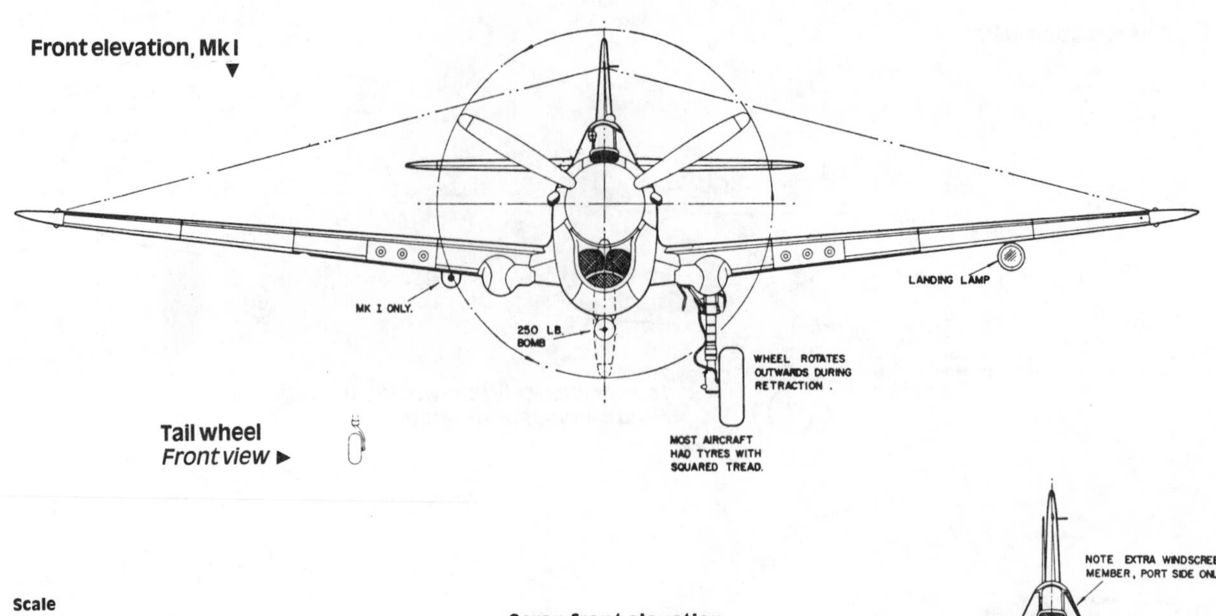

Tail wheel
Front view ►

Scale

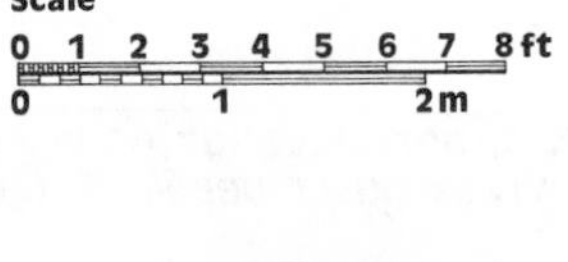

Scrap front elevation, late Mk III and Mk IV ►

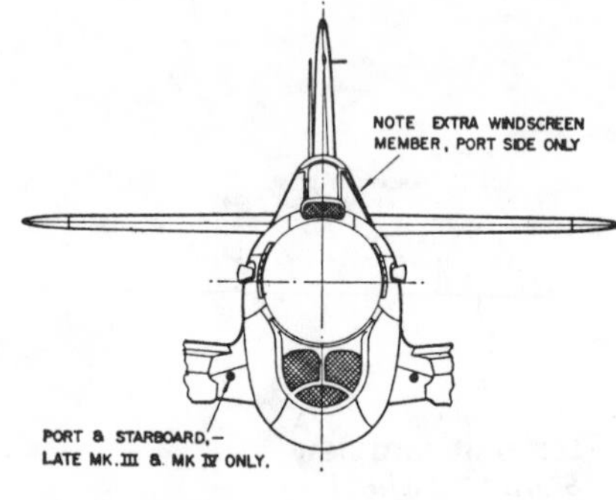

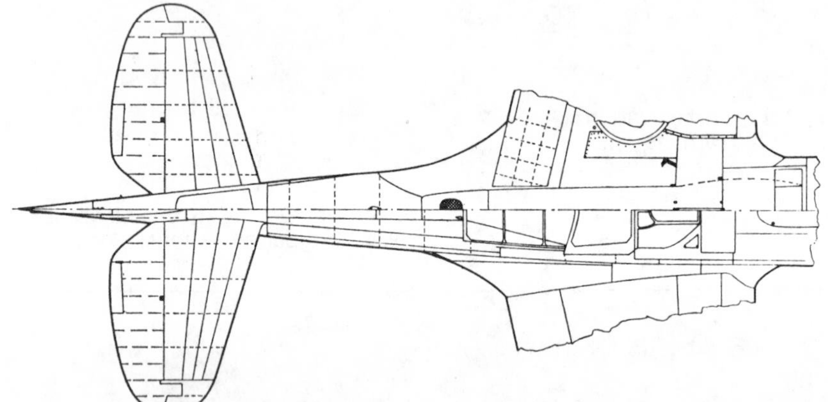

◄ **Scrap plan view/underplan, late Mk III and Mk IV**

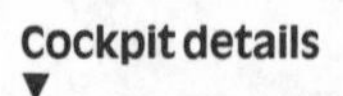

Cockpit details

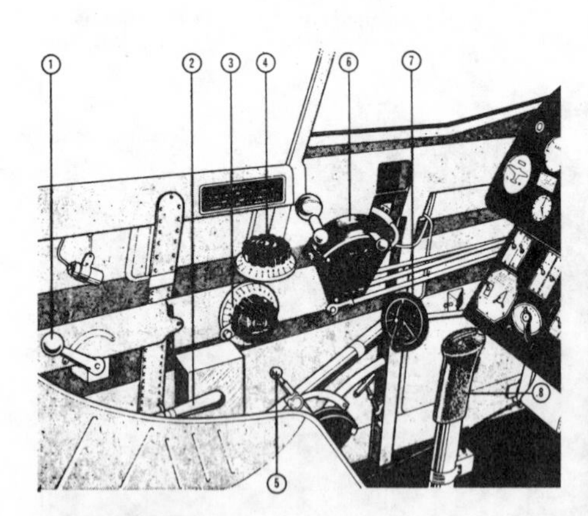

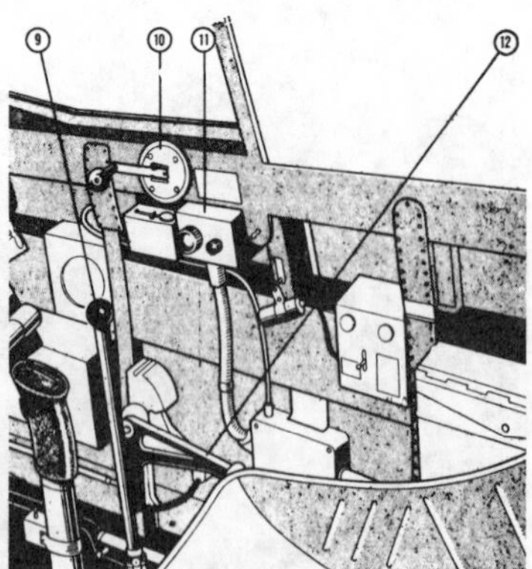

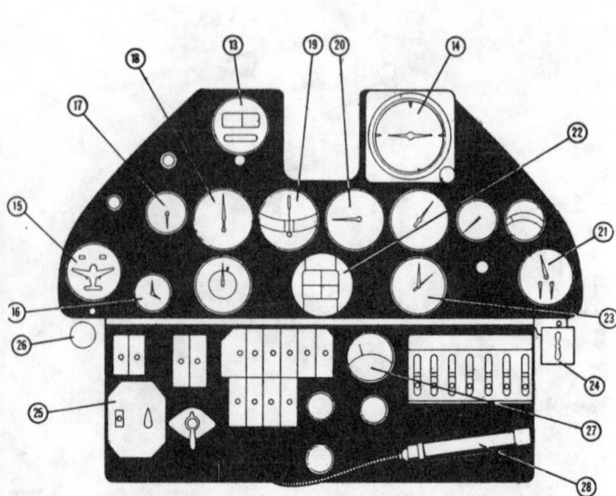

Numerical key

1. Flap control. **2.** Undercarriage lever. **3.** Elevator trim. **4.** Rudder trim. **5.** Bomb/belly tank release. **6.** Throttle/mixture/pitch controls. **7.** Fuel cock. **8.** Control column with gun trigger and flap actuator switch. **9.** Hydraulic hand pump, emergency pump at base. **10.** Canopy winding handle. **11.** Radio controls with morse key. **12.** Radiator flap control. **13.** Direction indicator. **14.** Artificial horizon. **15.** Flap/wheels indicator. **16.** Clock. **17.** Fuel gauge. **18.** Airspeed indicator. **19.** Turn and bank. **20.** Rate of climb/descent. **21.** Combined engine pressure/temperature gauge. **22.** Compass. **23.** RPM. **24.** Carburettor heat control. **25.** Propeller selector switches. **26.** Parking brake. **27.** Ammeter. **28.** Fluorescent lamp.
Note: Lower panel is angled towards pilot.

Messerschmitt Bf 110C-4, C-5, F and G

Country of origin: Germany.
Type: Two- or three-seat, land-based long-range fighter or (-G) three-seat, land-based, long-range night fighter.
Dimensions: Wing span (C-4, G-4/R3) 53ft 5in *16.28m*; length (C-4) 39ft 8½in *12.10m*, (G-4/R3) 41ft 6¾in *12.67m*; height (C-4) 11ft 6in *3.51m*, (G-4/R3) 13ft 1¼in *3.99m*; wing area (C-4, G-4/R3) 413 sq ft *38.36m²*.
Weights: Empty (G-4/R3) 11,220lb *5090kg*; normal loaded (C-4) 15,300lb *6942kg*, (G-4/R3) 20,700lb *9392kg*; maximum 21,800lb *9891kg*.
Powerplant: (C-4) Two Daimler-Benz DB 601A twelve-cylinder, liquid-cooled piston engines each rated at 1100hp, (G-4/R3) DB 605B rated at 1475hp.
Performance: Maximum speed (C-4) 349mph *562kph* at 22,950ft *7000m*, (G-4/R3) 342mph *551kph* at 22,950ft; initial climb rate (C-4) about 2200ft/min *670m/min*; service ceiling (C-4) 32,000ft *9750m*, (G-4/R3) 26,000ft *7925m*; range (C-4, clean) 565 miles *910km* at 301mph *485kph* at 22,950ft, (G-4/R3, maximum external fuel) 1305 miles *2100km*.
Armament: (C-4) Four fixed 7.9mm MG 17 machine guns, two fixed 20mm MG FF cannon and one flexibly mounted 7.9mm MG 15 machine gun; (G-4/R3) two fixed 30mm MK 108 cannon, two fixed 20mm MG 151 machine guns and one twin, flexibly mounted 7.9mm MG 81 machine gun.
Service: First flight (Bf 110V-1 prototype) 12 May 1936, (C-4) spring 1940, (G-4) summer 1942.

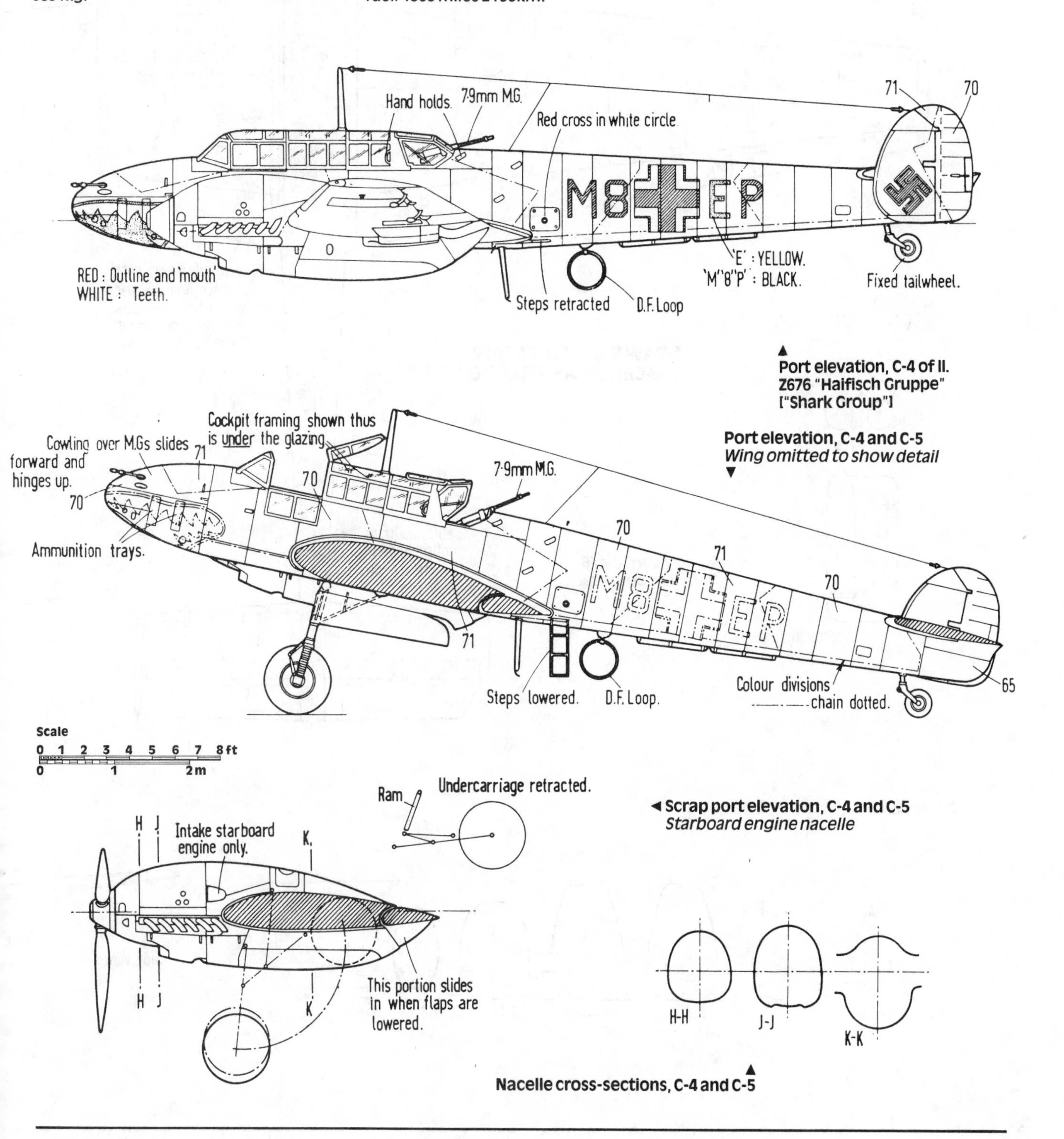

▲ **Port elevation, C-4 of II. ZG76 "Haifisch Gruppe" ["Shark Group"]**

Port elevation, C-4 and C-5
Wing omitted to show detail ▼

◄ **Scrap port elevation, C-4 and C-5**
Starboard engine nacelle

▲ **Nacelle cross-sections, C-4 and C-5**

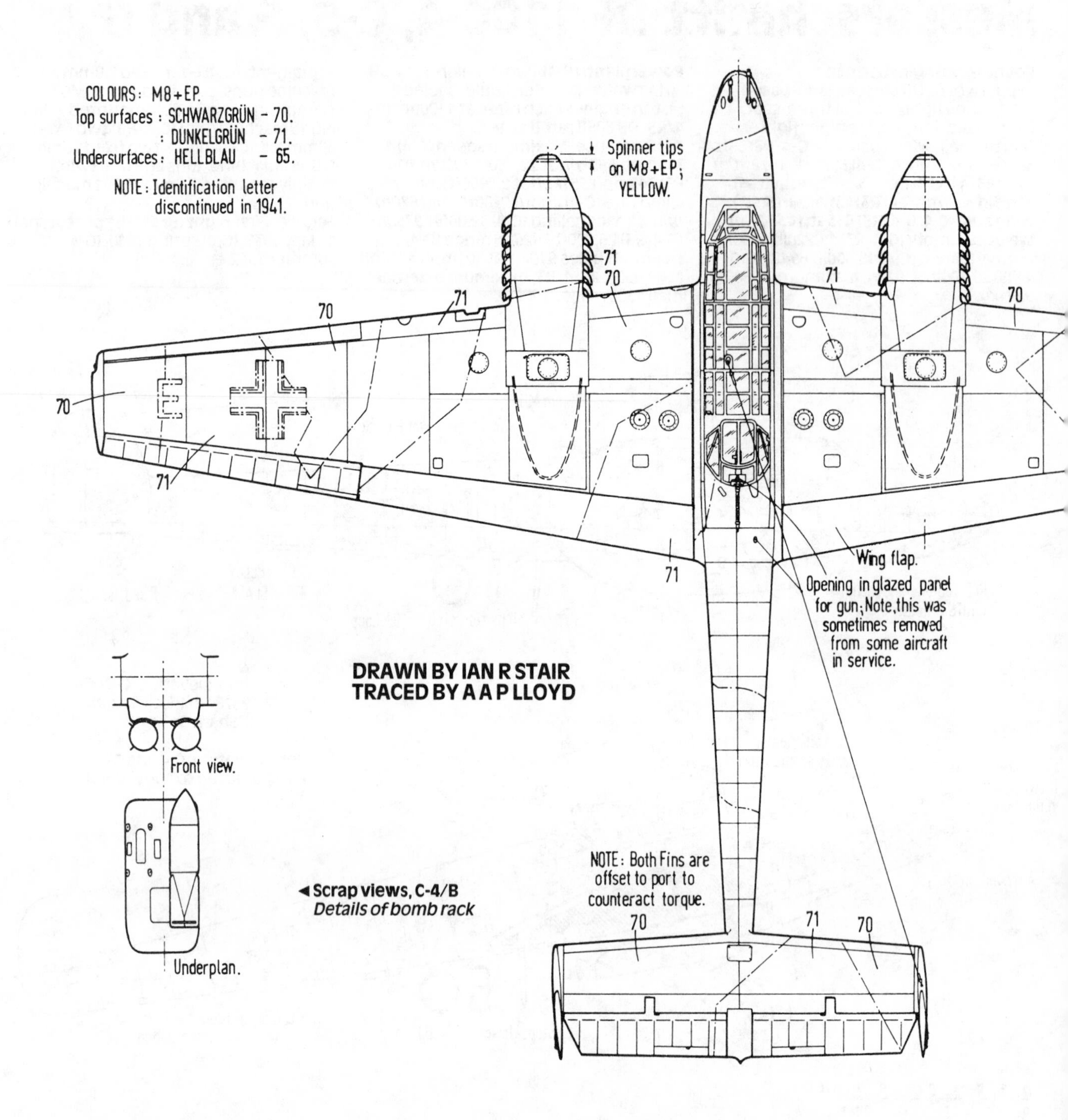

◄ **Scrap views, C-4/B**
Details of bomb rack

Fuselage cross-sections, C-4 and C-5
▼

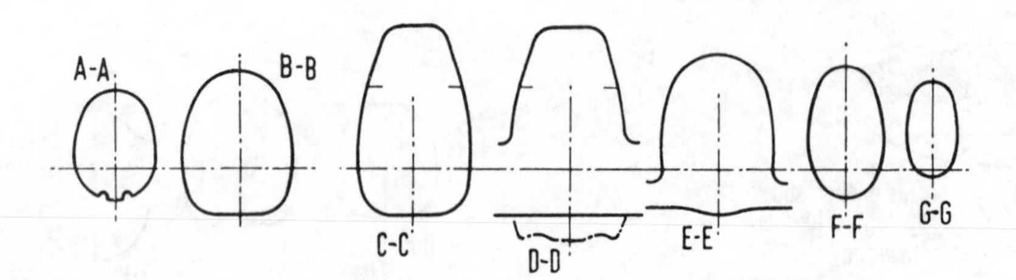

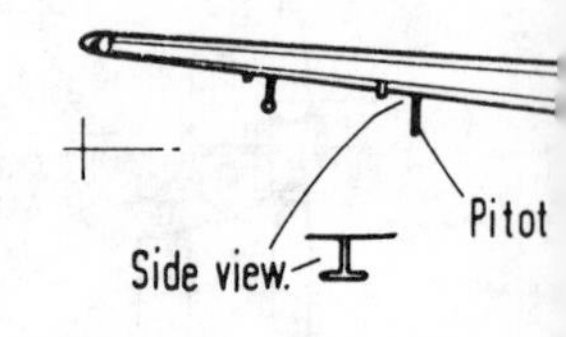

Captured Bf 110C-5, serial AX772, painted in RAF-style camouflage and markings. ►

◄ **Plan view, C-4 and C-5**

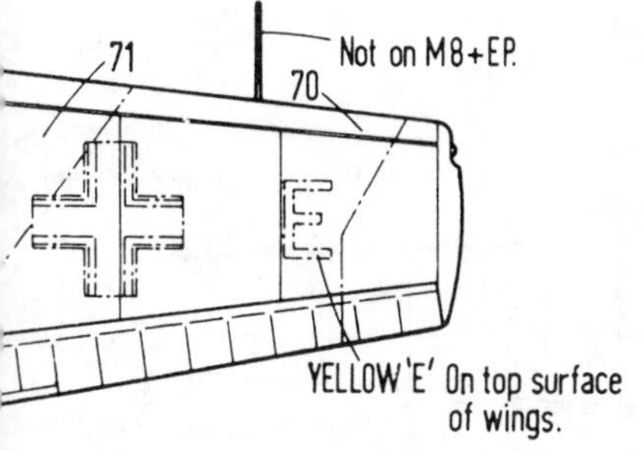

Starboard elevation, C-4/B
Wing omitted to show detail
▼

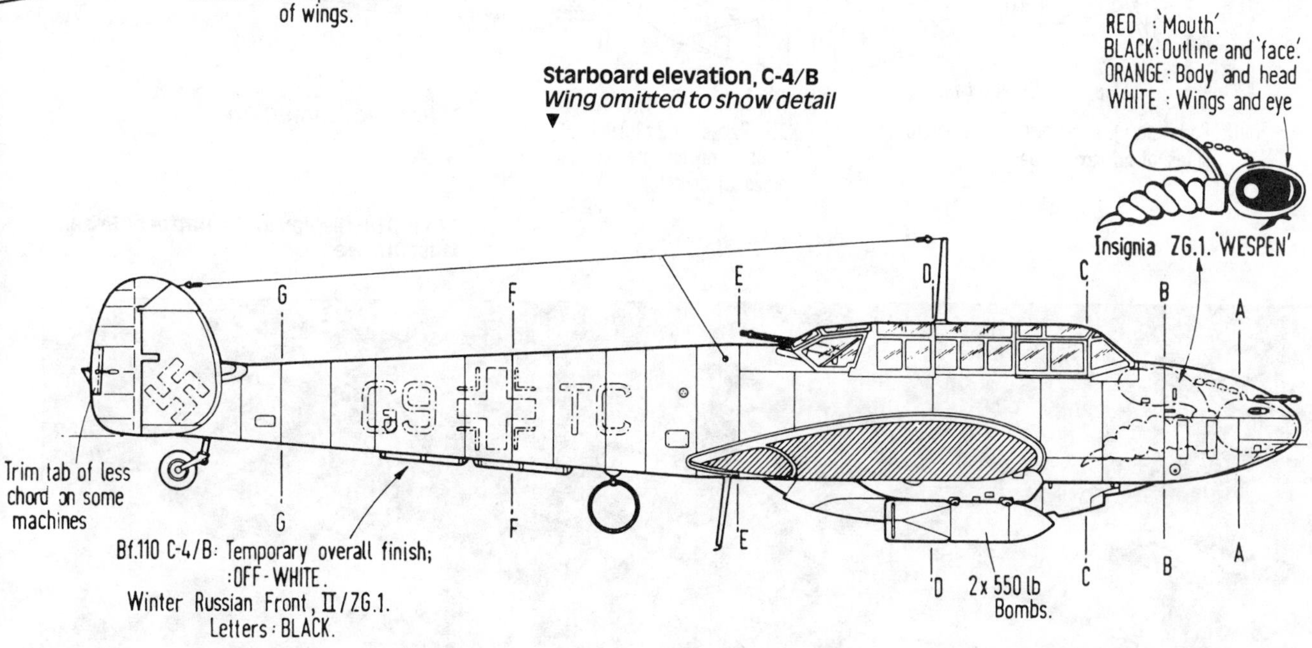

Front elevation, C-4 and C-5
▼

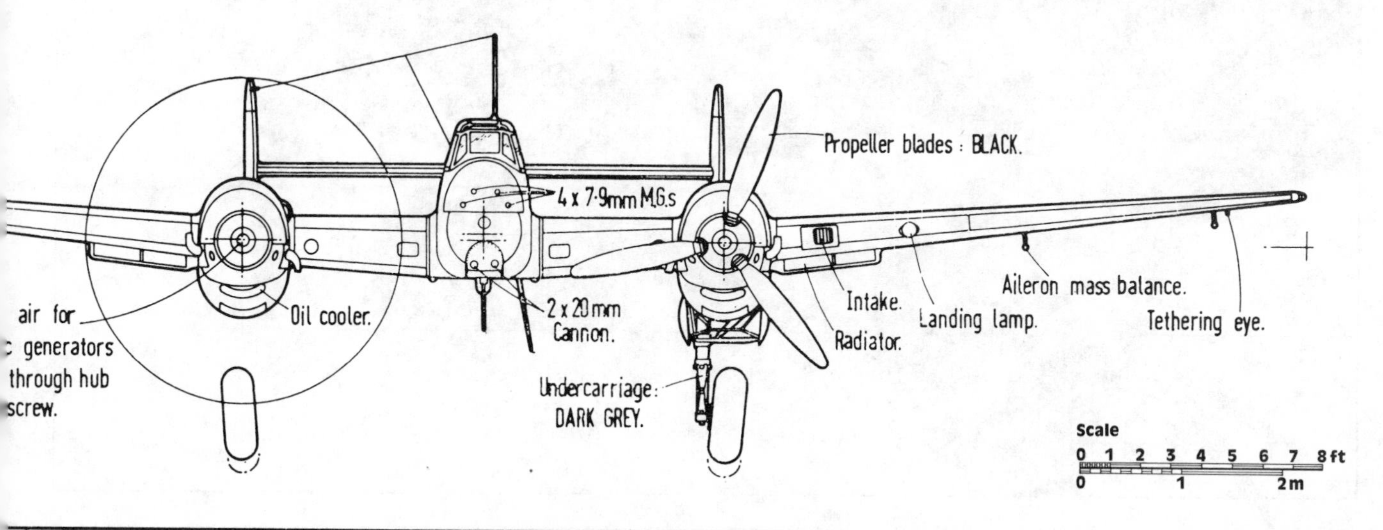

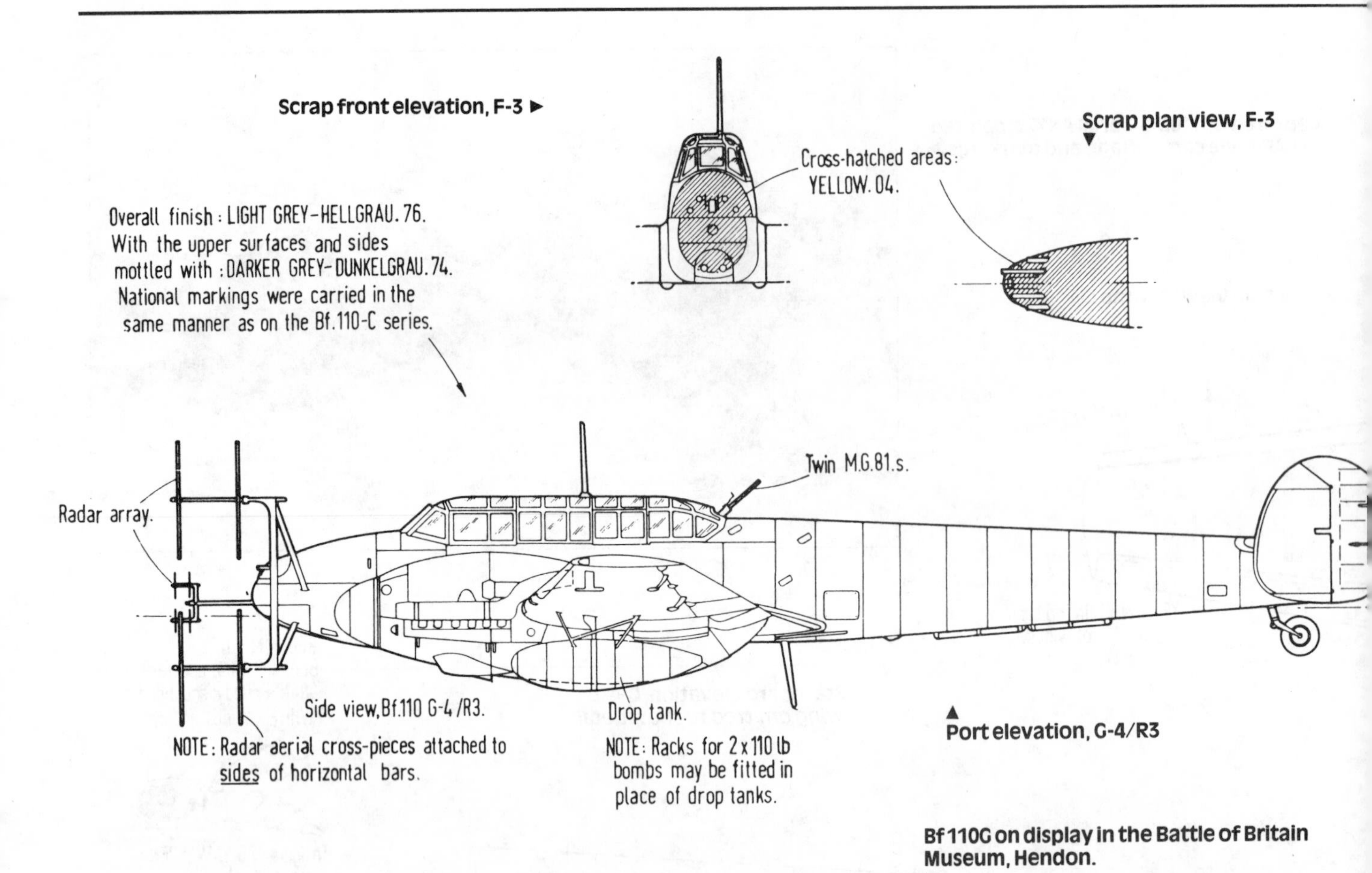

▲ Port elevation, G-4/R3

Bf 110G on display in the Battle of Britain Museum, Hendon. ▼

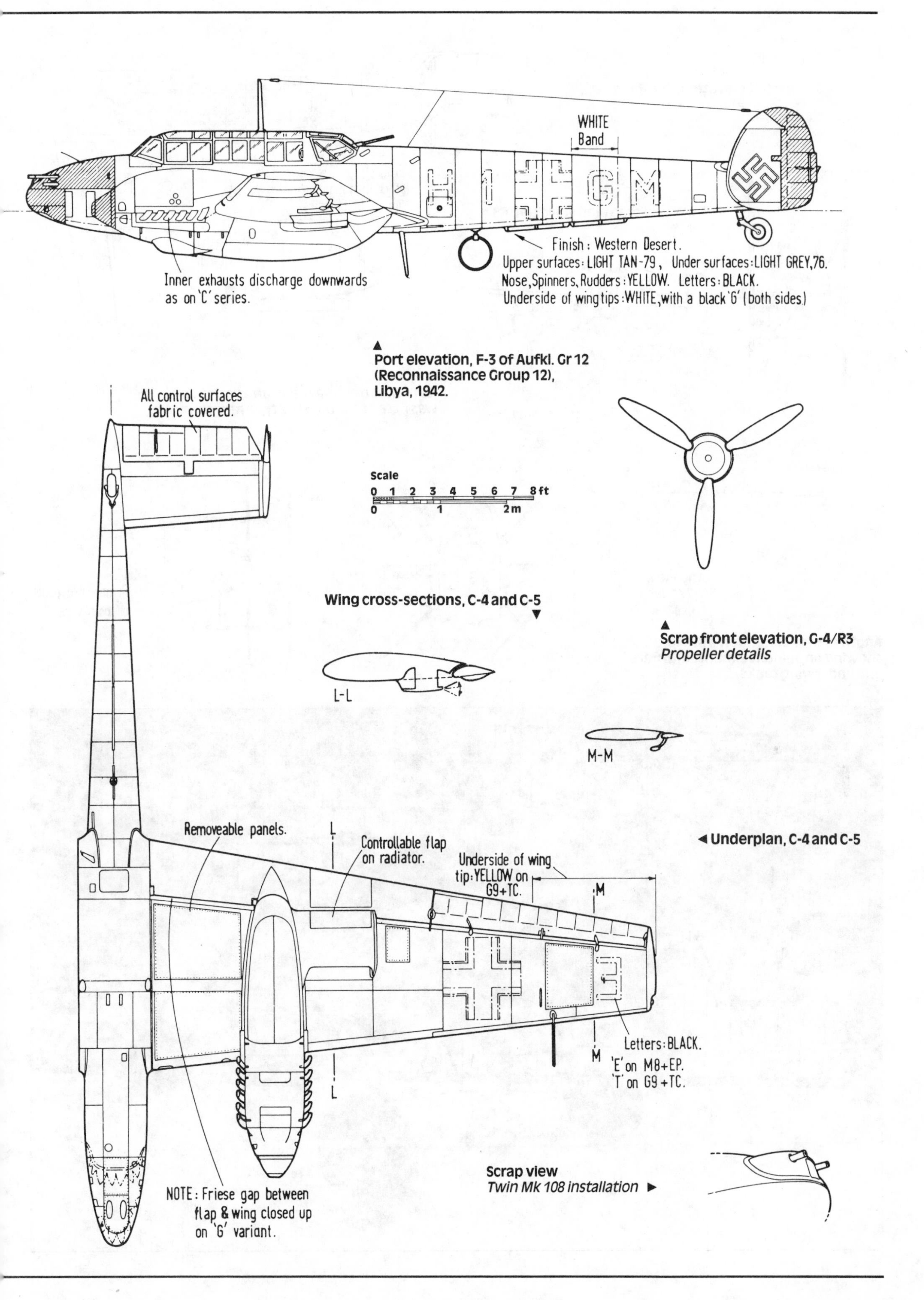

▲ **Port elevation, F-3 of Aufkl. Gr 12 (Reconnaissance Group 12), Libya, 1942.**

▲ **Scrap front elevation, G-4/R3**
Propeller details

Wing cross-sections, C-4 and C-5 ▼

◄ **Underplan, C-4 and C-5**

Scrap view
Twin Mk 108 installation ►

Scrap front elevation, G-4/R3 ▼

Scrap plan view, G-4/R3 ►

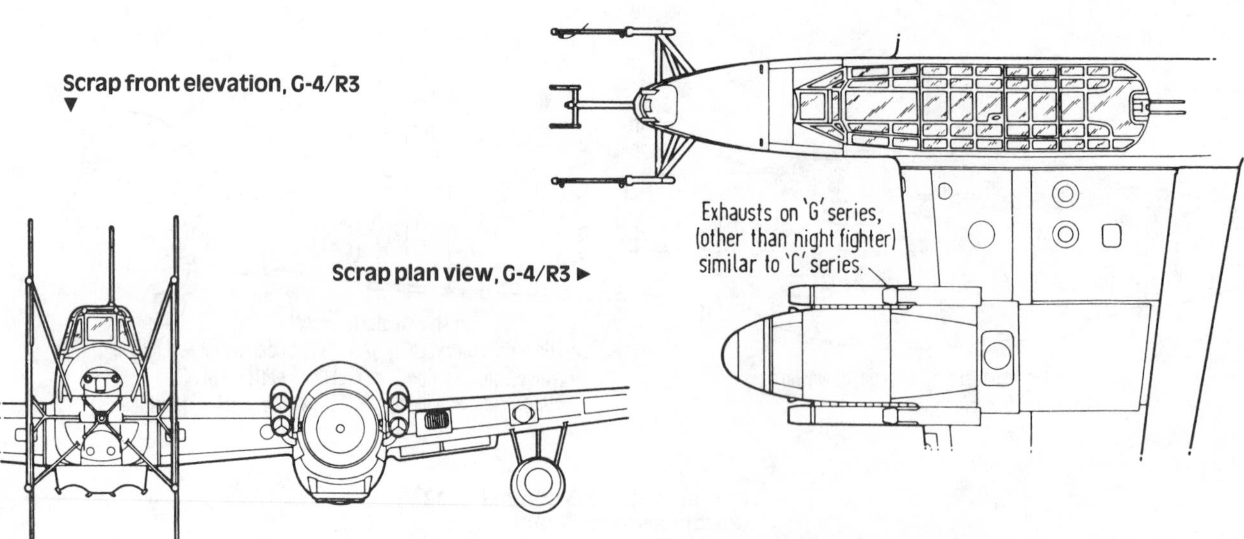

Note that the small central radar aerial was fitted to some SN-2 type radar arrays

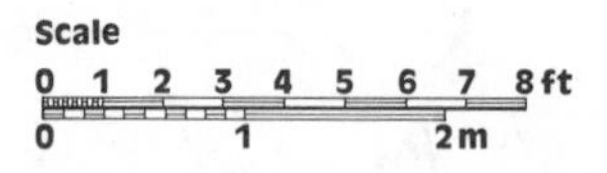

Scrap views *SN-2 radar* ►

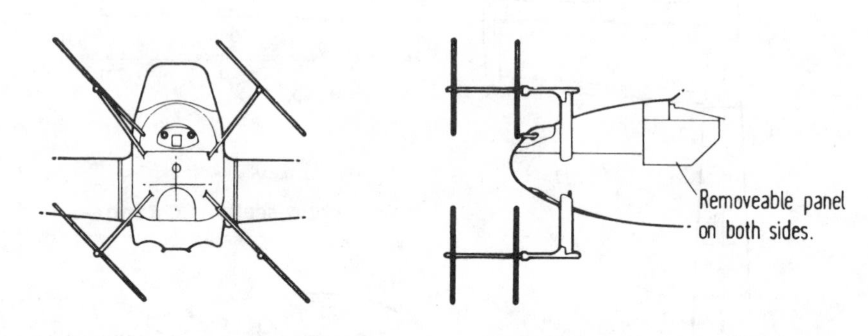

Another view of Hendon's Bf 110, showing prominent exhaust mufflers and underwing tanks. ▼

Hawker Typhoon Mk I

Country of origin: Great Britain.
Type: Single-seat, land-based fighter-bomber.
Dimensions: Wing span 41ft 7in *12.67m*; length 31ft 11in *9.73m*; height 15ft 3½in *4.66m*; wing area 279 sq ft *25.91m²*.
Weights: Empty 8800lb *3993kg*; loaded 11,400lb *5172kg*.
Powerplant: One Napier Sabre IIA 24-cylinder, liquid-cooled piston engine rated at 2180hp.
Performance: Maximum speed 405mph *652kph* at 18,000ft *5485m*; time to 15,000ft *4570m*, 6.2min; service ceiling 34,000ft *10,365m*; range (clean) 610 miles *982km* at 254mph *409kph* and 15,000ft, (maximum external fuel) about 1000 miles *1600km*.
Armament: (Mk IA) Twelve fixed 0.303in Browning machine guns; (Mk IB) four fixed 20mm Hispano cannon, plus two 1000lb *454kg* bombs or eight 60lb *27kg* underwing rocket projectiles.
Service: First flight (prototype) 24 February 1940, (Mk IA) 26 May 1941; service entry September 1941.

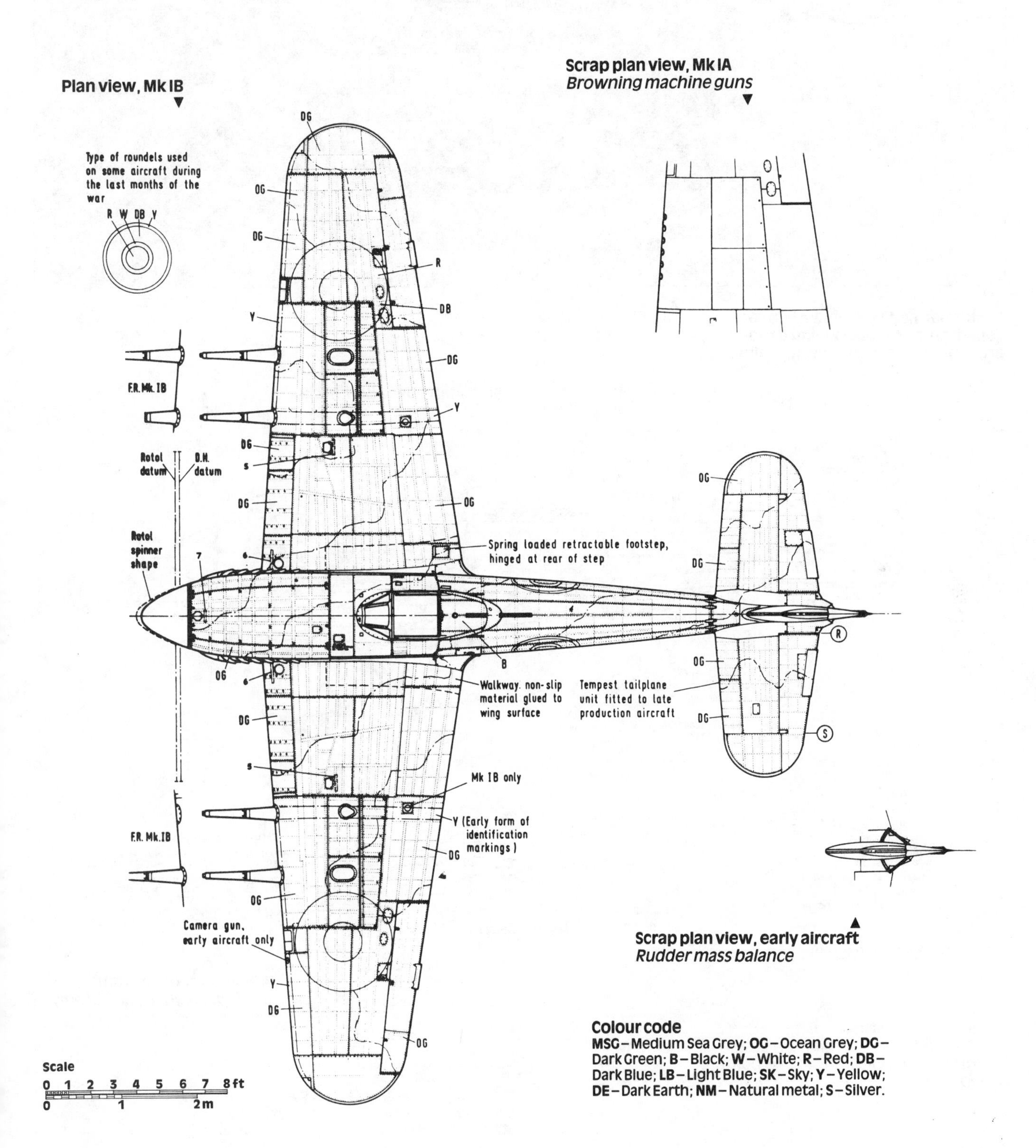

Colour code
MSG – Medium Sea Grey; **OG** – Ocean Grey; **DG** – Dark Green; **B** – Black; **W** – White; **R** – Red; **DB** – Dark Blue; **LB** – Light Blue; **SK** – Sky; **Y** – Yellow; **DE** – Dark Earth; **NM** – Natural metal; **S** – Silver.

▲
Cannon-armed Typhoons of No 56 Squadron. Note yellow wing bands prominent on two nearest machines.

Starboard elevation, Mk IB
▼

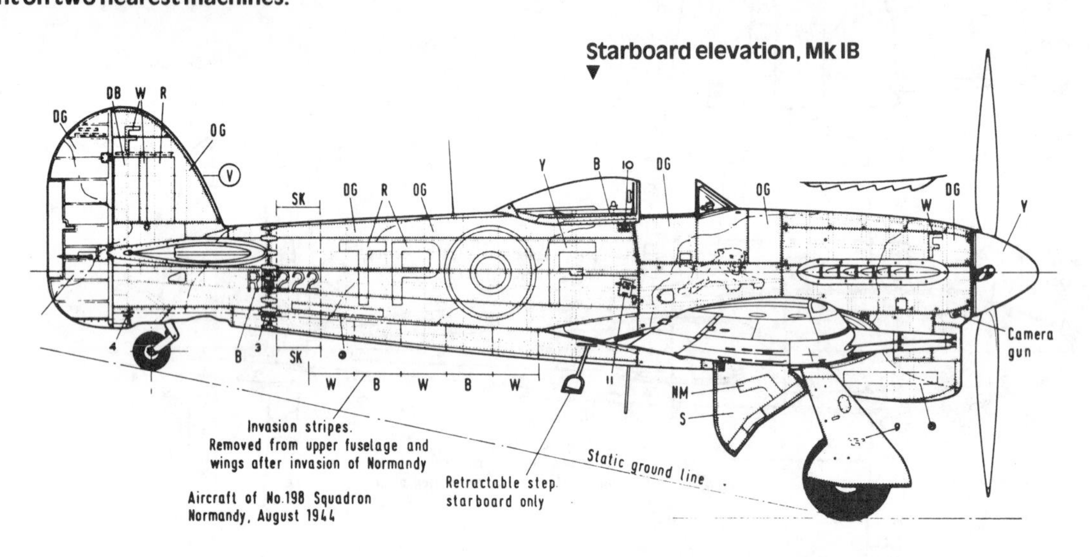

1. OIL X/X
CAPACITY OIL 16 GALLS
AIR SPACE 2 GALLS

2. FIRST AID

3. TRESTLE HERE

4. JACK HERE

5. FUEL 100 OCTANE (RED)

6. FUEL 100 OCTANE

7. COOLANT (BLUE)

8. TRESTLE HERE

▲
Stencilled instructions
Black lettering, 1in high, unless otherwise indicated; arrows point forward

9. PRESSURE 45 lbs

10. TO OPEN PULL DOWN STEP

11. HAND FOOT PUSH

Black lettering, ½in high

Port lower rear fuselage
IF FATE DECREES THAT I SHOULD FAIL
THEN FATE WILL NOT HAVE WATCHED MY TAIL

IF THIS ENGINE CATCHES FIRE ON STARTING
DON'T JUST WAVE YOUR ARMS AT THE PILOT–
TRY PUTTING THE BLOODY THING OUT AS WELL
Starboard radiator

▲
Hand-painted lettering
Black, 1in high, on RB222 only

Y&B

W

Port lower centre fuselage panel

◄ **Personal markings**
RB222 only

Wing and tailplane cross-sections ▼

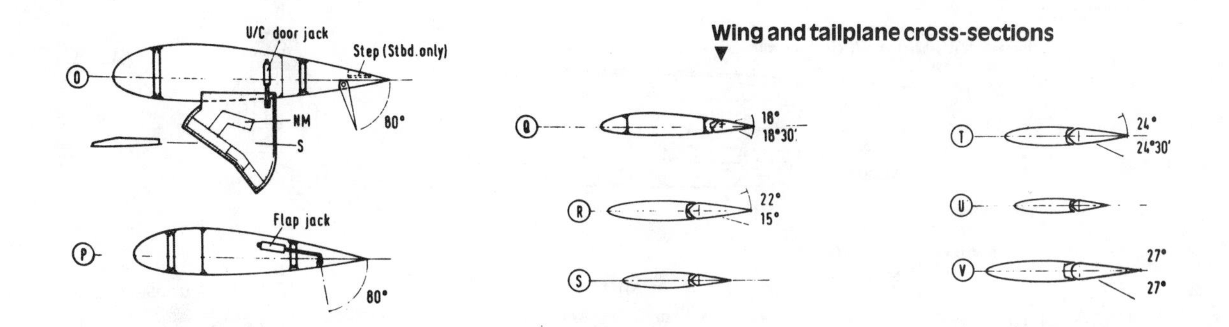

Wing incidence 0°
Tailplane incidence -0·5°

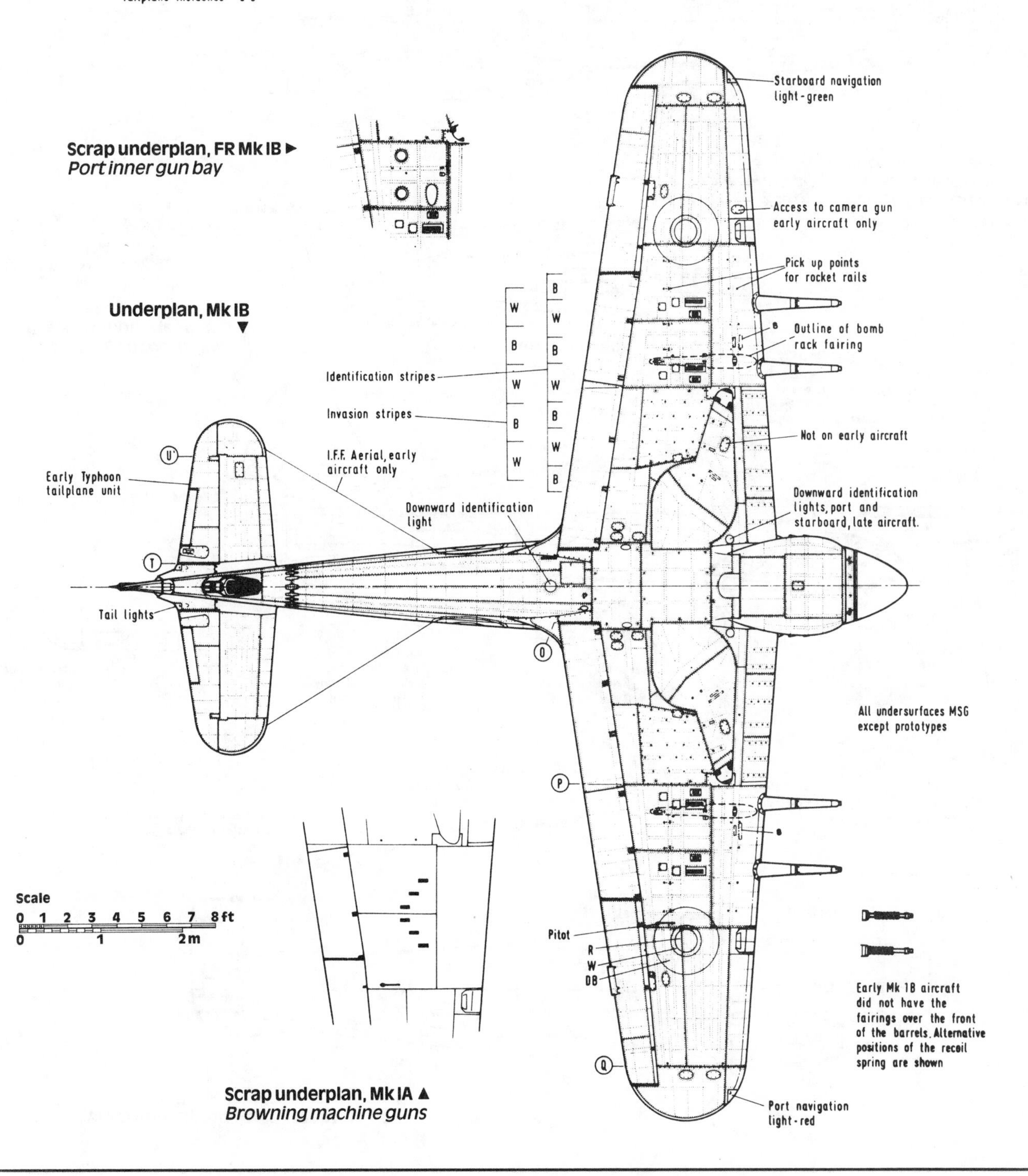

Scrap underplan, FR Mk IB ►
Port inner gun bay

Underplan, Mk IB ▼

Scrap underplan, Mk IA ▲
Browning machine guns

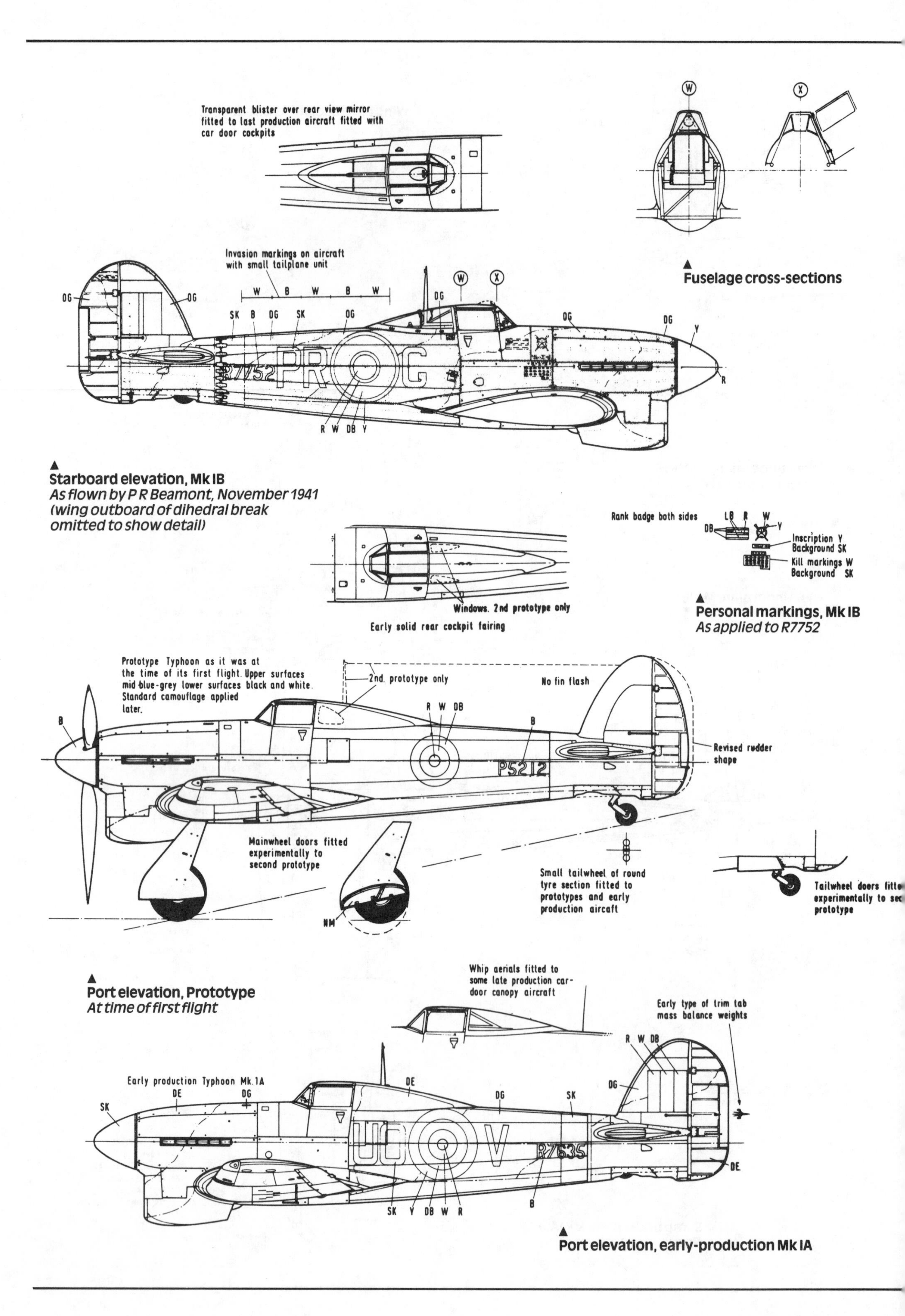

▲ **Fuselage cross-sections**

▲ **Starboard elevation, Mk IB**
As flown by P R Beamont, November 1941 (wing outboard of dihedral break omitted to show detail)

▲ **Personal markings, Mk IB**
As applied to R7752

▲ **Port elevation, Prototype**
At time of first flight

▲ **Port elevation, early-production Mk IA**

DRAWN BY A L BENTLEY

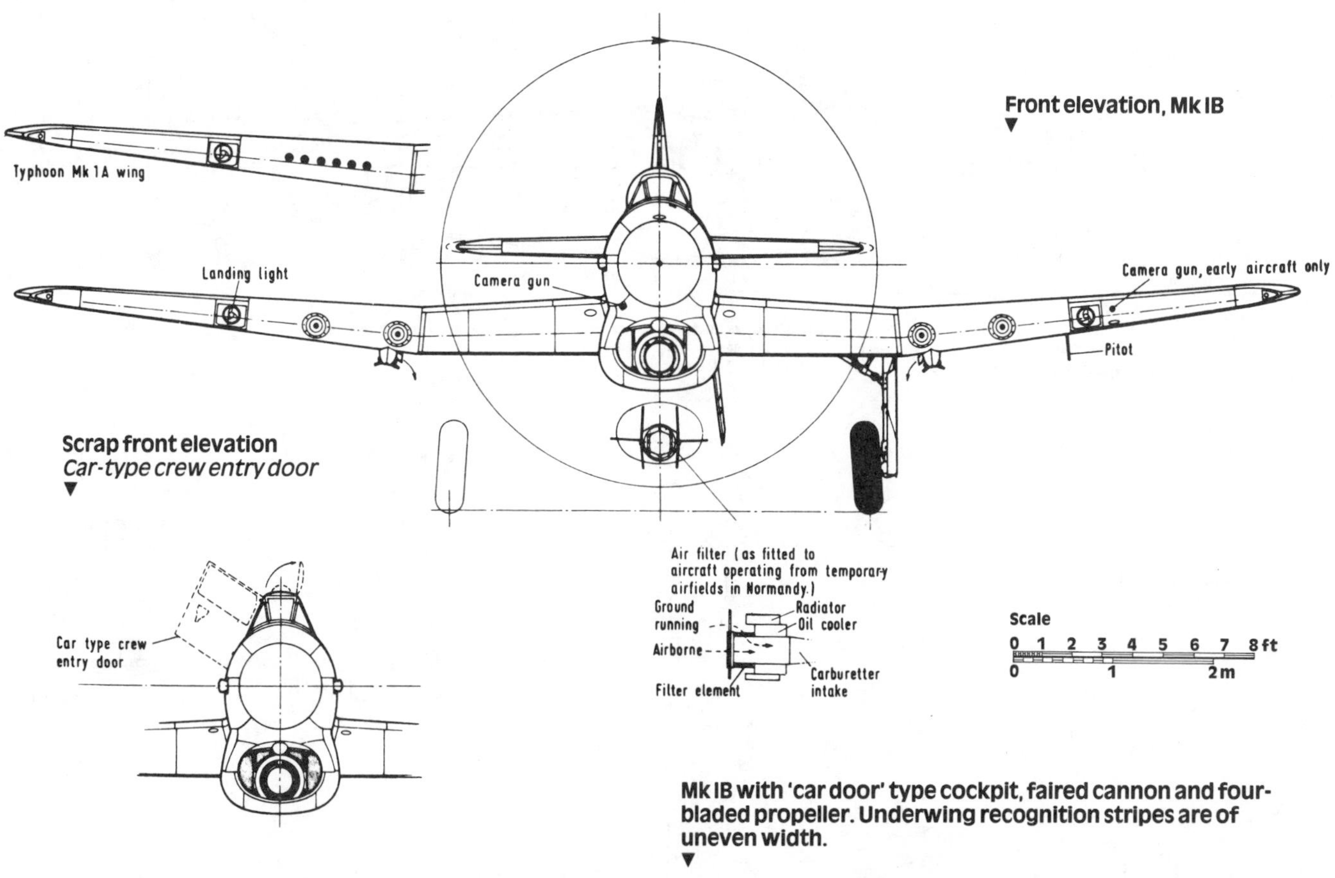

Mk IB with 'car door' type cockpit, faired cannon and four-bladed propeller. Underwing recognition stripes are of uneven width.

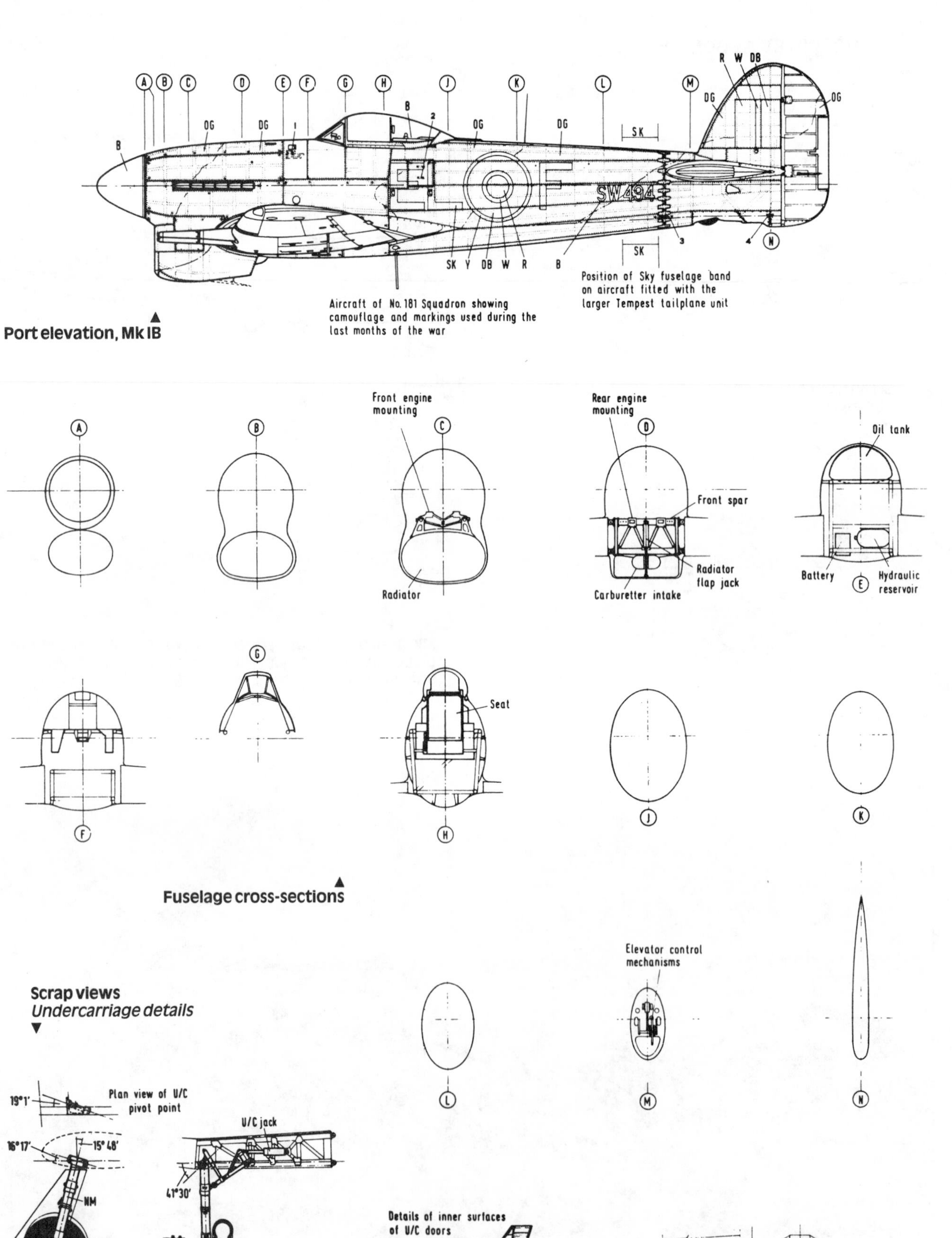

Port elevation, Mk IB

Fuselage cross-sections

Scrap views
Undercarriage details

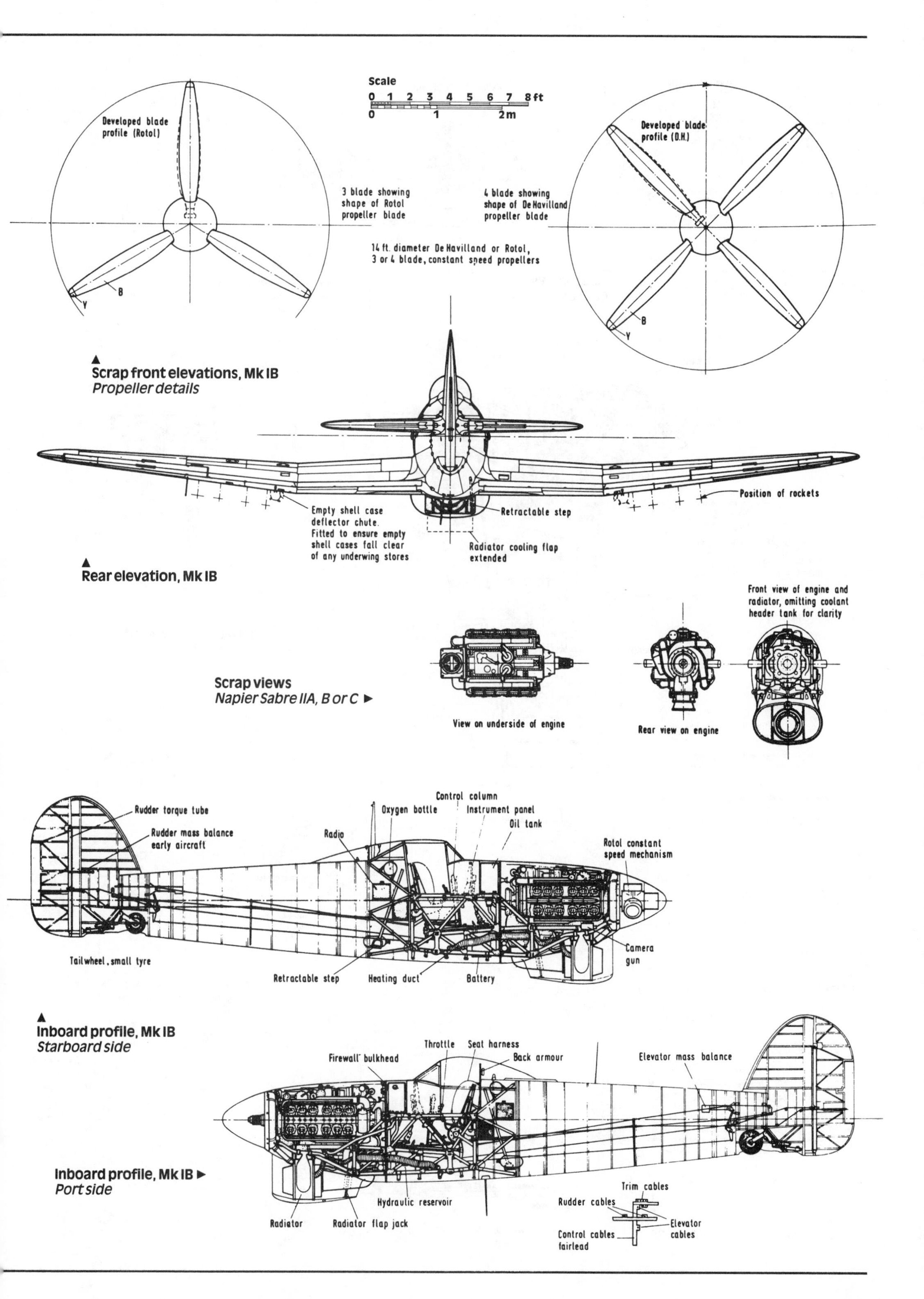

▲ **Scrap front elevations, Mk IB**
Propeller details

▲ **Rear elevation, Mk IB**

Scrap views
Napier Sabre IIA, B or C ►

▲ **Inboard profile, Mk IB**
Starboard side

Inboard profile, Mk IB ►
Port side

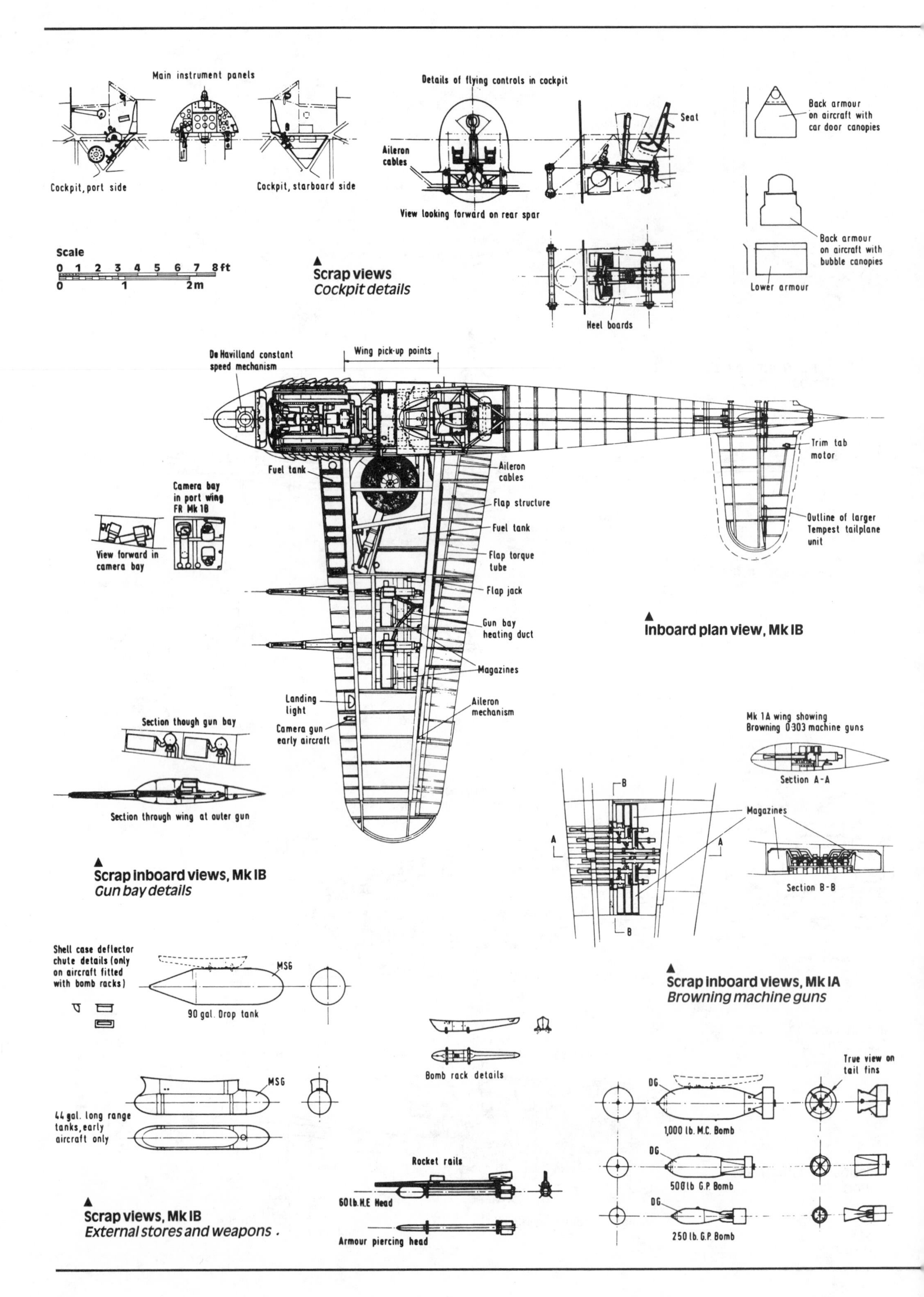
Main instrument panels
Cockpit, port side
Cockpit, starboard side
Details of flying controls in cockpit
Aileron cables
View looking forward on rear spar
Seat
Heel boards
Back armour on aircraft with car door canopies
Back armour on aircraft with bubble canopies
Lower armour
Scale
0 1 2 3 4 5 6 7 8ft
0 1 2m
Scrap views
Cockpit details
De Havilland constant speed mechanism
Wing pick-up points
Fuel tank
Aileron cables
Flap structure
Fuel tank
Flap torque tube
Flap jack
Gun bay heating duct
Magazines
Aileron mechanism
Landing light
Camera gun early aircraft
Trim tab motor
Outline of larger Tempest tailplane unit
Inboard plan view, Mk IB
Camera bay in port wing FR Mk IB
View forward in camera bay
Section though gun bay
Section through wing at outer gun
Scrap inboard views, Mk IB
Gun bay details
Mk 1A wing showing Browning 0·303 machine guns
Section A-A
Magazines
Section B-B
Scrap inboard views, Mk IA
Browning machine guns
Shell case deflector chute details (only on aircraft fitted with bomb racks)
MSG
90 gal. Drop tank
Bomb rack details
44 gal. long range tanks, early aircraft only
MSG
Rocket rails
60 lb. H.E Head
Armour piercing head
True view on tail fins
DG
1,000 lb. M.C. Bomb
500 lb G.P. Bomb
250 lb. G.P. Bomb
Scrap views, Mk IB
External stores and weapons .

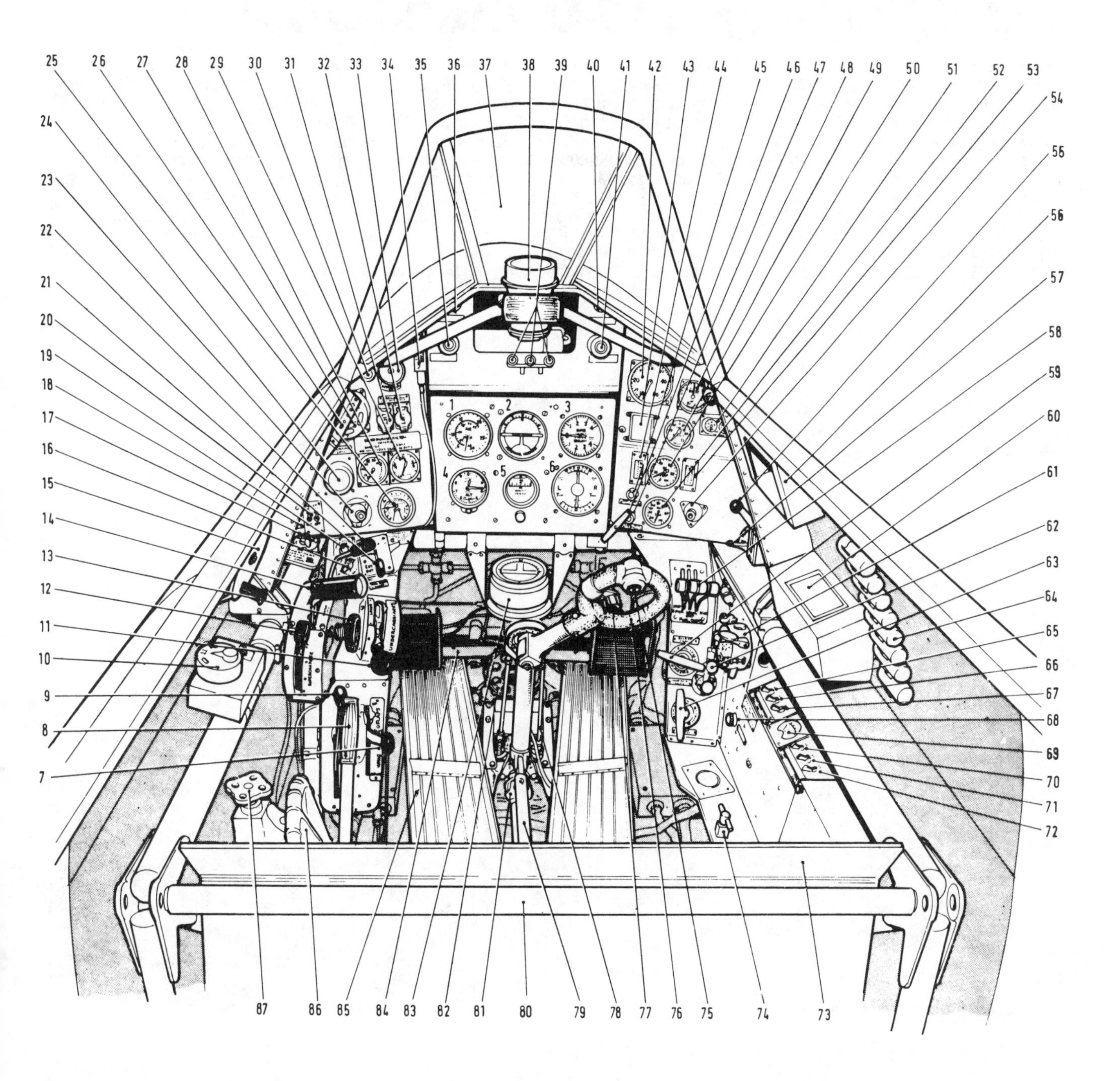

Numerical key

1. Airspeed indicator. **2.** Artificial horizon. **3.** Rate of climb indicator. **4.** Altimeter. **5.** Direction indicator. **6.** Turn and bank indicator. **7.** Flap lever. **8.** Hydraulic hand pump. **9.** Radiator shutter lever. **10.** Gunsight control weapons selector box. **11.** Undercarriage lever. **12.** Supercharger lever. **13.** Throttle friction knob. **14.** Throttle lever. **15.** Canopy winding handle. **16.** Reading lamp switch. **17.** Undercarriage emergency release switch. **18.** Undercarriage indicator lights. **19.** Beam approach button. **20.** Magnetic switches. **21.** Cut-out safety control. **22.** Propeller pitch lever. **23.** Punkah louvres (late models only). **24.** Watch holder. **25.** Wheel brake pressure indicators. **26.** T.R. 1143 control unit. **27.** Undercarriage indicators. **28.** Oxygen delivery indicator. **29.** Oxygen supply indicator. **30.** Contractor switch. **31.** Engine starting, boost coil switch. **32.** Engine starting starter switch. **33.** Remote contactor. **34.** Flap position indicator. **35.** Reflector sight switch. **36.** Cockpit light switch (port). **37.** Armoured windscreen. **38.** Gunsight. **39.** Spare bulbs for gunsight. **40.** Cockpit light switch (starboard). **41.** Compass light switch. **42.** Rev counter. **43.** Compass card. **44.** Oil pressure indicator. **45.** Fuel pressure indicator light. **46.** Hood jettison lever. **47.** Power failure warning light. **48.** Boost gauge. **49.** Fuel contents (main tank). **50.** Oil temperature indicator. **51.** Fuel contents (wing tanks). **52.** Radiator temperature indicator. **53.** Fuel pressure gauge. **54.** Punkah louvre (late models). **55.** Cockpit heating lever. **56.** Very pistol opening. **57.** Fuel tank pressure lever. **58.** Fuel cocks (inter, main and nose tanks). **59.** Cylinder priming pump. **60.** Engine data card. **61.** Signalling switch box. **62.** Windscreen anti-icing pumps. **63.** Carburettor priming pump. **64.** Very pistol cartridge stowage. **65.** Pressure head heating switch. **66.** T.R. 1143 master switch. **67.** Heated clothing switch. **68.** Dimmer switch. **69.** Voltmeter. **70.** Navigation light switch. **71.** Rising switch. **72.** Camera master switch. **73.** Lower seat armour plate (upper armour omitted for clarity). **74.** Cartridge starter reload handle. **75.** Gun button. **76.** Control column. **77.** Radio button. **78.** Push rods for aileron control. **79.** Elevator control push rod. **80.** Basic front fuselage structure of tubular steel. **81.** Universal joint, aileron torque tube. **82.** Handwheel for rudder bar adjustment. **83.** Compass. **84.** Rudder bar. **85.** Heel boards (no floor as such to cockpit). **86.** Elevator trim wheel. **87.** Rudder trim wheel.

Republic P-47B and D Thunderbolt

Country of origin: USA.
Type: Single-seat, long-range fighter or (D) escort fighter or fighter-bomber.
Dimensions: Wing span 40ft 9¾in *12.20m*; length 35ft 3¼in *10.75m*, (D) 36ft 1¾in *11.02m*; height 14ft 1¾in *4.31m*, (D) 14ft 7in *4.45m*; wing area 300 sq ft *27.87m²*.
Weights: Empty 9346lb *4240kg*, (D-22) 9900lb *4492kg*, (D-35) 10,000lb *4537kg*; normal loaded 12,245lb *5556kg*, (D-22) 13,500lb *6125kg*, (D-35) 14,000lb *6352kg*; maximum 13,360lb *6062kg*, (D-22) 15,000lb *6806kg*, (D-35) 17,500lb *7940kg*.
Powerplant: One Pratt & Whitney R-2800-21 eighteen-cylinder radial engine rated at 2000hp (D-22) R-2800-21 rated at 2300hp, (D-35) R-2800-59 rated at 2535hp.
Performance: Maximum speed 429mph *691kph* at 27,000ft *8230m*, (D-22) 433mph *697kph* at 30,000ft *9150m*, (D-35) 426mph *686kph* at 30,000ft; initial climb rate about 2600ft/min *800m/min*; service ceiling 42,000ft *12,800m*, (D-22) 40,000ft *12,200m*; range (clean) 550 miles *885km* at 10,000ft *3050m*, (D-22) 640 miles *1030km* at 25,000ft *7620m*, (D-35) 590 miles *950km* at 25,000ft.
Armament: Eight fixed 0.5in Browning machine guns, plus (D-22) one 500lb *227kg* bomb or (D-35) three 500lb bombs or ten 5in *127mm* rockets.
Service: First flight (XB-47B) 6 May 1941; service entry (P-47B) June 1942.

'Razorbacks' in OD and 'bubble-hoods' in natural metal: P-47s in the snow. Note bomb on wing pylon of nearest aircraft. ▼

DRAWN BY G R DUVAL

Colour code
NG – Neutral Gray; OD – Olive Drab; B – Black; BL – Blue; R – Red; CY – Chrome yellow; W – White; GD – Dark green; LG – Light grey; DSG – Dark Sea Grey; AB – Azure blue; DB – Dark blue; NM – Natural metal.

Scale

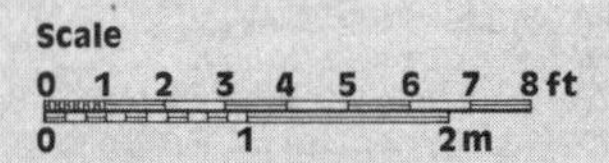

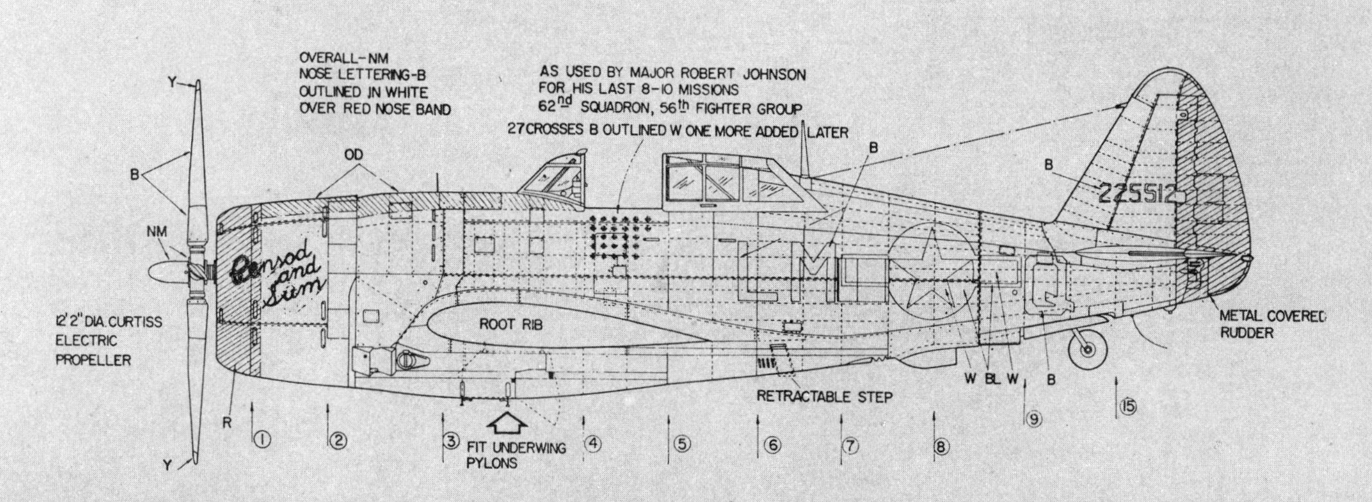

Port elevation, P-47D-22-RE

Note that machines prior to P-47D-25 had fabric-covered rudder and elevators; modification was made to metal-covered surfaces, as shown, in the field

Fuselage cross-sections

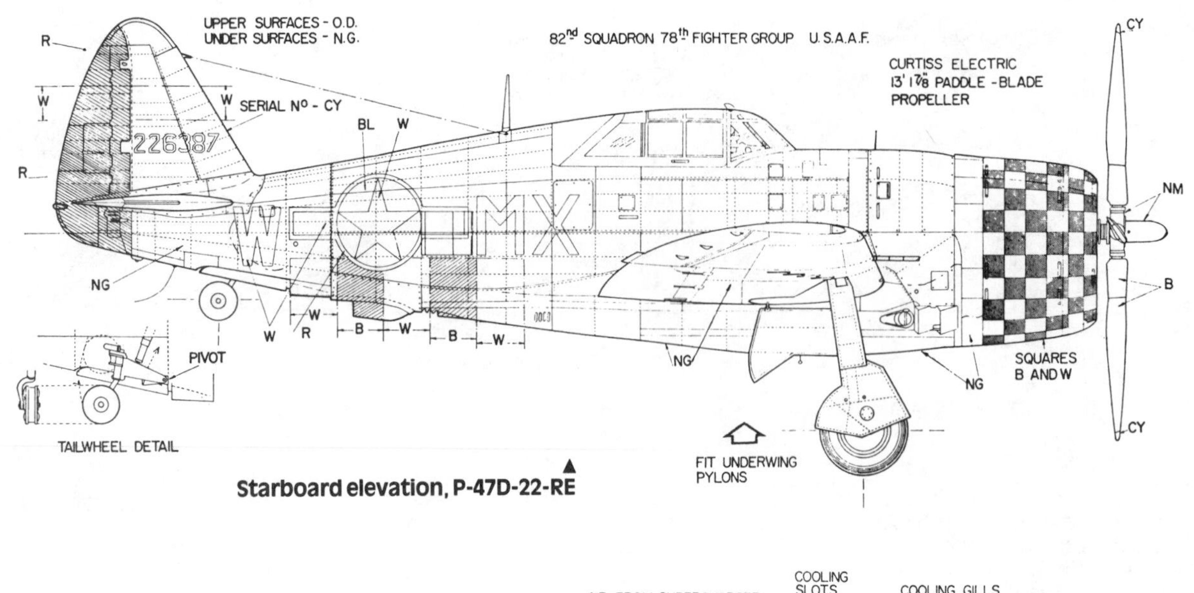

▲ **Starboard elevation, P-47D-22-RE**

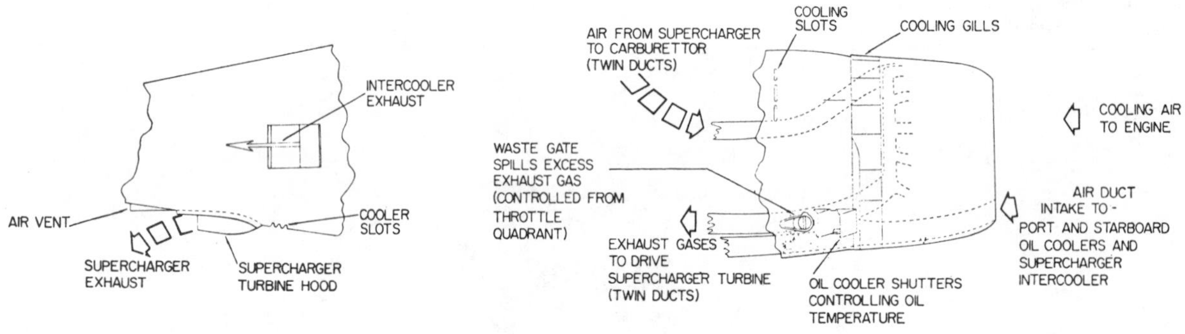

▲ **Scrap views**
Engine details

High-set bubble canopy gave pilots of late-type P-47s a much improved all-round view. Fin fillet is evident on this aircraft.
▼

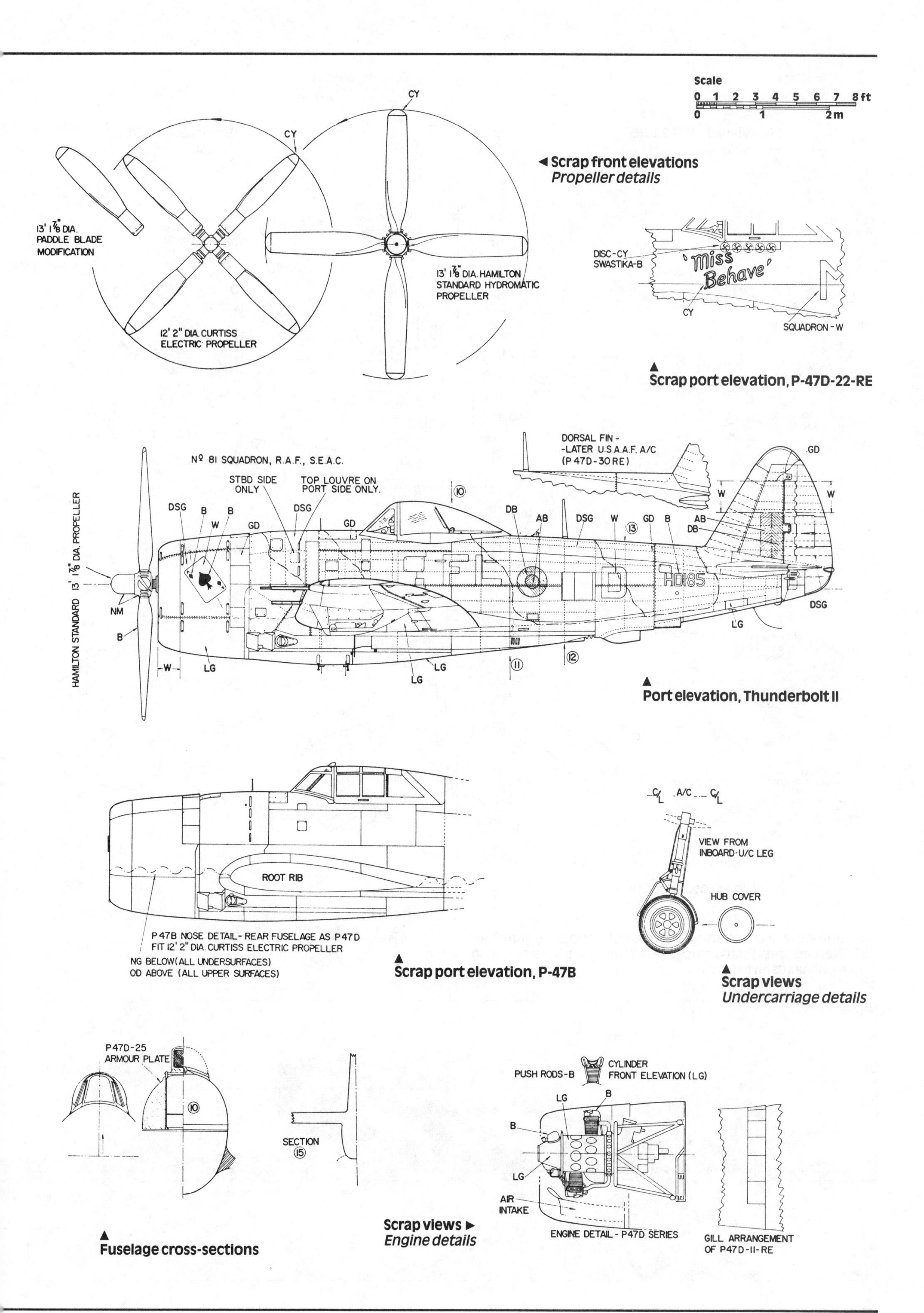

◄ **Scrap front elevations**
Propeller details

▲ **Scrap port elevation, P-47D-22-RE**

▲ **Port elevation, Thunderbolt II**

▲ **Scrap port elevation, P-47B**

▲ **Scrap views**
Undercarriage details

▲ **Fuselage cross-sections**

Scrap views ►
Engine details

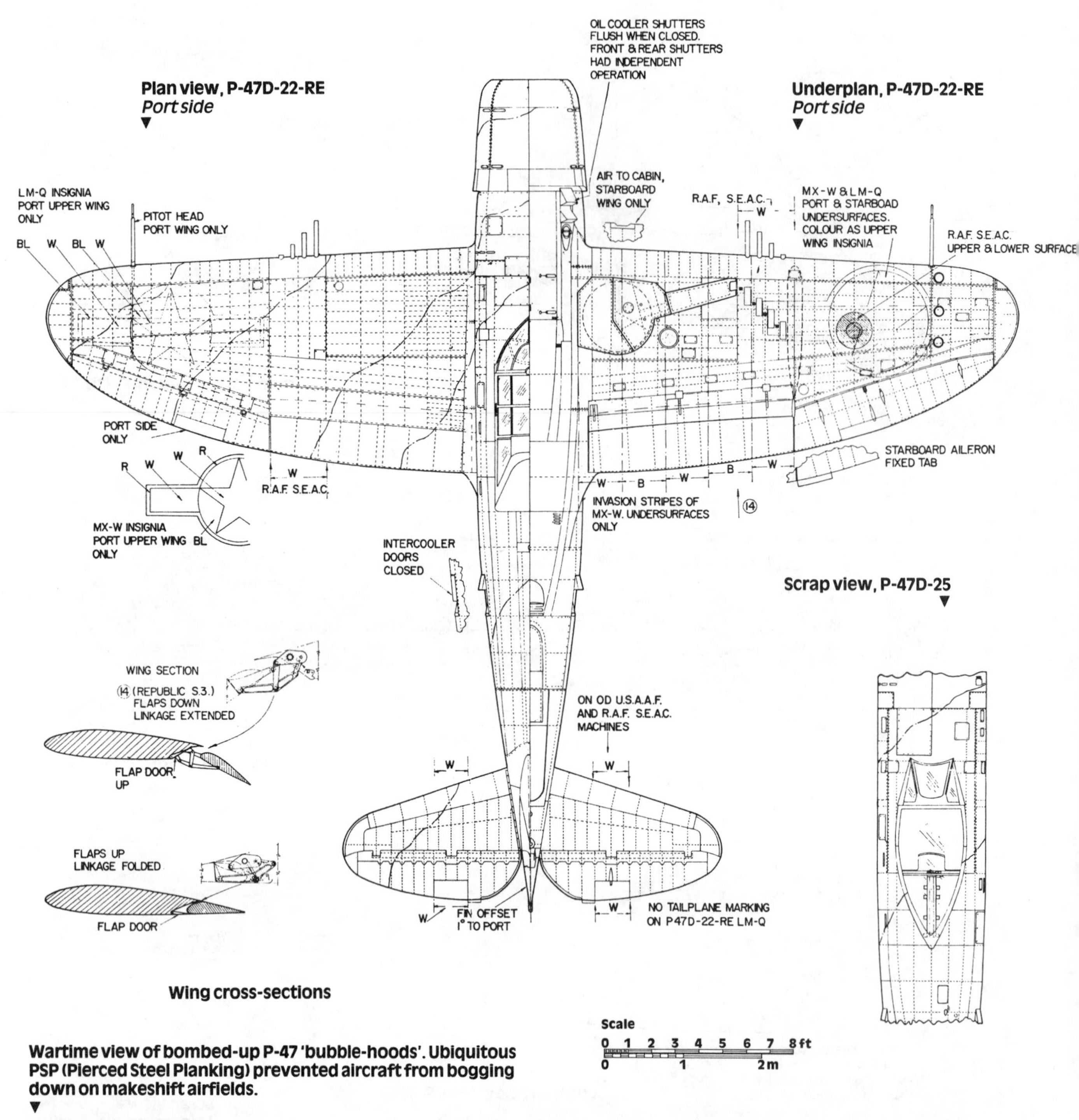

Wartime view of bombed-up P-47 'bubble-hoods'. Ubiquitous PSP (Pierced Steel Planking) prevented aircraft from bogging down on makeshift airfields.

▲
The sheer brute size of the P-47 Thunderbolt is obvious in this photo taken in the Far East. Note white cowling band and staggered wing guns.

Front elevation, P-47D-22-RE
▼

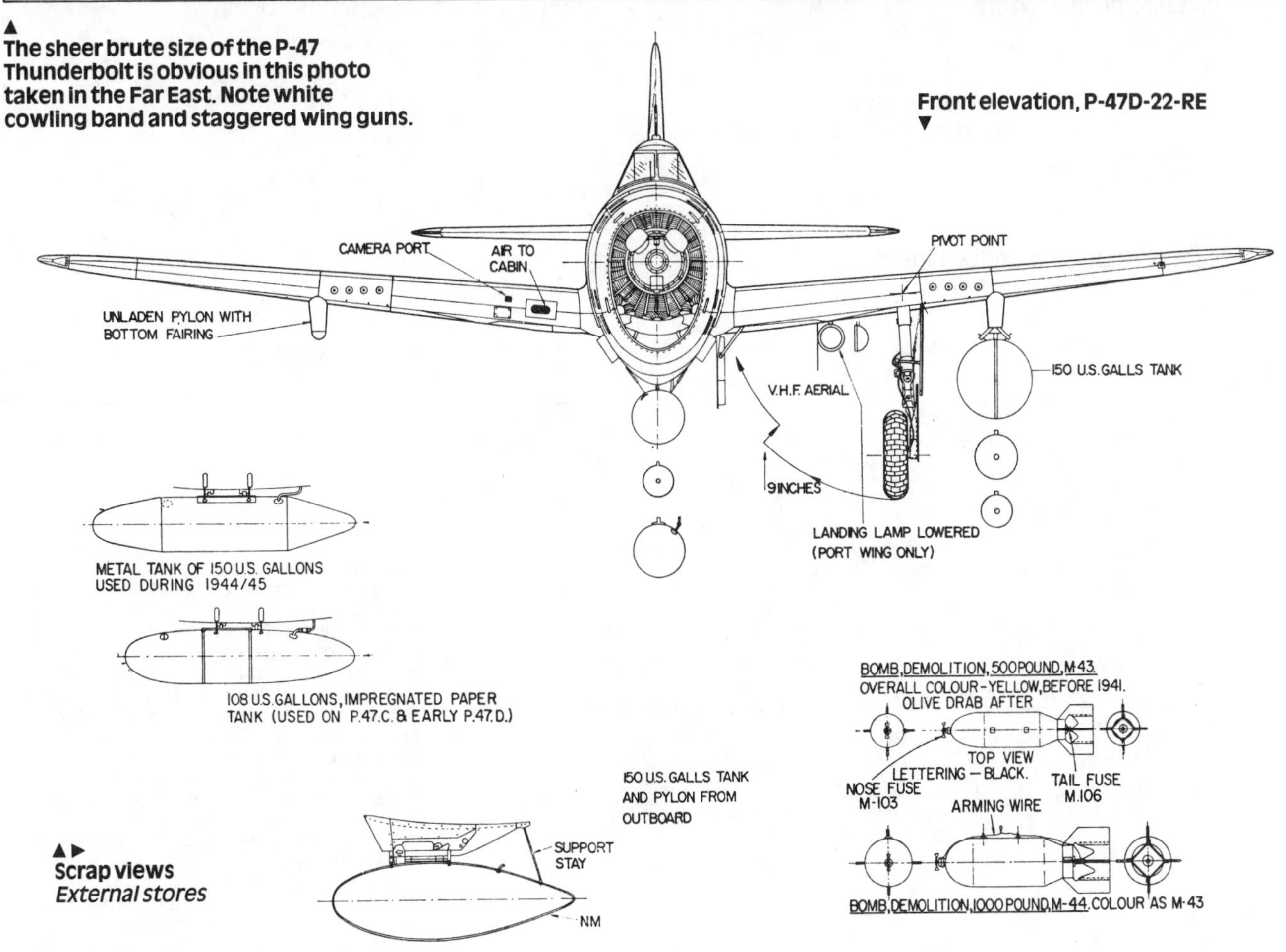

▲▶
Scrap views
External stores

Flamboyant markings characterised P-47 schemes as the end of the war approached, as shown in this view of a preserved aircraft. ►

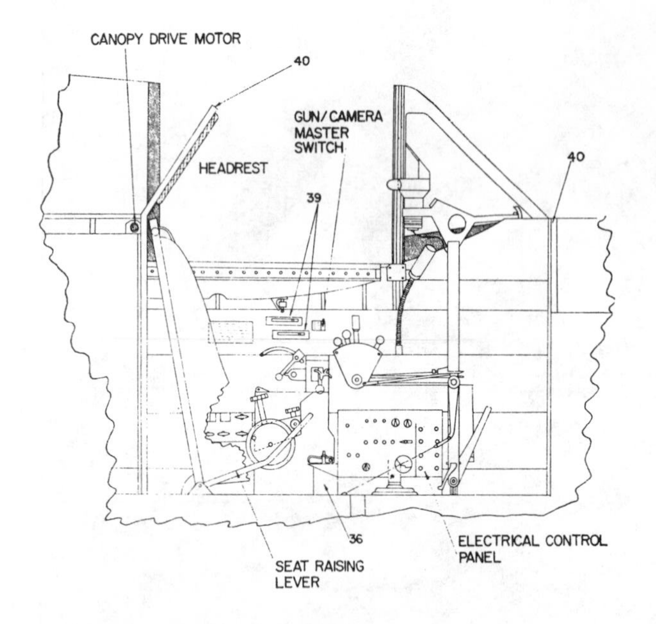

▲
Cockpit details
Port side, bubble canopy

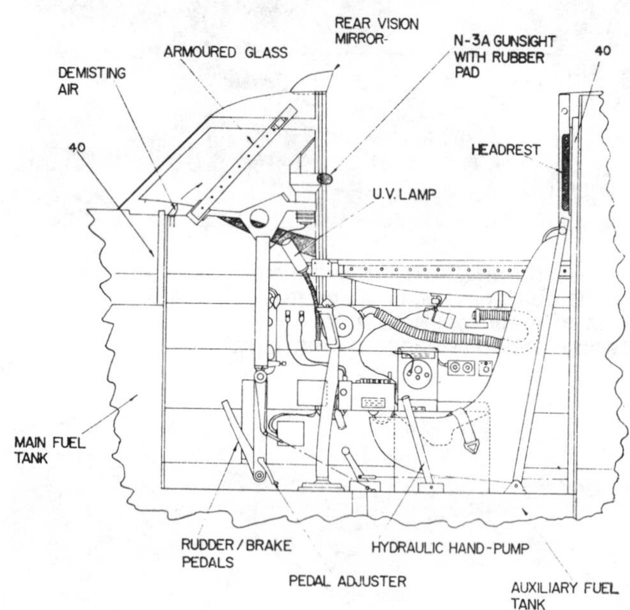

Cockpit details
Starboard side, framed canopy ►

Cockpit details, P-47 series (typical)
General view, framed canopy
▼

Numerical key

1. Airspeed indicator. **2.** Altimeter. **3.** Data plate. **4.** Artificial horizon. **5.** Vertical speed indicator. **6.** Starter switch. **7.** Suction gauge. **8.** Carburettor temperature. **9.** RPM. **10.** Oil pressure temperature. **11.** Priming pump. **12.** Gills control. **13.** Oxygen pressure. **14.** Oxygen regulator. **15.** VHF radio control. **16.** Detrola radio (radio range). **17.** Tailwheel lock. **18.** Destructor buttons. **19.** Map and data case. **20.** Cylinder head temperature. **21.** Manifold pressure. **22.** Fuel pressure. **23.** Compass. **24.** Turn and bank. **25.** Directional gyro. **26.** Cylinder head temperature. **27.** Supercharger RPM. **28.** Propeller de-icing. **29.** Fuel change. **30.** Trimmers. **31.** Bomb/tank release. **32.** Throttle. **33.** Mixture. **34.** Pitch. **35.** Supercharger. **36.** Fuel cock control. **37.** Flap and undercarriage controls. **38.** Ignition switch. **39.** Oil cooler and intercooler shutter plate. **40.** Armour plate. **41.** Parking brake. **42.** Elevator trim.

Supermarine Spitfire Mks IX and XVI

Country of origin: Great Britain.
Type: Single-seat, land-based fighter and fighter-bomber.
Dimensions: Wing span (Mk IX standard) 36ft 10in *11.23m*, (Mk IX clipped, Mk XVI) 32ft 7in *9.93m*; length (Mk IX) 31ft 3½in *9.54m*, (Mk XVI) 31ft 3in *9.53m*; height (maximum) 12ft 7¾in *3.84m*; wing area (Mk IX standard) 242 sq ft *22.48m²*, (Mk IX clipped, Mk XVI) 231 sq ft *21.46m²*.
Weights: Empty 5800lb *2632kg*, maximum loaded 7500lb *3403kg*.
Powerplant: (F Mk IX) One Rolls-Royce Merlin 61 or 63 V12, liquid-cooled piston engine rated at 1710hp, (LF Mk IX) Merlin 66 rated at 1720hp, (HF Mk IX) Merlin 70 rated at 1710hp, (Mk XVI) Merlin 266 rated at 1720hp.
Performance: Maximum speed (F/LF Mk IX, Mk XVI) 404mph *650kph* at 21,000ft *6400m*, (HF Mk IX) 416mph *670kph* at 27,500ft *8380m*; time to 20,000ft *6100m*, 6.4min; service ceiling (F/LF Mk IX, Mk XVI) 42,500ft *12,950m*, (HF Mk IX) 45,000ft *13,720m*; range (normal) 434 miles *700km*, (maximum external fuel) 980 miles *1575km*..
Armament: Two fixed 20mm Hispano cannon and ('C' wing) four fixed 0.303in or ('E' wing) two fixed 0.5in Browning machine guns; (optional) one 500lb *227kg* plus two 250lb *113kg* bombs.
Service: Service entry (Mk IX) July 1942, (Mk XVI) 1944.

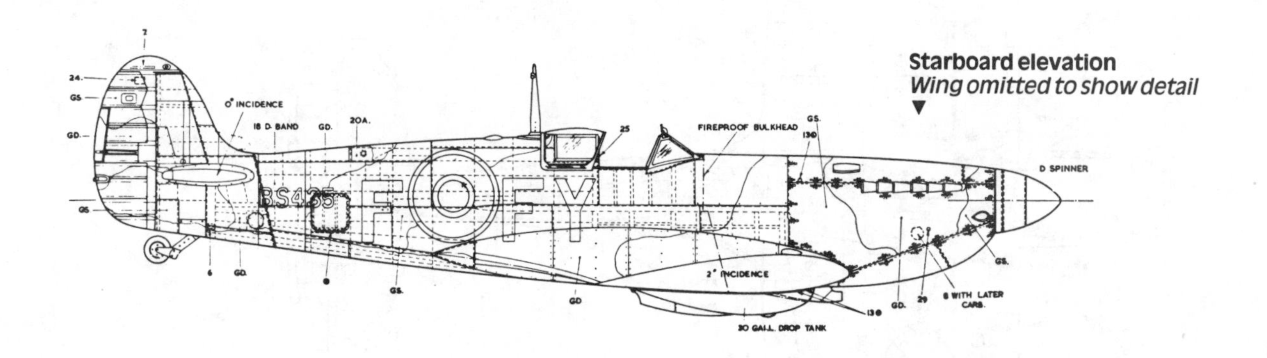

Starboard elevation
Wing omitted to show detail

Spitfire Mk VIIIs of No 136 Squadron, South-East Asia Command; national markings are dark and light blue. The Mk VIII differed little from the Mk IX in external appearance, apart from the shape of the fin tip.

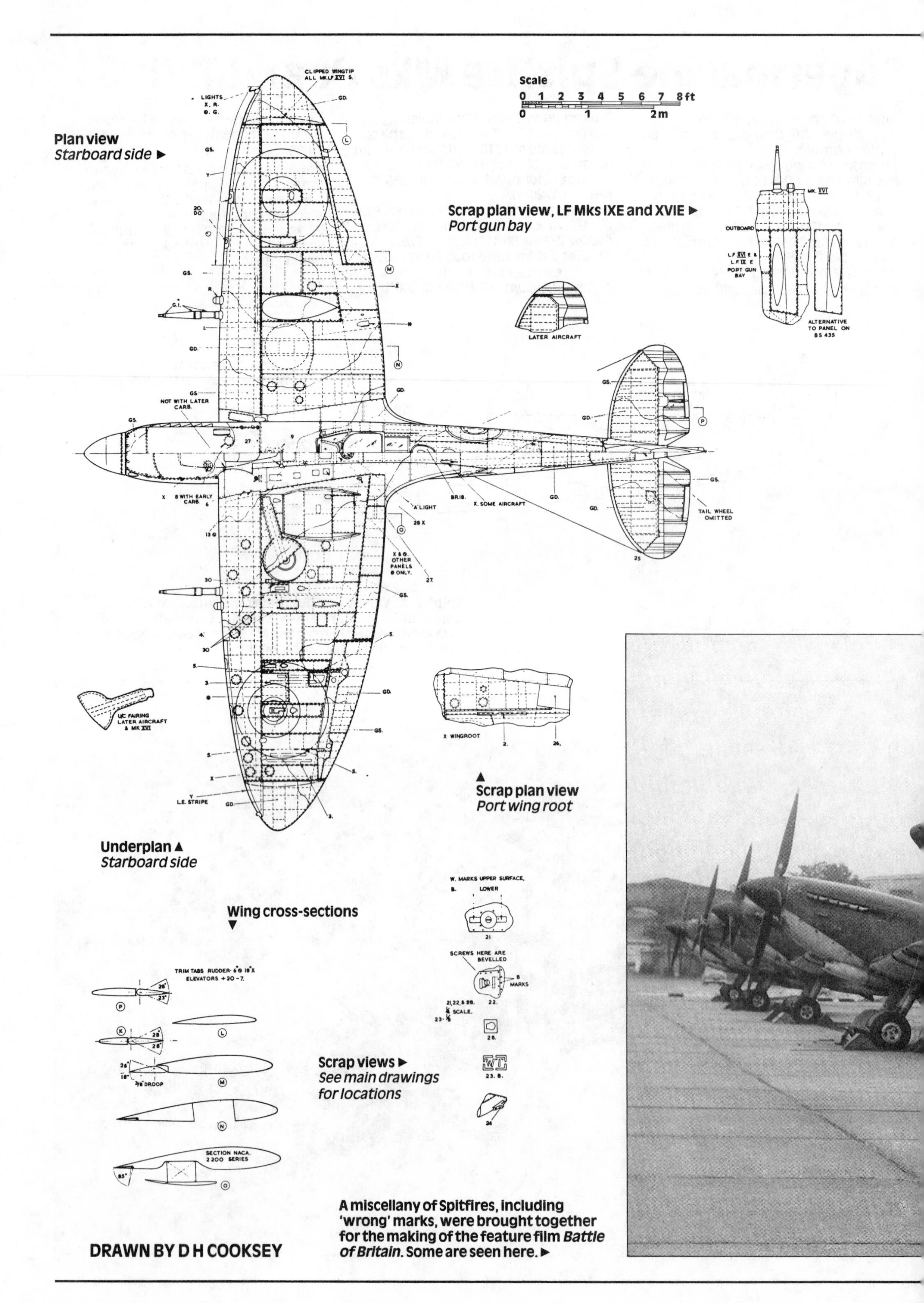

A miscellany of Spitfires, including 'wrong' marks, were brought together for the making of the feature film *Battle of Britain*. Some are seen here. ►

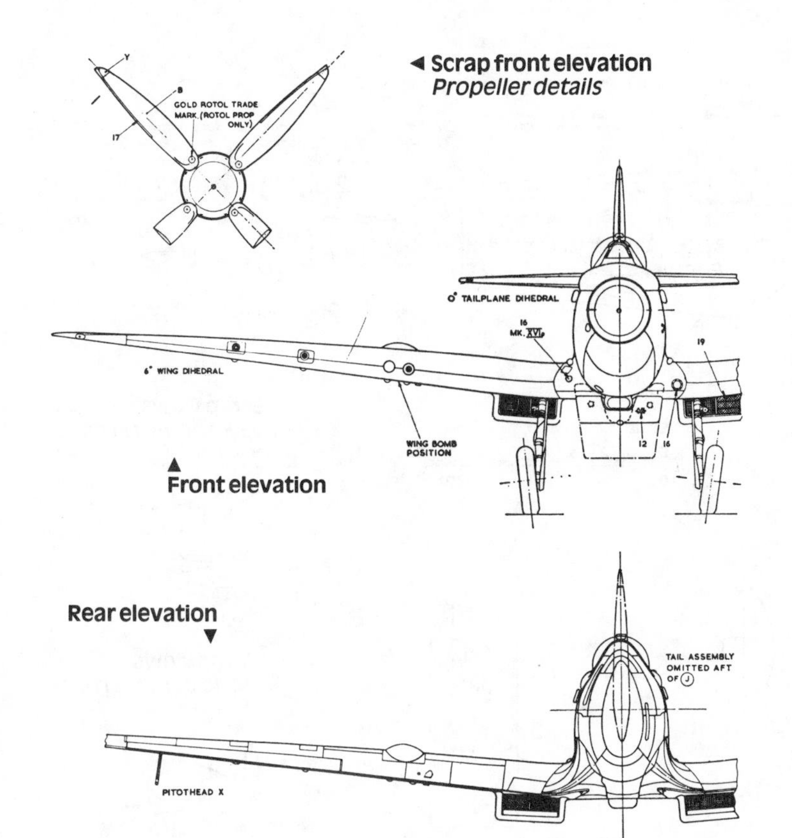

◄ **Scrap front elevation**
Propeller details

▲
Front elevation

Rear elevation
▼

Numerical key

1. Walkway forward. **2.** Walkway inboard. **3.** Location for wingtip steadying trestle. **4.** B dotted lines ¼in × ¾in. **5.** B dotted lines 1in × ½in. **6.** Jack here. **7.** 68/168917. **8.** Engine starting plug. **9.** 100 octane, capacity 85 galls. **10, 11.** Electrical and radio socket. **12.** Fuel, octane 100, 30 galls. **13.** Small B pipes. **14.** Cockpit cover emergency release. **15.** Mirror. **16.** Camera gunport. **17.** Brass strip, Jablo prop only. **18.** BR fibre aerial insulator. **19.** Hexagonal honeycomb. **20, 20A.** DO patches over gunports. **25.** Armour plate. **26.** B foothold sheet like sandpaper. **27.** Drop tank attachment points. **29.** 1in dia flush pipe angled back. **30.** Wing bomb attachment points.
Note: All stencilling black.

Colour code

A – Amber; **B** – Black; **BR** – Brown; **D** – Duck Egg Blue; **DO** – Dope; **G** – Green; **GD** – Dark Green; **GL** – Light grey; **GM** – Mid-grey; **GS** – Dark Sea Grey; **W** – White; **Y** – Yellow; **R** – Red; **BM** – Bare metal (all drop tanks).

Notes

Aircraft are matt overall, then wax polished. All camouflage divisions sprayed. Entire undersides, undercarriage and undercarriage wells – GL; No 611 Squadron code letters – GL; serial – B. X = port only; ⊘ = starboard only; * = hinged and sprung; ● = hinged.

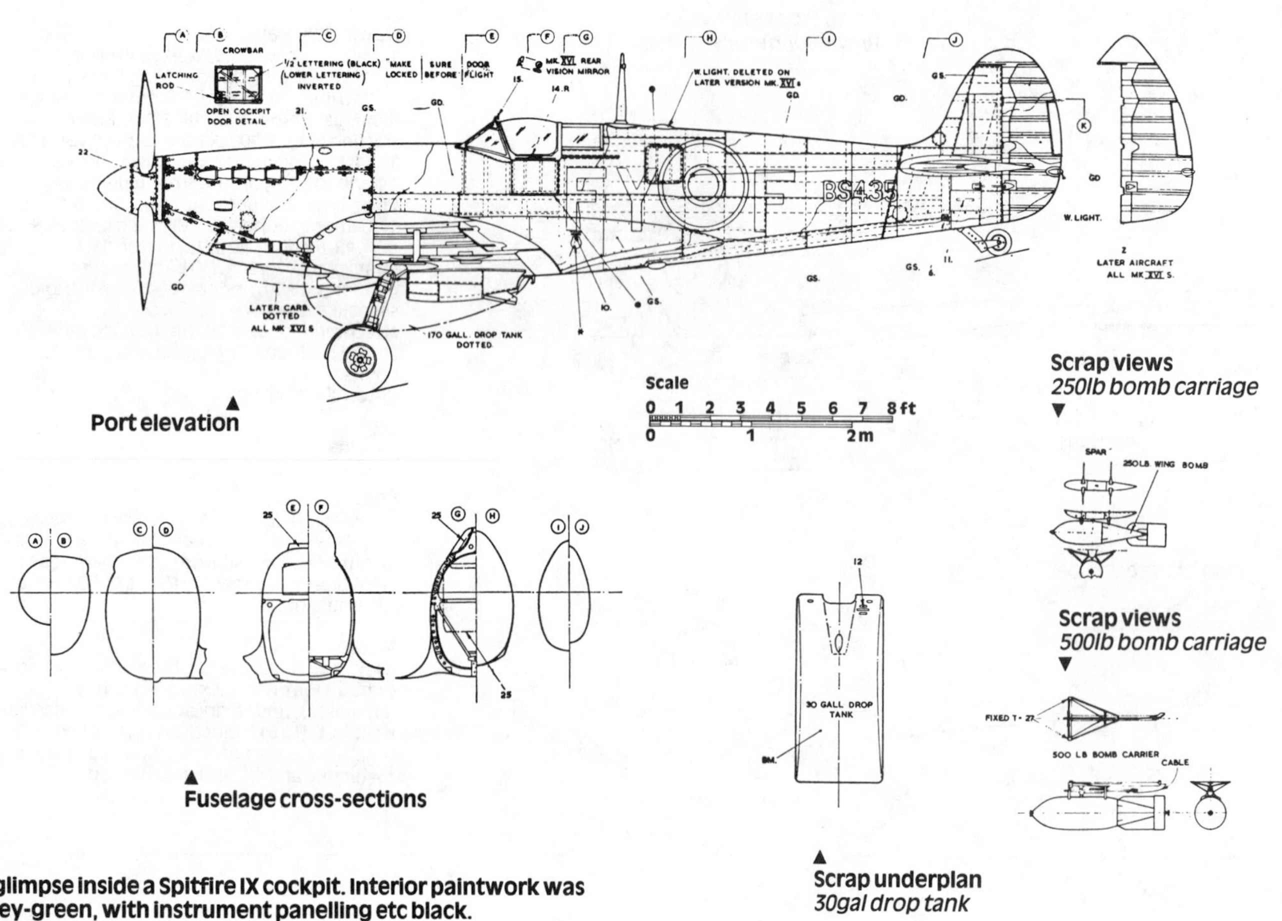

▲
Port elevation

Scale
0 1 2 3 4 5 6 7 8 ft
0 1 2 m

Scrap views
250lb bomb carriage
▼

Scrap views
500lb bomb carriage
▼

▲
Fuselage cross-sections

▲
Scrap underplan
30gal drop tank

A glimpse inside a Spitfire IX cockpit. Interior paintwork was grey-green, with instrument panelling etc black.
▼

De Havilland Mosquito Mks II, IV and VI

Country of origin: Great Britain.
Type: Two-seat, land-based fighter, (NF Mk II) night fighter, (B Mk IV) bomber and (FB Mk VI) fighter-bomber.
Dimensions: Wing span 54ft 2in *16.51m*; length (F Mk II, FB Mk VI) 41ft 2in *12.55m*, (B Mk IV) 40ft 9½in *12.43m*; height 15ft 3½in *4.66m*; wing area 420 sq ft *39.01m²*.
Weights: (FB Mk VI) Empty 14,300lb *6488kg*; normal loaded 19,500lb *8848kg*; maximum 22,300lb *10,118kg*.
Powerplant: (F Mk II, B Mk IV) Two Rolls-Royce Merlin 21 or 23 V12, liquid-cooled piston engines each rated at 1460hp at 6250ft *1905m*, (FB Mk VI) Merlin 21, 23 or 25 rated at 1460hp or 1635hp.
Performance: Maximum speed (Mk II) 407mph *655kph* at 28,000ft *8535m*, (FB Mk VI) 380mph *612kph* at 13,000ft *3960m*; initial climb rate (FB Mk VI) 1870ft/min *570m/min*; time to 15,000ft *4570m*, (Mk II) 6.75min (FB Mk VI) 9.5min; service ceiling (Mk II) 34,500ft *10,515m*, (FB Mk VI) 33,000ft *10,060m*; range (Mk II, clean) 1520 miles *2445km* at 255 mph *410kph* and 15,000ft, (FB Mk VI, clean) 1270 miles *2045km*.
Armament: (Mk II) Four fixed 20mm Hispano cannon; (B Mk IV) up to 4000lb *1815kg* of bombs; (FB Mk VI) four fixed 20mm Hispano cannon and four fixed 0.303in Browning machine guns plus up to 2000lb *907kg* of bombs and eight 60lb *27kg* rocket projectiles.
Service: First flight (prototype) 25 November 1940, (Mk II) 15 May 1941; service entry (Mk II, B Mk IV) May 1942, (FB Mk VI) May 1943.

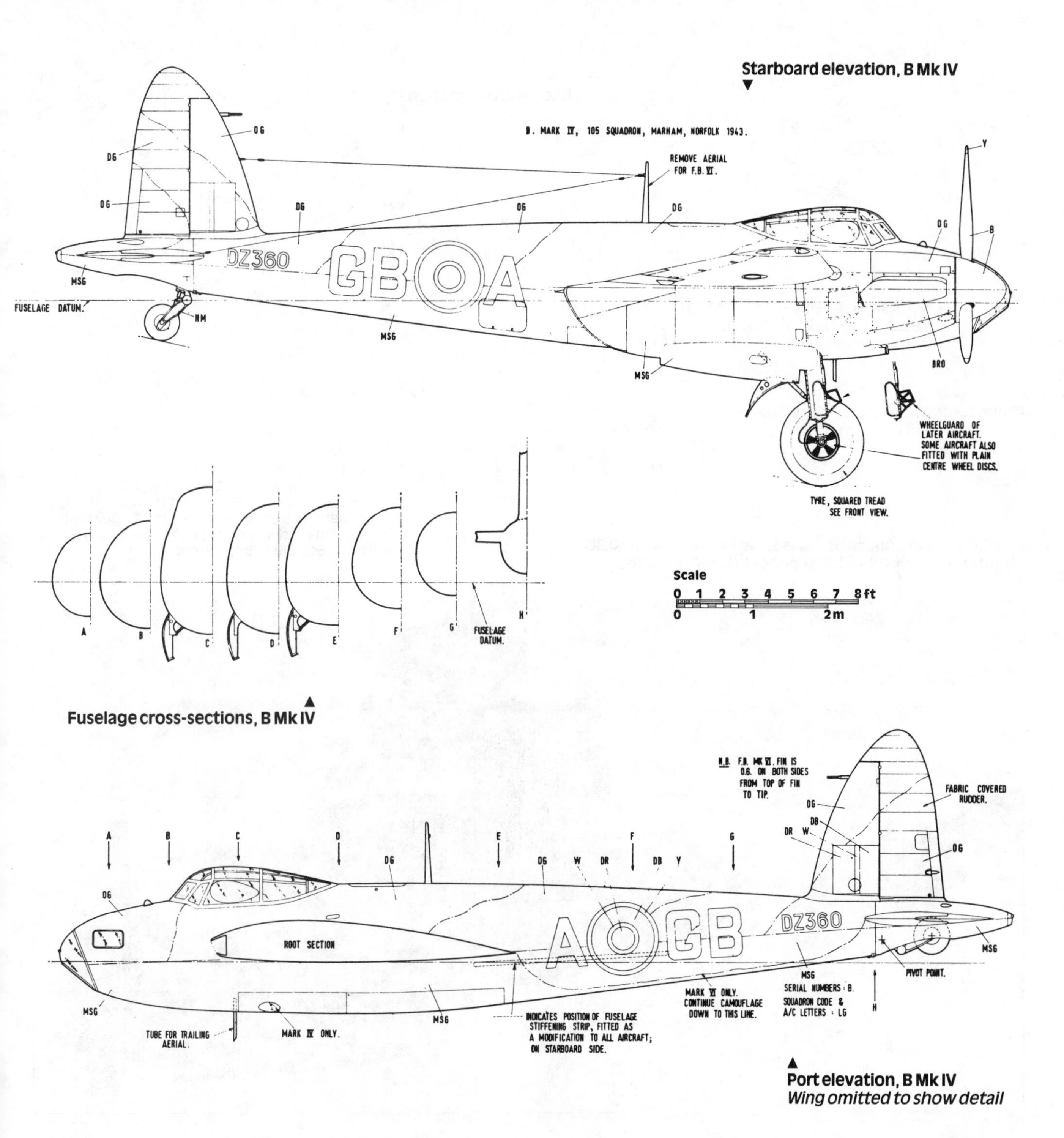

Starboard elevation, B Mk IV

Fuselage cross-sections, B Mk IV

Port elevation, B Mk IV
Wing omitted to show detail

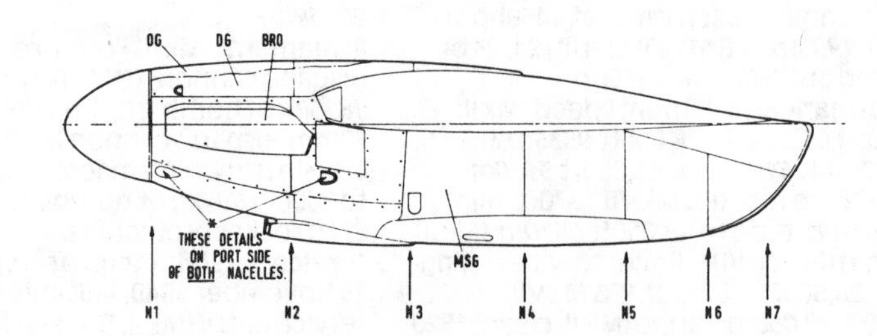

◀ **Scrap port elevation, B Mk IV**
*Starboard nacelle (for port inboard view, delete details marked *)*

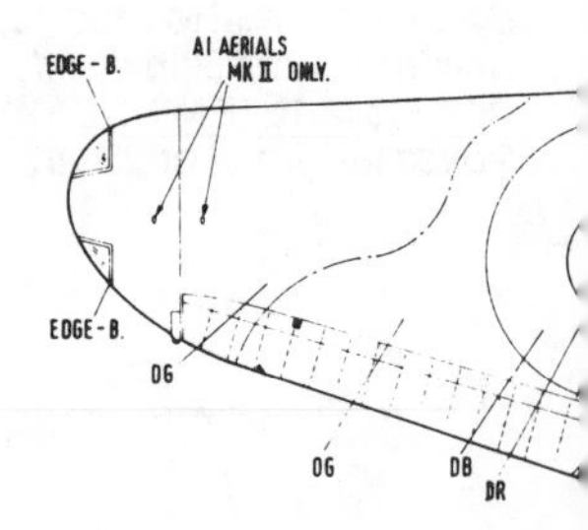

Nacelle cross-sections
▼

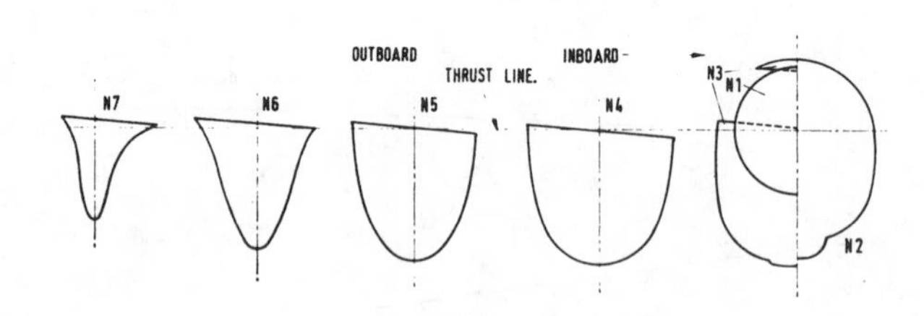

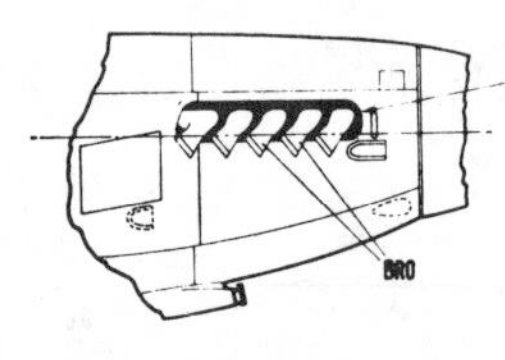

▲
Scrap starboard elevation, FB Mk VI
Note that some Mk IVs also had unshrouded exhausts

Scale
0 1 2 3 4 5 6 7 8 ft
0 1 2 m

Colour code
DG–Dark Green; **OG**–Ocean Grey; **MSG**–Medium Sea Grey; **Si**–Silver; **NM**–Natural metal; **LG**–Light grey; **B**–Black; **DB**–Dull Blue; **DR**–Dull Red; **W**–White; **Y**–Yellow; **S**–Sky (Duck Egg Blue); **BRO**–Bronze.

Official wartime photo of a Mosquito FB Mk VI, with 500lb bombs underwing. Markings denote No 487 Squadron.
▼

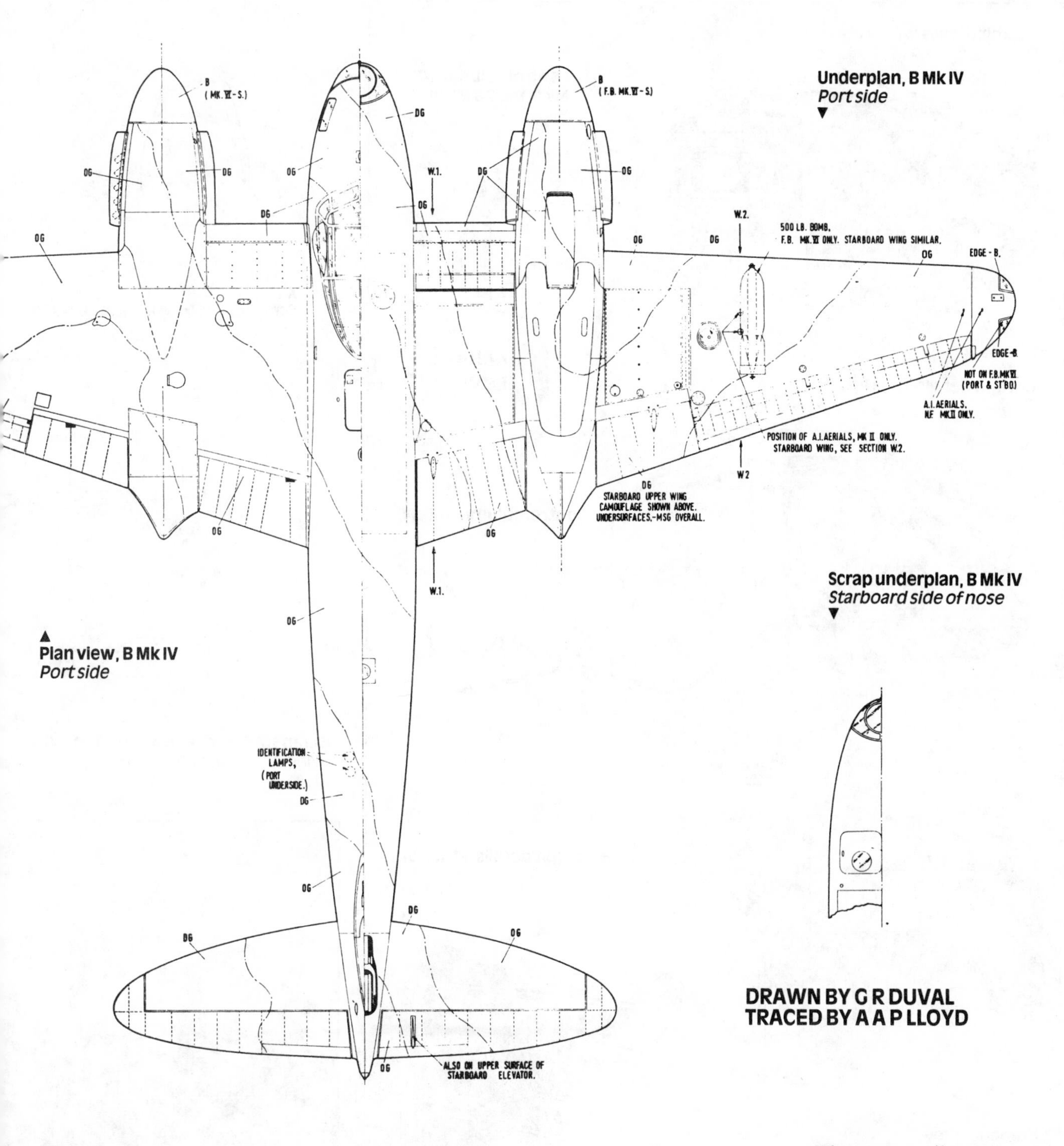

Underplan, B Mk IV
Port side

Plan view, B Mk IV
Port side

Scrap underplan, B Mk IV
Starboard side of nose

DRAWN BY G R DUVAL
TRACED BY A A P LLOYD

Wing cross-sections

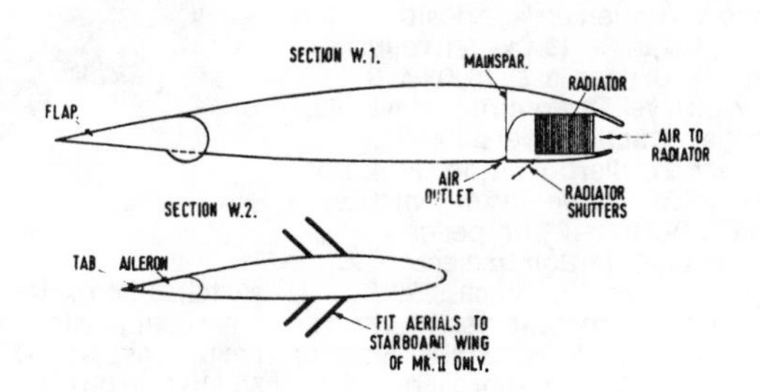

Colour notes

NF Mk II: Overall semi-matt Night black; standard national markings; serial numbers Dull Red, and also squadron code letters which were applied at a later date. Representative serial number – DD750.

FB Mk VI: Camouflage as B Mk IV; squadron codes Sky; spinner Sky; 18in Sky band around rear fuselage, from leading edge of fin fillet forward. These details apply to aircraft HP927, SY-B, of No 613 Squadron.

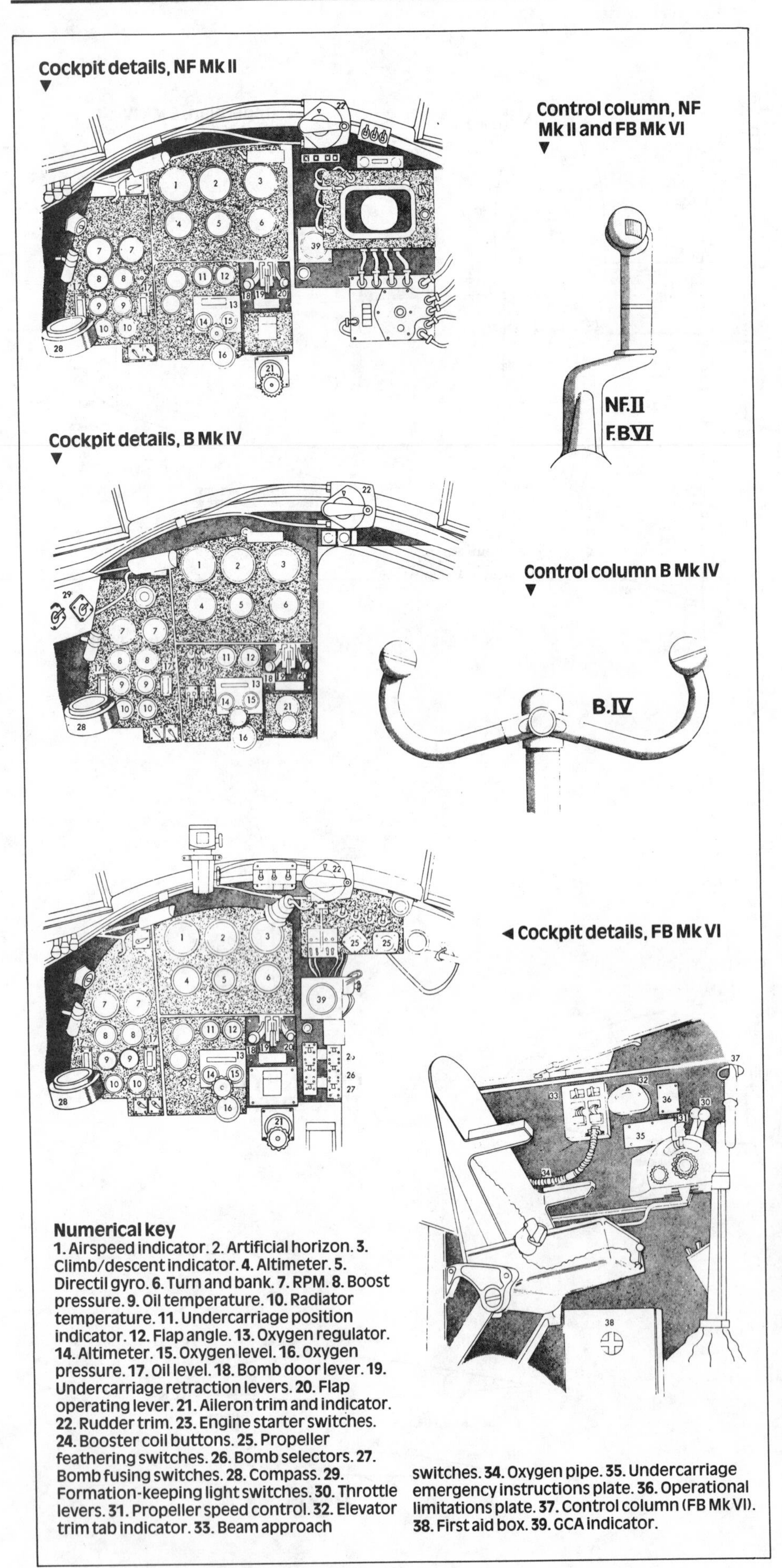

Cockpit details, NF Mk II ▼

Control column, NF Mk II and FB Mk VI ▼

Cockpit details, B Mk IV ▼

Control column B Mk IV ▼

◄ Cockpit details, FB Mk VI

Numerical key
1. Airspeed indicator. **2.** Artificial horizon. **3.** Climb/descent indicator. **4.** Altimeter. **5.** Directil gyro. **6.** Turn and bank. **7.** RPM. **8.** Boost pressure. **9.** Oil temperature. **10.** Radiator temperature. **11.** Undercarriage position indicator. **12.** Flap angle. **13.** Oxygen regulator. **14.** Altimeter. **15.** Oxygen level. **16.** Oxygen pressure. **17.** Oil level. **18.** Bomb door lever. **19.** Undercarriage retraction levers. **20.** Flap operating lever. **21.** Aileron trim and indicator. **22.** Rudder trim. **23.** Engine starter switches. **24.** Booster coil buttons. **25.** Propeller feathering switches. **26.** Bomb selectors. **27.** Bomb fusing switches. **28.** Compass. **29.** Formation-keeping light switches. **30.** Throttle levers. **31.** Propeller speed control. **32.** Elevator trim tab indicator. **33.** Beam approach switches. **34.** Oxygen pipe. **35.** Undercarriage emergency instructions plate. **36.** Operational limitations plate. **37.** Control column (FB Mk VI). **38.** First aid box. **39.** GCA indicator.

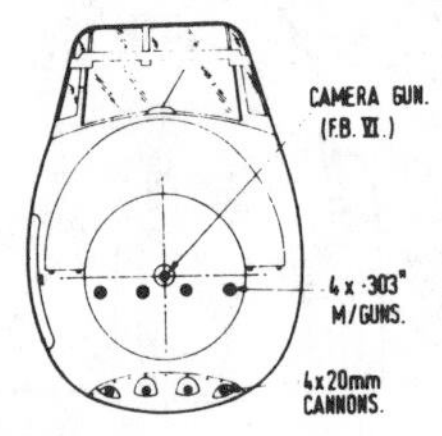

▲► Scrap views, NF Mk II and FB Mk VI

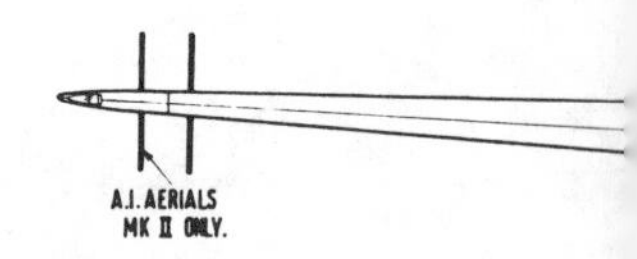

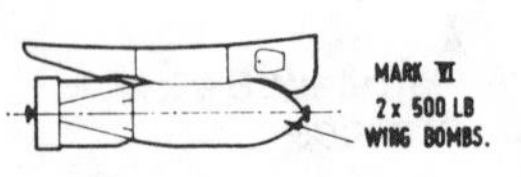

Scrap starboard elevation, FB Mk VI ▲
Wing bomb carriage

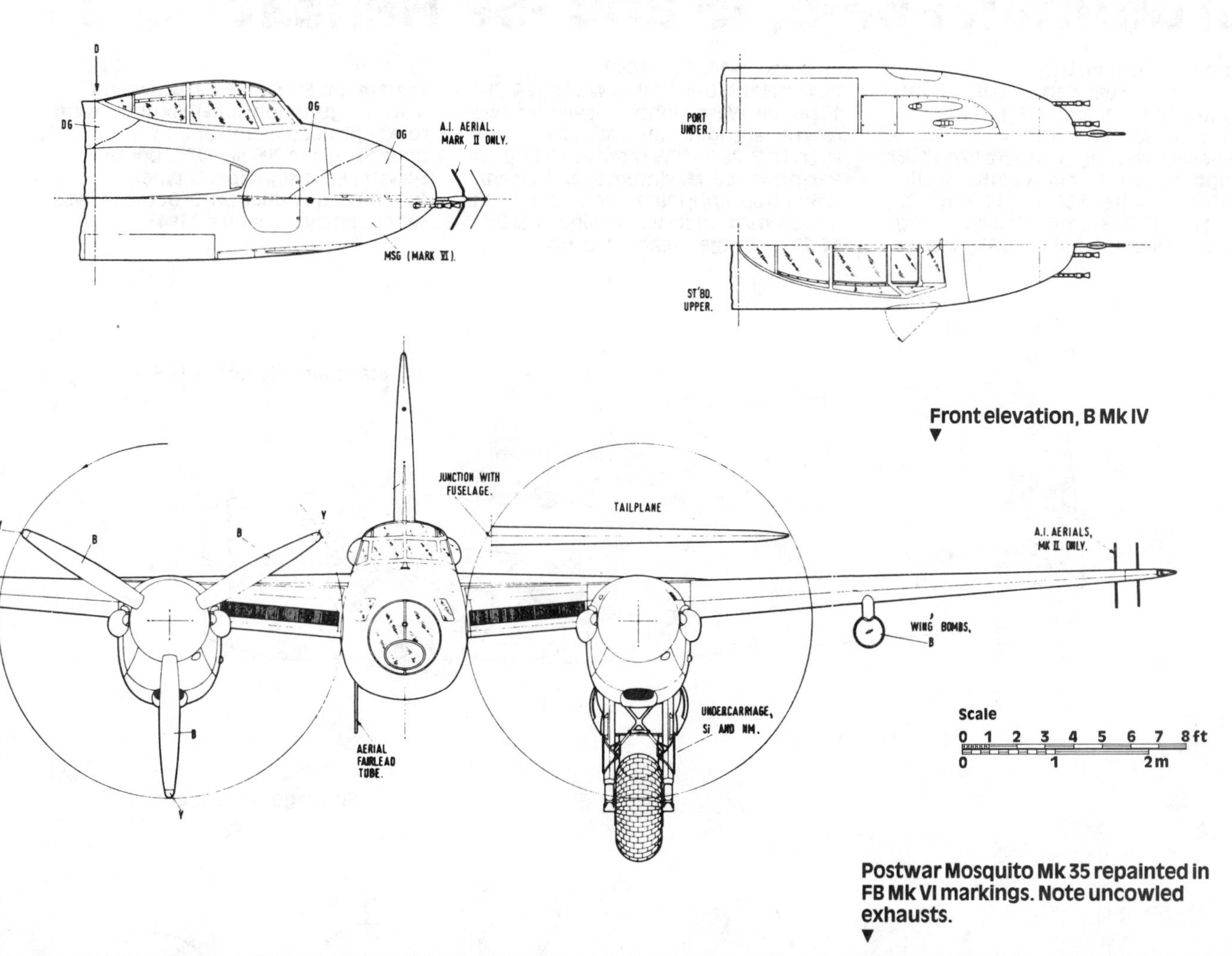

Front elevation, B Mk IV

Postwar Mosquito Mk 35 repainted in FB Mk VI markings. Note uncowled exhausts.

Grumman F6F-3, -5 and -5P Hellcat

Country of origin: USA.
Type: Single-seat, carrier-based fighter, fighter-bomber and (-5P) photo-reconnaissance fighter.
Dimensions: Wing span 42ft 10in *13.05m*; length 33ft 7in *10.24m*; height 13ft 1in *3.99m*; wing area 334 sq ft *31.03m²*.
Weights: (F6F-3) Empty 9042lb *4101kg*; loaded (clean) 12,186lb *5528kg*; loaded (maximum) 13,228lb *6000kg*.
Powerplant: One Pratt & Whitney R-2800-10 Double Wasp eighteen-cylinder, two-row radial engine rated at 2000hp, (later aircraft) R-2800-10W rated at 2200hp.
Performance: Maximum speed (clean) 376mph *605kph*; initial climb rate 3240ft/min *990m/min*; service ceiling 37,500ft *11,450m*; range (clean) 1100 miles *1770km*.
Armament: Six fixed 0.5in Browning machine guns; (optional) six underwing rocket projectiles and one underfuselage 2000lb *907kg* bomb.
Service: First flight (prototype) June 1942, (production -3) October 1942; service entry (-3) January 1943.

Starboard elevation, F6F-5

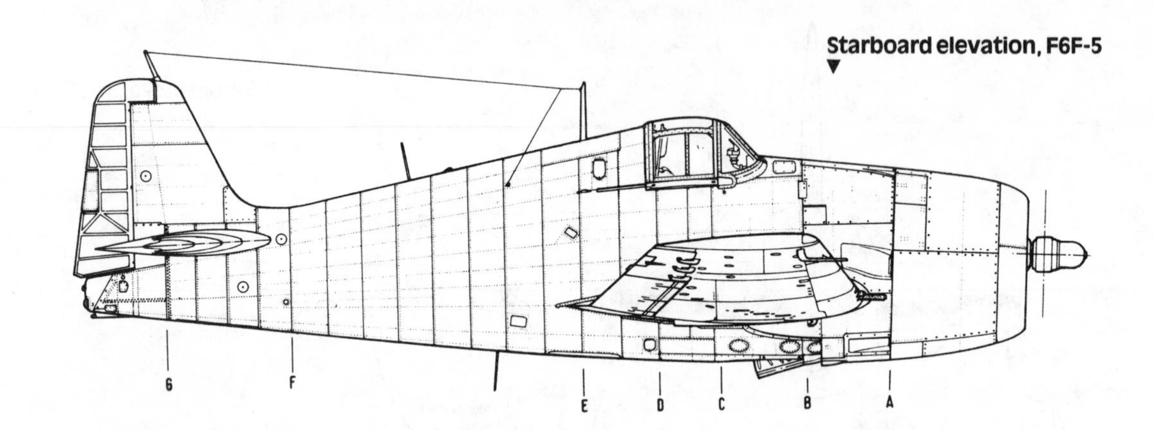

Fuselage cross-sections

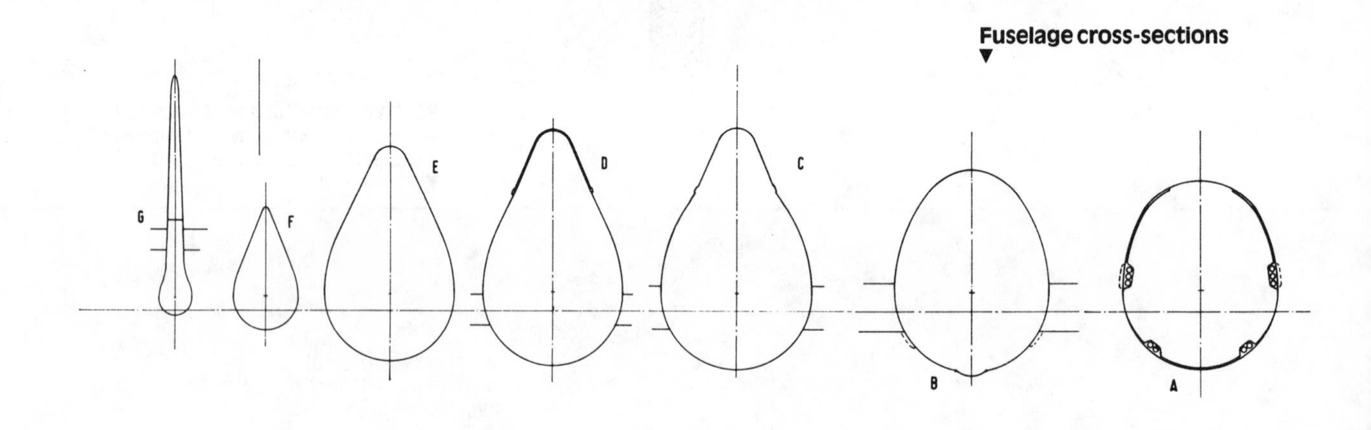

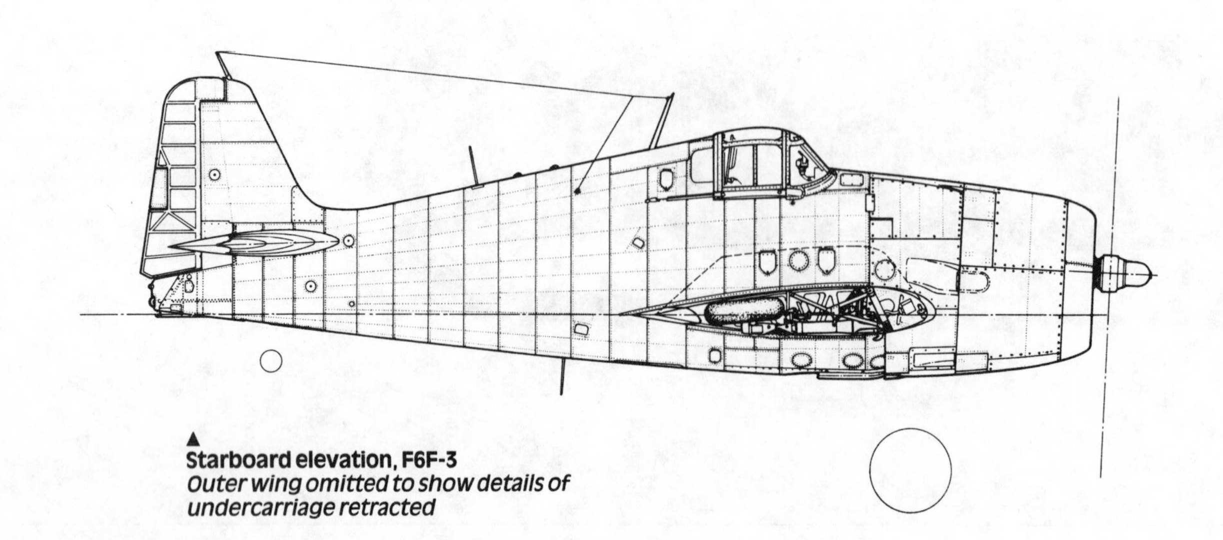

Starboard elevation, F6F-3
Outer wing omitted to show details of undercarriage retracted

▲
One of the most successful carrier fighters of the war, the Hellcat was used in vast numbers by the US Navy, whose shipboard F6Fs accounted for no fewer than 4947 enemy aircraft in air-to-air combat.

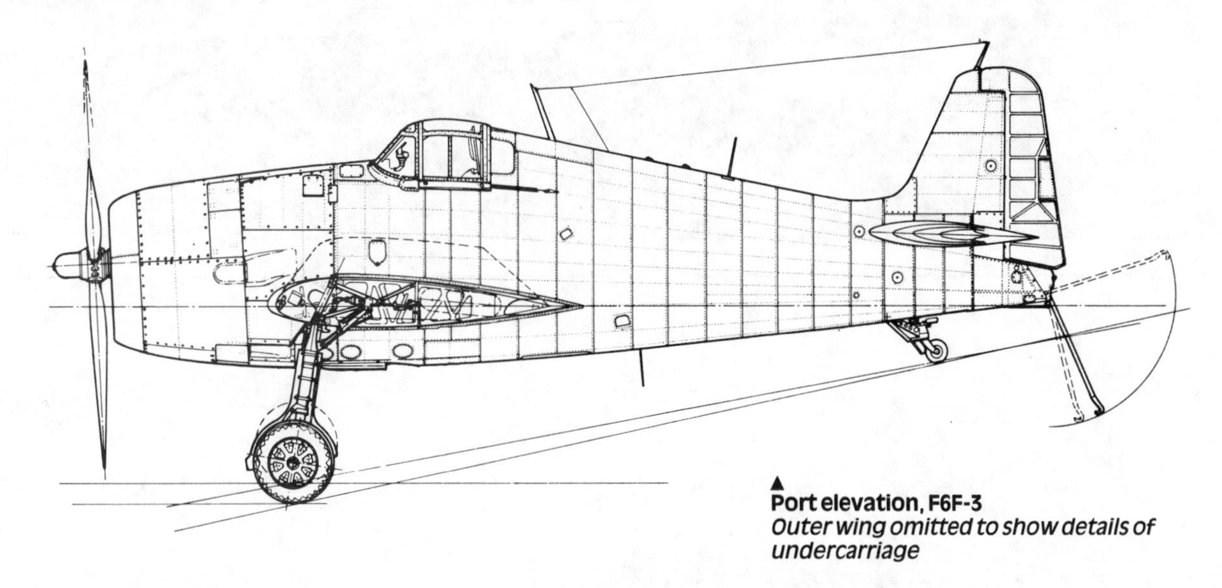

▲
Port elevation, F6F-3
Outer wing omitted to show details of undercarriage

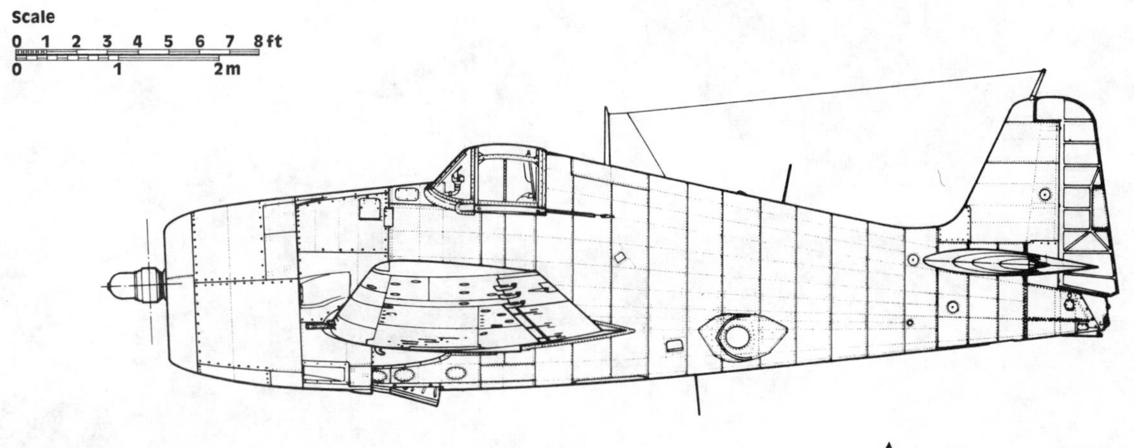

▲
Port elevation, F6F-5P

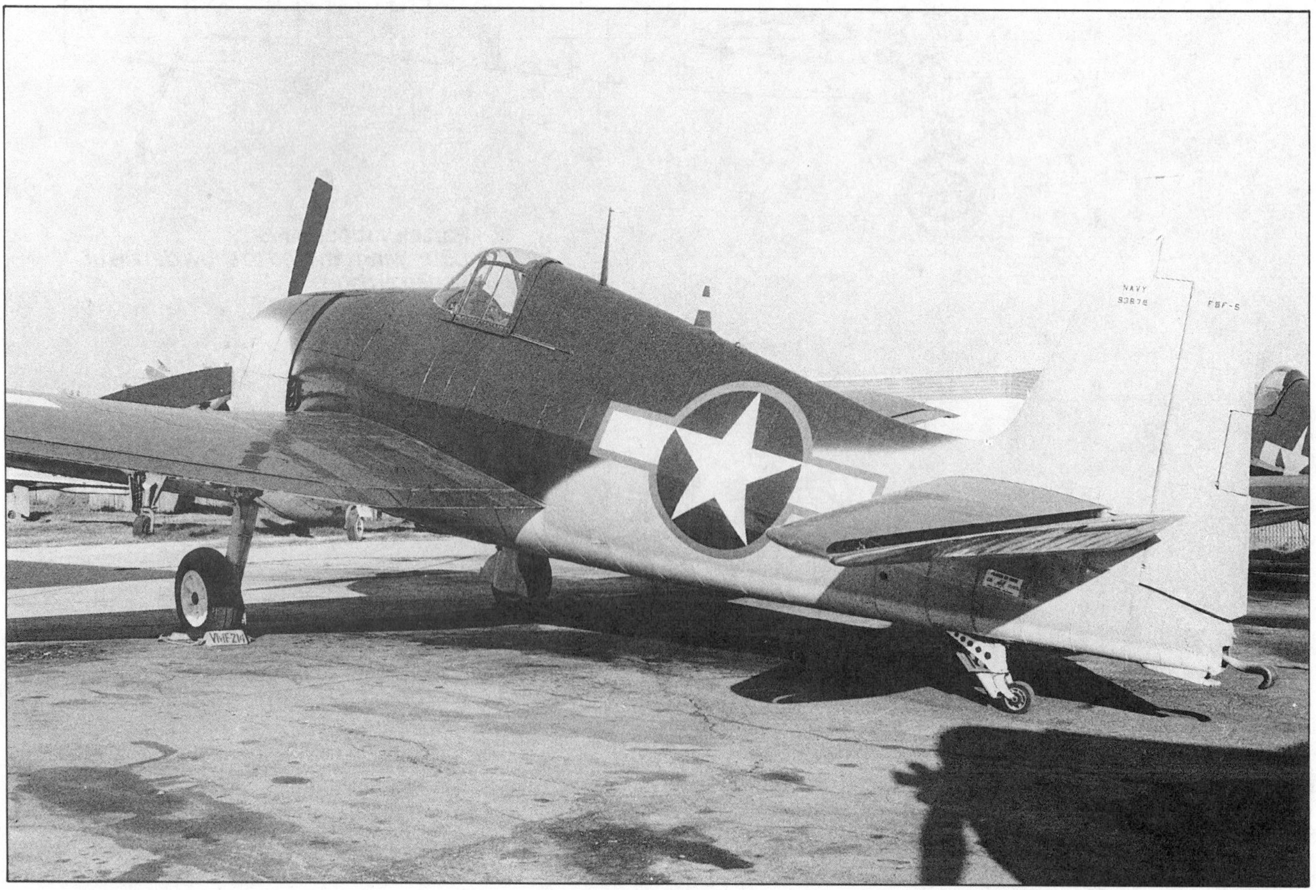
NAVY
F6F-5

◀ Wing-folding reduced the Hellcat's span considerably, aiding stowage on board ship. Finish of this example is glossy 'Midnite Blue'.

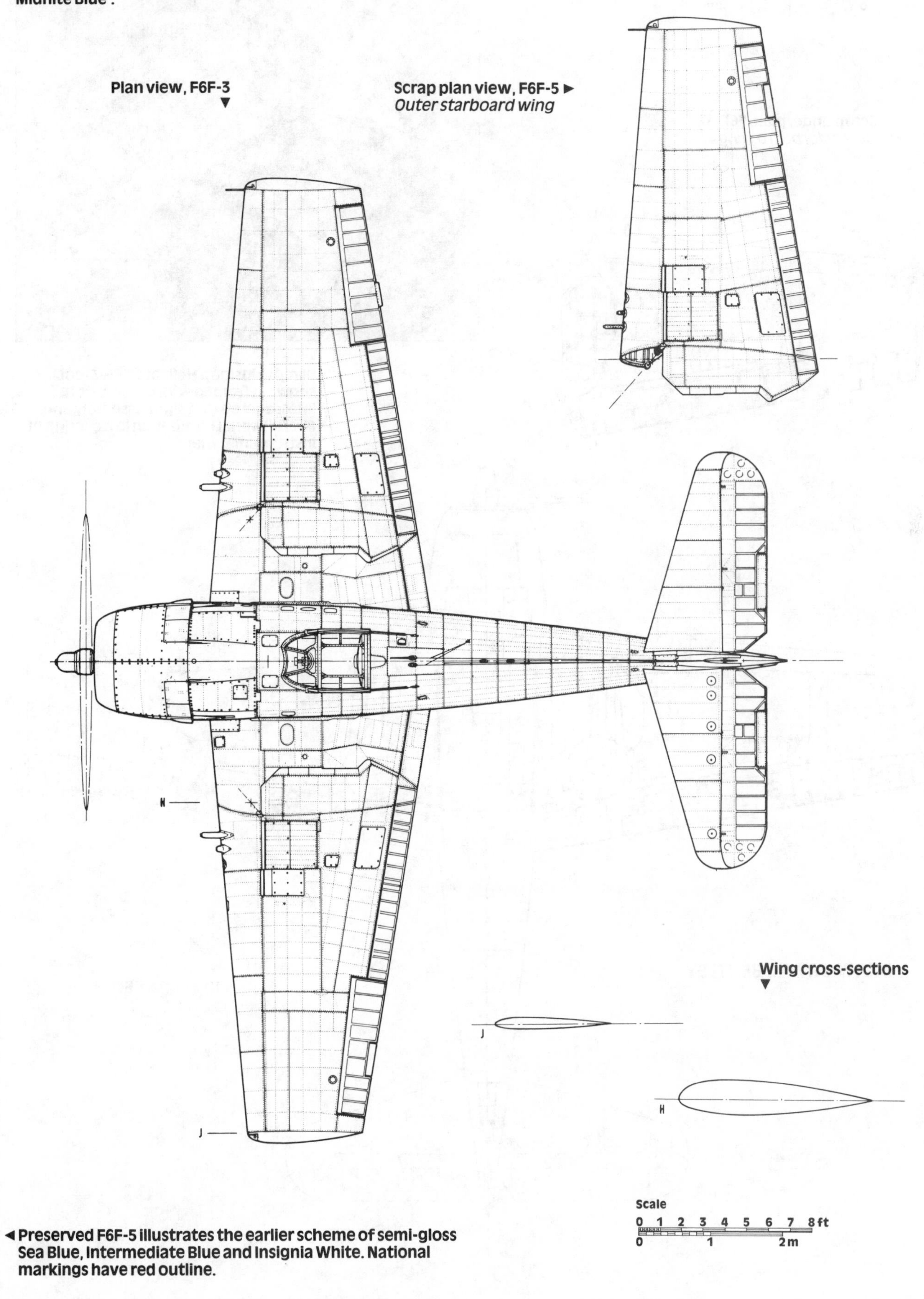

◀ Preserved F6F-5 illustrates the earlier scheme of semi-gloss Sea Blue, Intermediate Blue and Insignia White. National markings have red outline.

▲
Glimpse inside a Hellcat I (F6F-3) cockpit, showing framed windscreen. Note 'message' on gun sight assembly and aircraft serial number on lower edge of instrument panel.

Scrap underplan, F6F-5
Outer starboard wing
▼

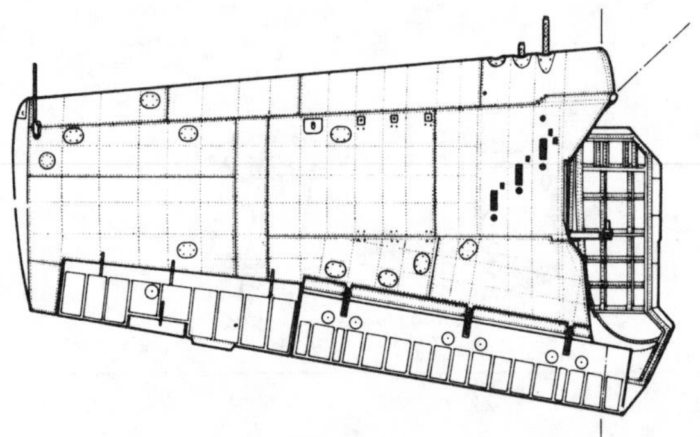

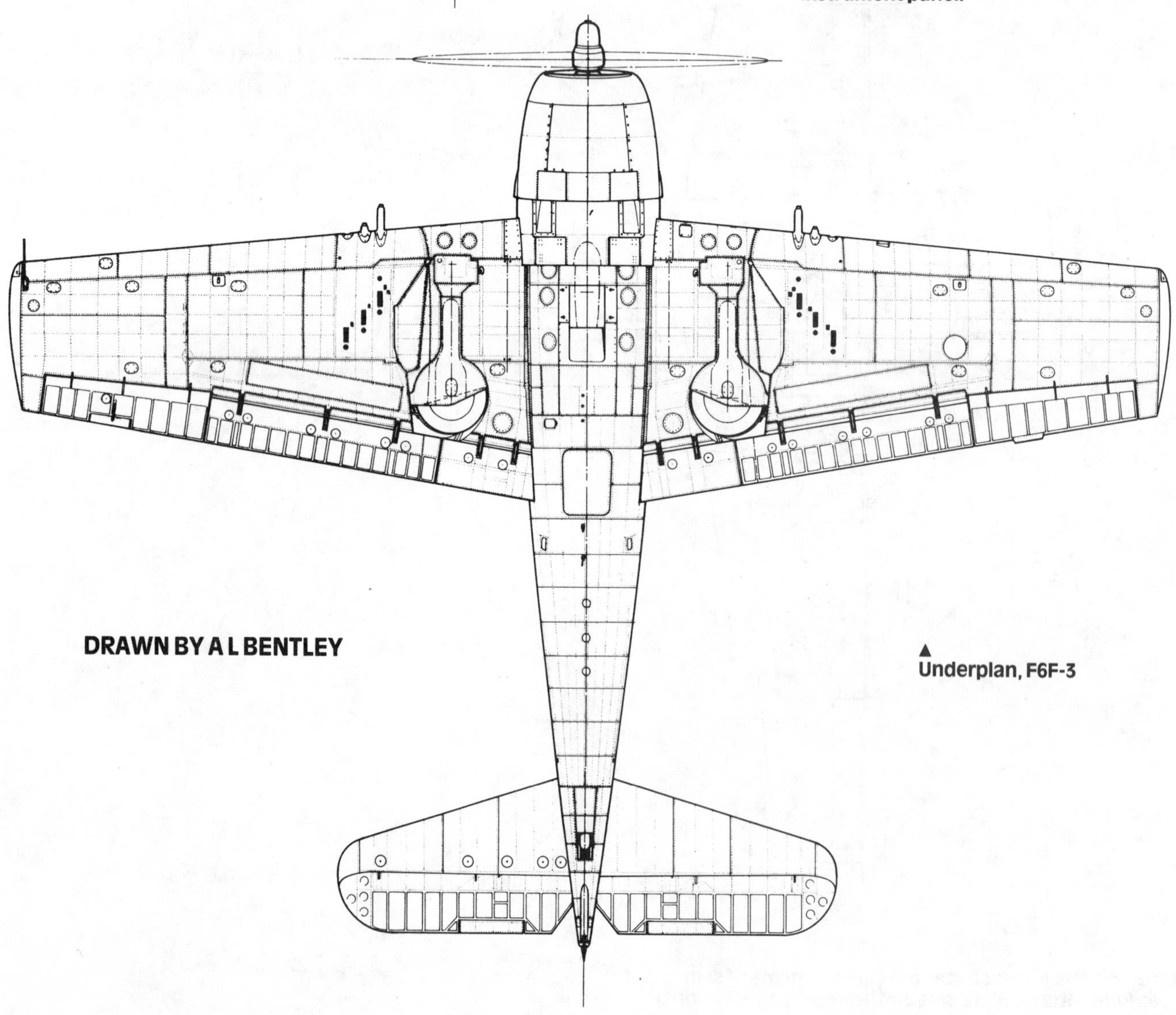

DRAWN BY A L BENTLEY

▲
Underplan, F6F-3

Front elevation, F6F-3

Rear elevation, F6F-3

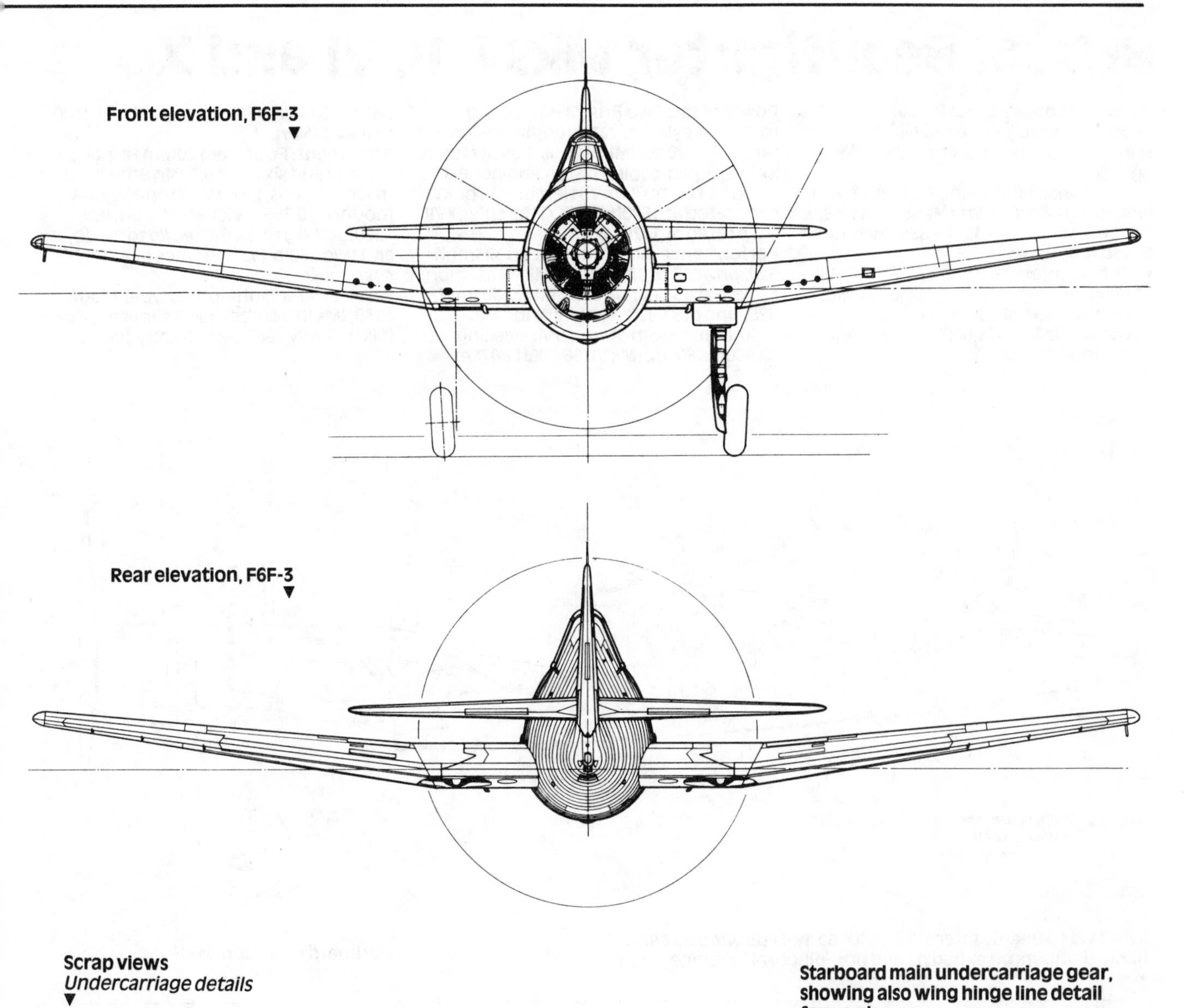

Scrap views
Undercarriage details

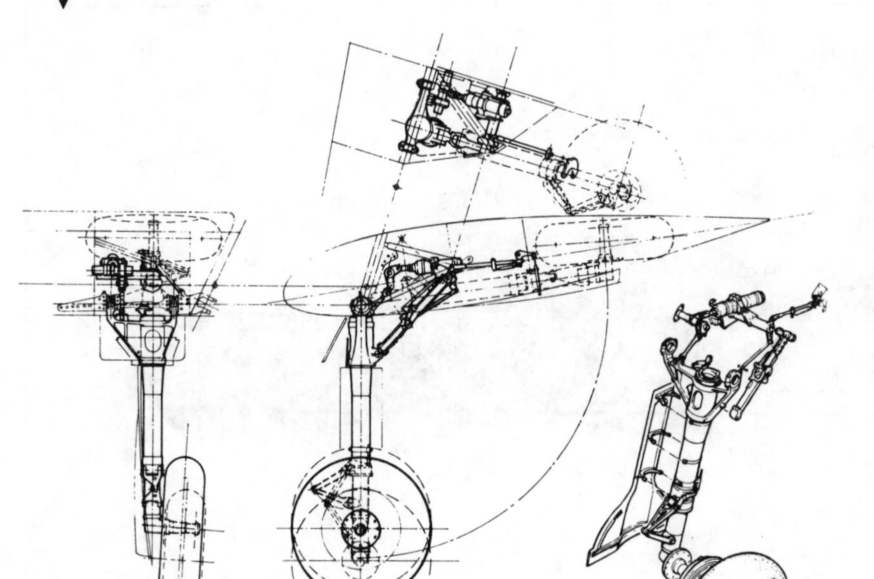

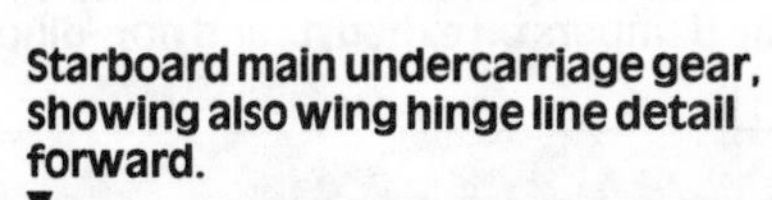

Starboard main undercarriage gear, showing also wing hinge line detail forward.

Bristol Beaufighter Mks I, II, VI and X

Country of origin: Great Britain.
Type: Two-seat, land based night-fighter or (Mks VI, X) long-range strike fighter.
Dimensions: Wing span 57ft 10in *17.63m*; length 41ft 4in *12.60m*, (Mks VI, X) 41ft 8in *12.70m*; height 15ft 10in *4.83m*; wing area 503 sq ft *46.72m²*.
Weights: Empty 14,069lb *6383kg*, (Mk VI) 14,600lb *6624kg*, (Mk X) 15,600lb *7078kg*; normal loaded 20,800lb *9437kg*; maximum loaded 21,600lb *6584kg*, (Mk X) 25,200lb *11,434kg*.
Powerplant: Two Bristol Hercules XI fourteen-cylinder radial engines each rated at 1590hp, (Mk II) Rolls-Royce Merlin XX V12, liquid-cooled piston engines each rated at 1280hp, (Mk VI) Hercules VI or XVI each rated at 1670hp, (Mk X) Hercules XVII each rated at 1770hp.
Performance: Maximum speed 323mph *520kph* at 15,000ft *4570m*, (Mk VI) 333mph *536kph* at 15,600ft *4750m*, (Mk X) 303mph *488kph* at 15,600ft; initial climb rate 1850ft/min *565m/min*; service ceiling 28,900ft *8800m*, (Mk VI) 26,500ft *8075m*, (Mk X) 15,000ft *4570m*; range about 1500 miles *2415km*.
Armament: Four fixed 20mm Hispano cannon and six fixed 0.303in Browning machine guns, plus (Mk X) one flexibly mounted 0.303in Vickers 'K' gun, one 1650lb *749kg* or 2127lb *965kg* torpedo, and two 250lb *113kg* bombs or eight 90lb *41kg* rockets.
Service: First flight (prototype) 17 July 1939, (Mk II) October 1940; service entry (Mk I) 27 July 1940, (Mk VI) early 1942.

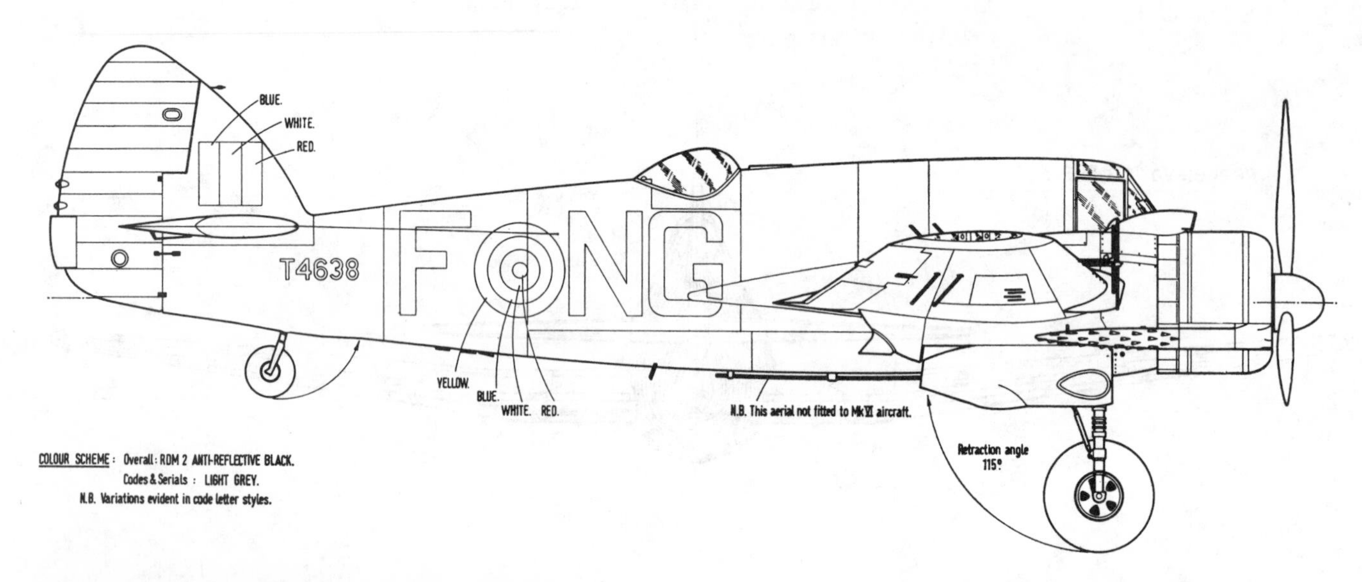

▲ Starboard elevation, Mk IF

X7543 was a Beaufighter Mk IF, with early-type windscreen, flame dampers on exhausts and non-dihedral tailplane. ▼

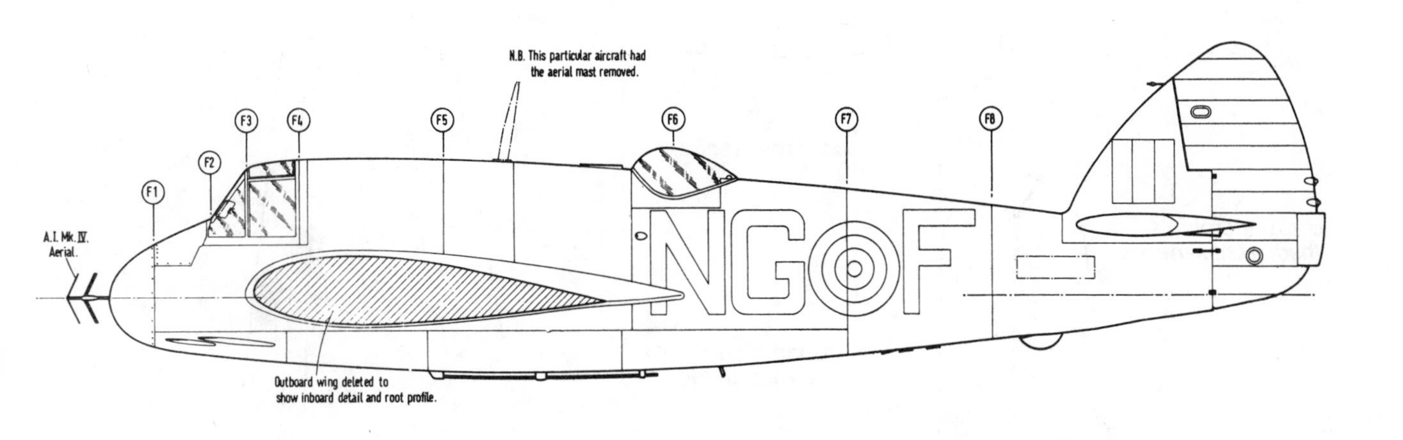

▲ **Port elevation, Mk IF**
Wing omitted to show detail

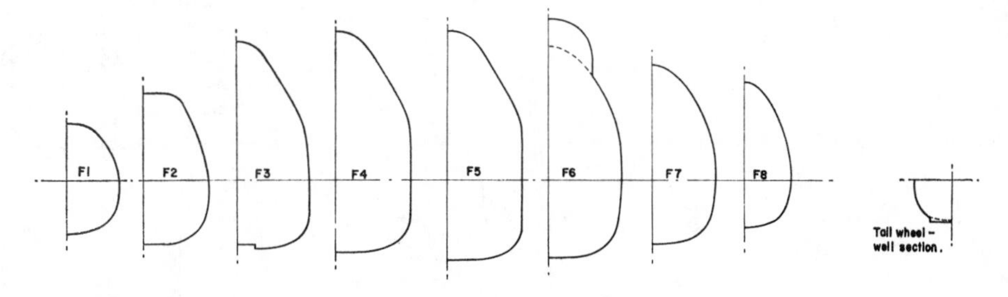

DRAWN BY G R DUVAL

▲ **Fuselage cross-sections**

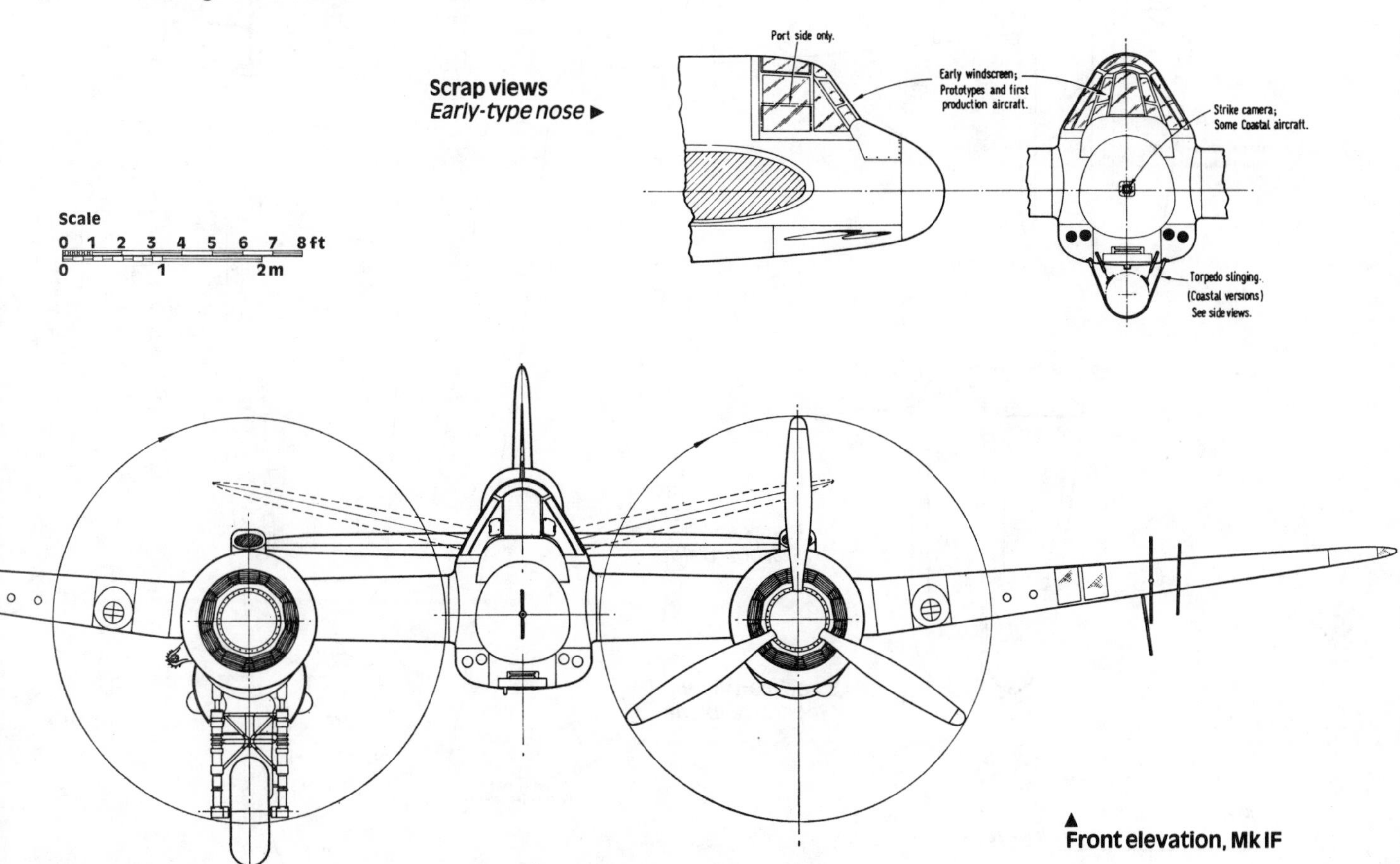

▲ **Front elevation, Mk IF**

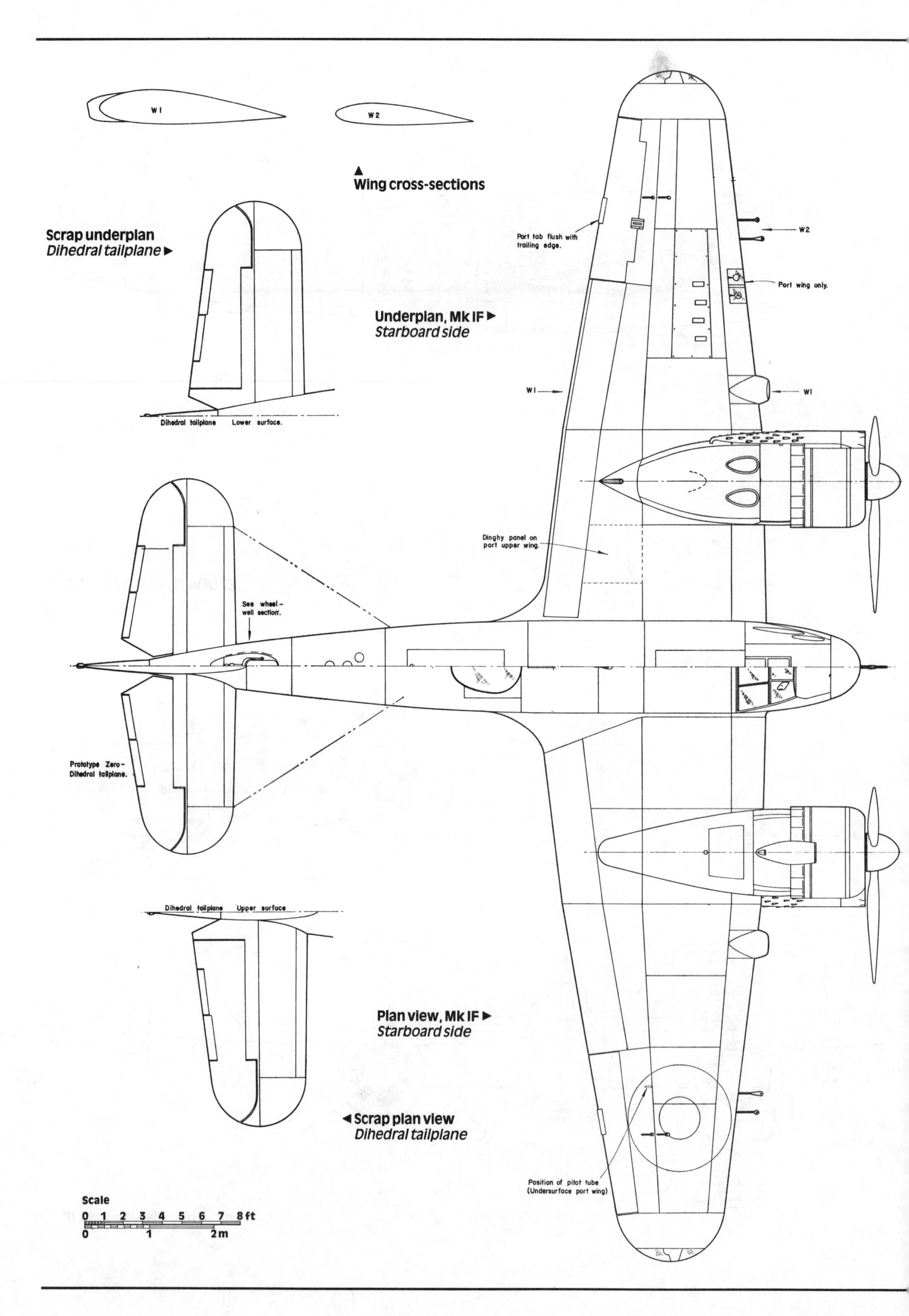
W1
W2
Wing cross-sections
Scrap underplan
Dihedral tailplane
Dihedral tailplane Lower surface.
Port tab flush with trailing edge.
W2
Port wing only.
Underplan, Mk IF
Starboard side
W1
W1
Dinghy panel on port upper wing.
See wheel-well section.
Prototype Zero-Dihedral tailplane.
Dihedral tailplane Upper surface
Plan view, Mk IF
Starboard side
Scrap plan view
Dihedral tailplane
Position of pitot tube (Undersurface port wing)
Scale
0 1 2 3 4 5 6 7 8 ft
0 1 2 m

▲
'Whispering Death' – a TF Mk X, armed with a torpedo and showing a feathered starboard propeller, makes a low pass over the airfield.

Port elevation, Mk IIF
▼

Port elevation, TF Mk X
Wing omitted to show detail
▼

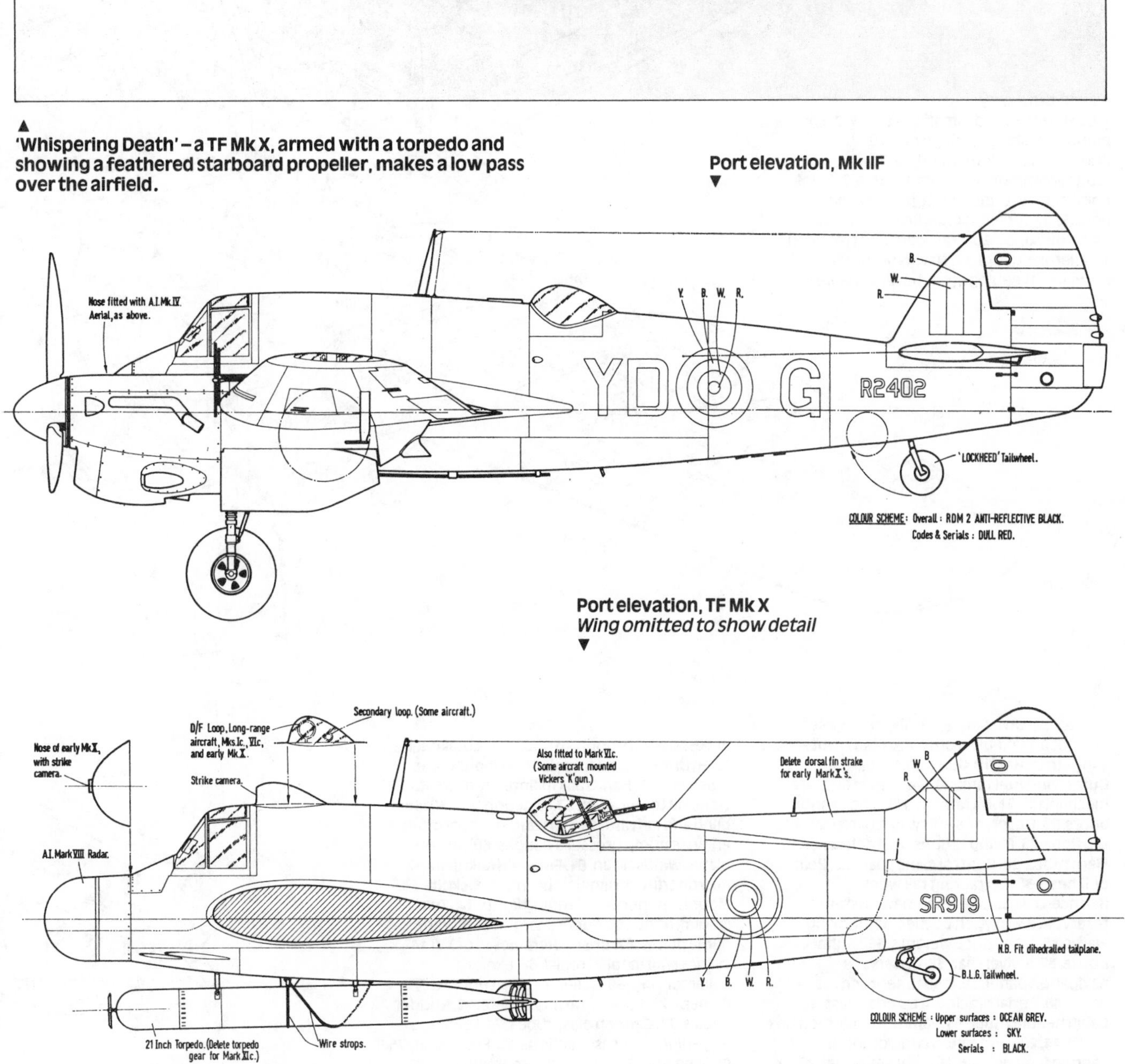

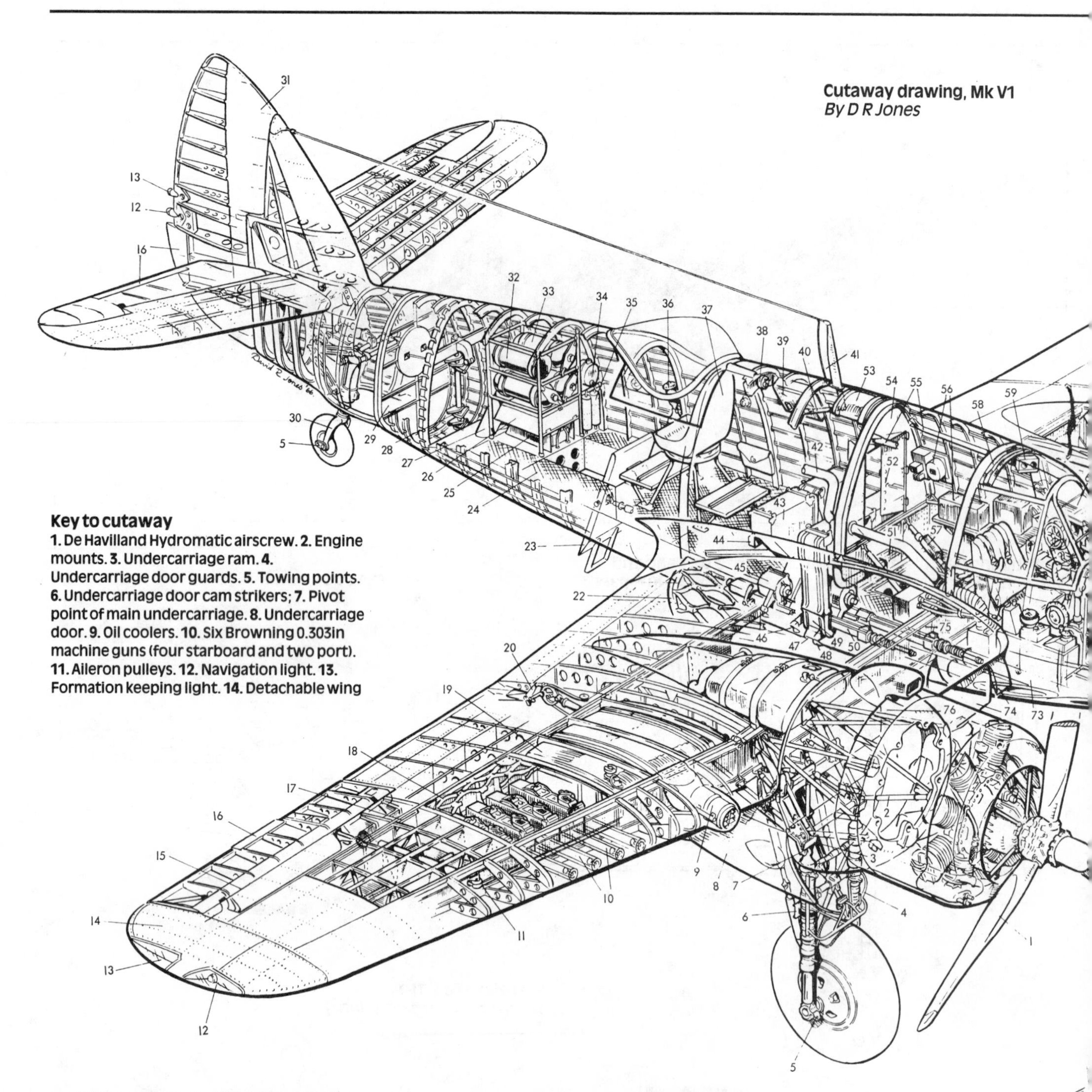

Cutaway drawing, Mk V1
By D R Jones

Key to cutaway

1. De Havilland Hydromatic airscrew. **2.** Engine mounts. **3.** Undercarriage ram. **4.** Undercarriage door guards. **5.** Towing points. **6.** Undercarriage door cam strikers; **7.** Pivot point of main undercarriage. **8.** Undercarriage door. **9.** Oil coolers. **10.** Six Browning 0.303in machine guns (four starboard and two port). **11.** Aileron pulleys. **12.** Navigation light. **13.** Formation keeping light. **14.** Detachable wing tip. **15.** Aileron balance. **16.** Aileron adjusting tab (not adjustable from cockpit). **17.** Outer wing structure. **18.** Gun detachable panel. **19.** Outer wing fuel tank. **20.** Flap operating mechanism. **21.** Oil tank. **22.** Hinging cannon doors. **23.** Observer's entry/exit hatch. **24.** Non-slip floor. **25.** Flying rations. **26.** Tool locker. **27.** Flare tubes. **28.** Control cable shaft. **29.** Rear bulkhead. **30.** Retracting tail wheel. **31.** Balanced rudder. **32.** Pneumatic system reservoir. **33.** Oxygen bottles. **34.** Drinking water. **35.** CG balance weights. **36.** Sanitary bottle. **37.** Swivel seat. **38.** Observer's navigation panel. **39.** Instrument and fuse panel. **40.** Aerial bracing. **41.** Aerial mast. **42.** Cabin heating duct. **43.** 20mm ammunition box (4 off). **44.** 20mm cannon control unit. **45.** Cannon feed unit. **46.** Link chutes outlet. **47.** Empty shell case outlet. **48.** Wood fairing. **49.** Cannon feed chute. **50.** Four 20mm Hispano cannon. **51.** Step over cannon heating duct. **52.** Access door through armour plate bulkhead. **53.** Hydraulic header tank. **54.** Armour plate bulkhead. **55.** Hand rails (painted red). **56.** Radio transmitter receiver. **57.** Junction box. **58.** Sun blind and lanyard. **59.** Port and starboard engines pump pressure gauges. **60.** Armour-plated windscreen. **61.** Firewall bulkhead. **62.** Aileron trim tab (adjustable from cockpit). **63.** Mounting tripod for landing lights. **64.** Two landing lights. **65.** Supercharger. **66.** Engine baffle plates. **67.** Bristol Hercules VI or XVI 14-cylinder, air-cooled radial. **68.** Exhaust collector ring. **69.** Collector ring supports. **70.** Camera. **71.** Forward armour plate. **72.** Rudder pedals. **73.** Cannon blast tubes. **74.** Leading edge hinged access sections. **75.** Front spar. **76.** Cooling gills. **77.** Shock absorber bungee. **78.** Fuel jettison pipe. **79.** Undercarriage door hinge tube. **80.** Undercarriage door cam. **81.** Undercarriage door activation cable.

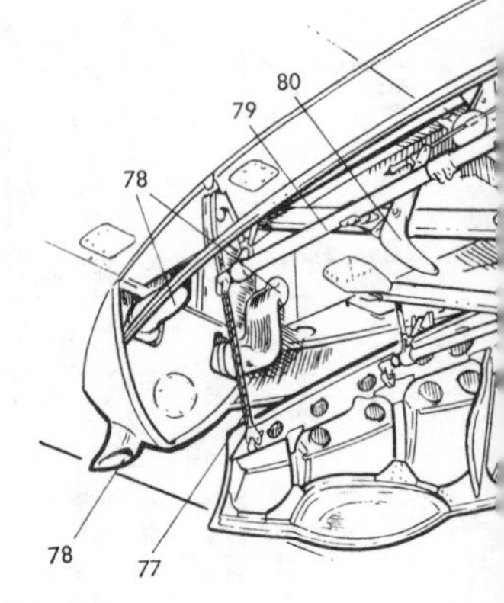

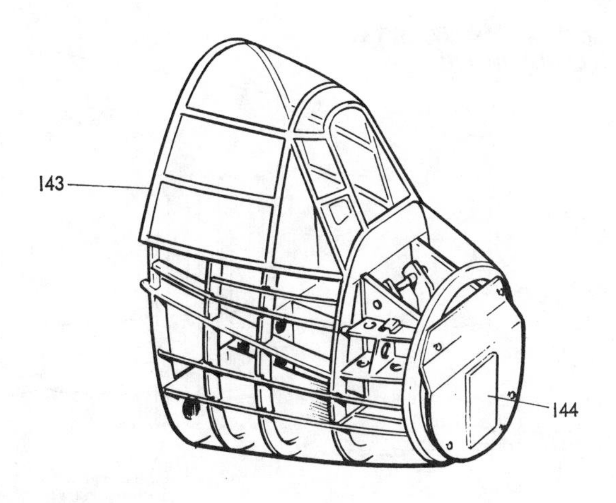

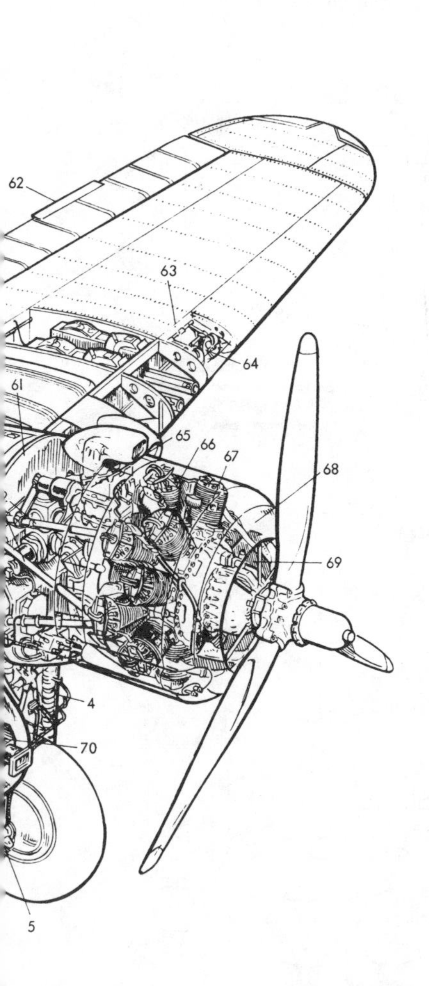

Key to cockpit details

82. Carburettor cut-out controls. 83. Two-speed supercharger controls. 84. Air intake control. 85. Fuel balance lever. 86. Port fuel tank cocks handwheel. 87. Starboard fuel tank cocks handwheel. 88. Mixture control. 89. Propeller speed controls. 90. Throttle controls. 91. Flap lever. 92. Flap indicator. 93. Cockpit heating control. 94. Emergency hatch lever. 95. Hydraulic emergency selector. 96. Escape hand rail (painted red). 97. Oxygen regulator. 98. Fuel contents port. 99. Cockpit lamp. 100. Undercarriage position indicators. 101. Clock. 102. Beam approach indicator. 103. Reflector sight socket. 104. Propeller feathering buttons. 105. Altimeter. 106. Airspeed indicator. 107. Reflector sight mounting. 108. Reflector sight. 109. Artificial horizon. 110. Rate of climb. 111. Gun firing push button. 112. Direct vision window. 113. Brake lever. 114. Turn and bank indicator. 115. Engine speed indicators. 116. Engine management panel. 117. Landing flare buttons. 118. Switchbox for identification lamps. 119. Rudder trimming tab control. 120. Trimming tab indicator. 121. Release handle – knock-out panel. 122. Switchbox for formation keeping lights. 123. Compass. 124. Propeller de-icer control. 125. Fuel contents starboard. 126. Cabin heating duct. 127. Aileron trimming control. 128. Camera gun switch. 129. Sutton harness release lever. 130. Hydraulic handpump. 131. Elevator trimming control. 132. Seat (shown collapsed). 133. Rudder pedals. 134. Pneumatic pressure gauge. 135. Vacuum pump control. 136. Seat adjustment lever. 137. Map case. 138. Undercarriage selection lever. 139. Landing lamps dipping lever. 140. Landing lamps switch. 141. Cowling gills indicators. 142. Front wing spar. 143. Early-type canopy frame. 144. Sevicing panel in armour plate.

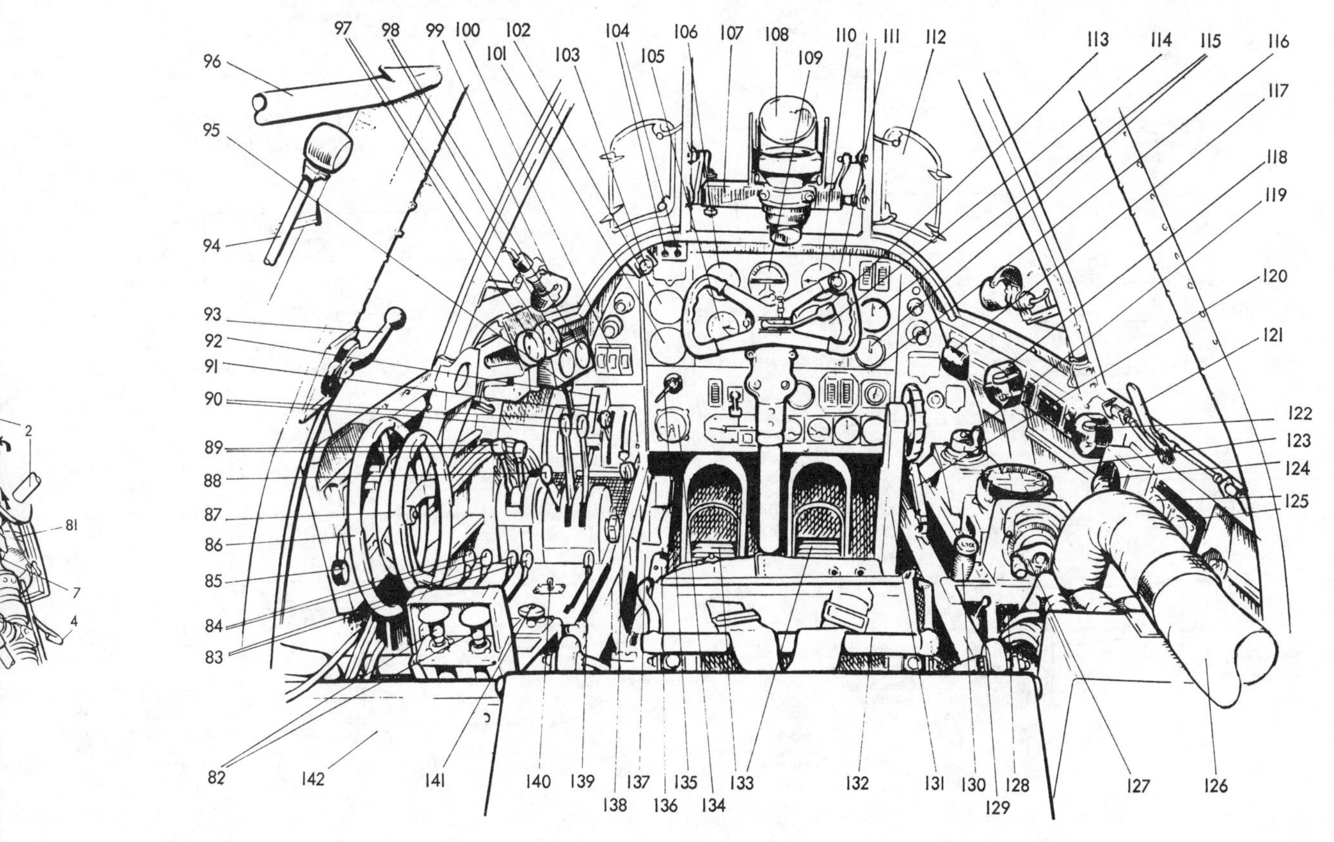

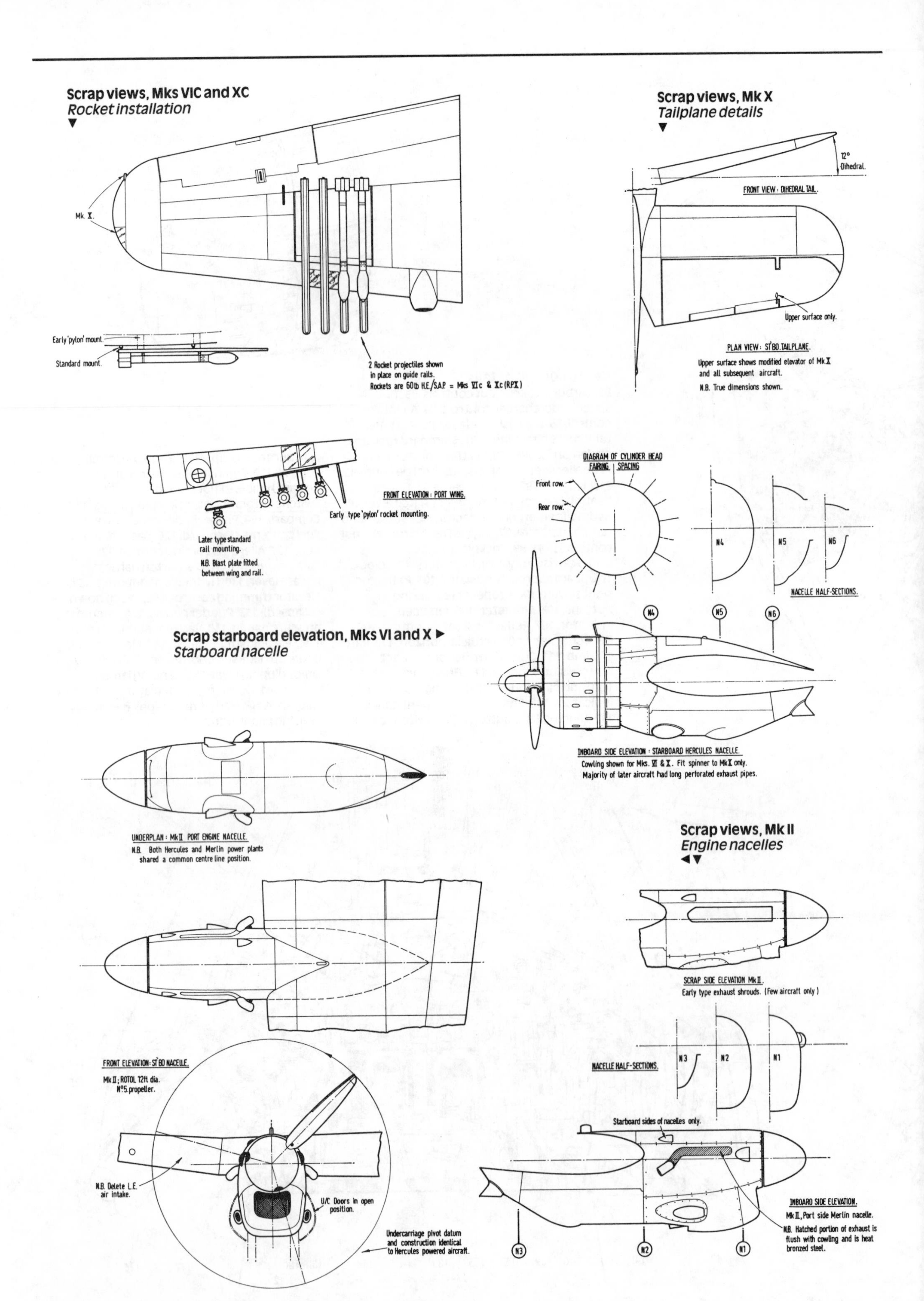
Scrap views, Mks VIC and XC
Rocket installation
Mk. X.
Early 'pylon' mount.
Standard mount.
2 Rocket projectiles shown in place on guide rails.
Rockets are 60lb H.E./S.A.P. = Mks VIc & Xc (R.P.X)
Scrap views, Mk X
Tailplane details
12°
Dihedral.
FRONT VIEW: DIHEDRAL TAIL.
Upper surface only.
PLAN VIEW: ST'BD. TAILPLANE.
Upper surface shows modified elevator of Mk.X and all subsequent aircraft.
N.B. True dimensions shown.
FRONT ELEVATION: PORT WING.
Early type 'pylon' rocket mounting.
Later type standard rail mounting.
N.B. Blast plate fitted between wing and rail.
DIAGRAM OF CYLINDER HEAD
FAIRING | SPACING
Front row.
Rear row.
N4
N5
N6
NACELLE HALF-SECTIONS.
Scrap starboard elevation, Mks VI and X
Starboard nacelle
INBOARD SIDE ELEVATION: STARBOARD HERCULES NACELLE.
Cowling shown for Mks. VI & X. Fit spinner to Mk X only.
Majority of later aircraft had long perforated exhaust pipes.
UNDERPLAN: Mk II PORT ENGINE NACELLE.
N.B. Both Hercules and Merlin power plants shared a common centre line position.
Scrap views, Mk II
Engine nacelles
SCRAP SIDE ELEVATION Mk II.
Early type exhaust shrouds. (Few aircraft only)
NACELLE HALF-SECTIONS.
N3
N2
N1
FRONT ELEVATION: ST'BD NACELLE.
Mk II; ROTOL 12ft dia.
N°5 propeller.
N.B. Delete L.E. air intake.
U/C Doors in open position.
Undercarriage pivot datum and construction identical to Hercules powered aircraft.
Starboard sides of nacelles only.
INBOARD SIDE ELEVATION.
Mk II, Port side Merlin nacelle.
N.B. Hatched portion of exhaust is flush with cowling and is heat bronzed steel.

Lavochkin La-5FN and La-7

Country of origin: USSR.
Type: Single-seat, land-based fighter and fighter bomber.
Dimensions: Wing span 32ft 1¾in *9.80m*; length 27ft 10¾in *8.50m*, (La-7) 27ft 4in *8.33m*; height 8ft 4in *2.54m*, (La-7) 11ft 9in *3.58m*; wing area 188.4 sq ft *17.5m*^{2}.
Weights: Empty (La-5FN) 6170lb *2800kg*; loaded 7405lb *3360kg*, (La-7) 7495lb *3400kg*.
Powerplant: One Shvetsov M-82FN fourteen-cylinder, two-row radial engine rated at 1700hp, (La-7) M-82FNU or FNV rated at 1700hp or 1870hp.
Performance: Maximum speed 402mph *647kph* at 16,400ft *5000m*, (La-7) 422mph *680kph* at 21,000ft *6400m*; climb to 3280ft *1000m* (La-5FN), 18.5sec; service ceiling 32,800ft *10,000m*; range 435 miles *700km*.
Armament: Two fixed 20mm ShVak cannon, plus (optional) four 3.2in *82mm* RS82 rockets or 330lb *150kg* of bombs; (La-7) three fixed 20mm ShVak or 23mm NS cannon, plus (optional) six 3.2in RS82 rockets or 330lb of bombs.
Service: First flight (modified LaGG-3) late 1941; service entry (La-5FN, La-7) 1943.

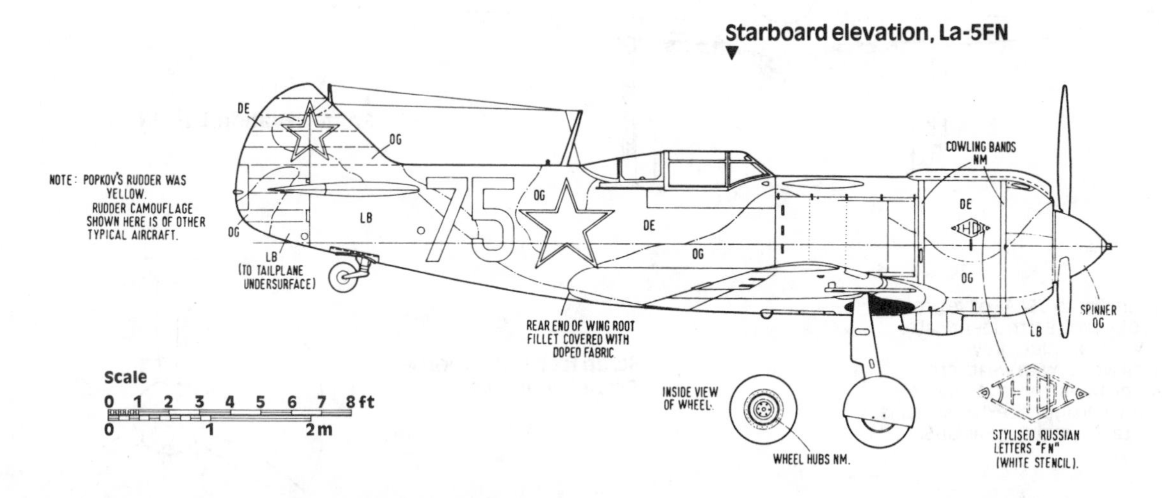

DRAWN BY G R DUVAL

Reconstructed La-7 on display in the Air Force Museum in Prague. Note gun apertures atop engine cowling; the weapons were synchronised to fire through the spinning propeller.

Construction data
Wings, tailplane and fuselage aft of section 'C' – covered with bonded plywood; control surfaces – fabric-covered metal; flaps – metal; fuselage forward of section 'C', wing-root fairings, inspection panels and undercarriage fairings – metal.

Colour code
OG – Olive green (similar to USAAF olive green used in Europe); **DE** – Dark Earth (identical to RAF shade); **LB** – Very pale blue-grey.
Note: Aircraft 'well worn', with weathered paint, mud stains on undercarriage, smoke stains on upper cowling (guns), exhaust stains behind cowl gills. La-7 camouflage as La-5FN.

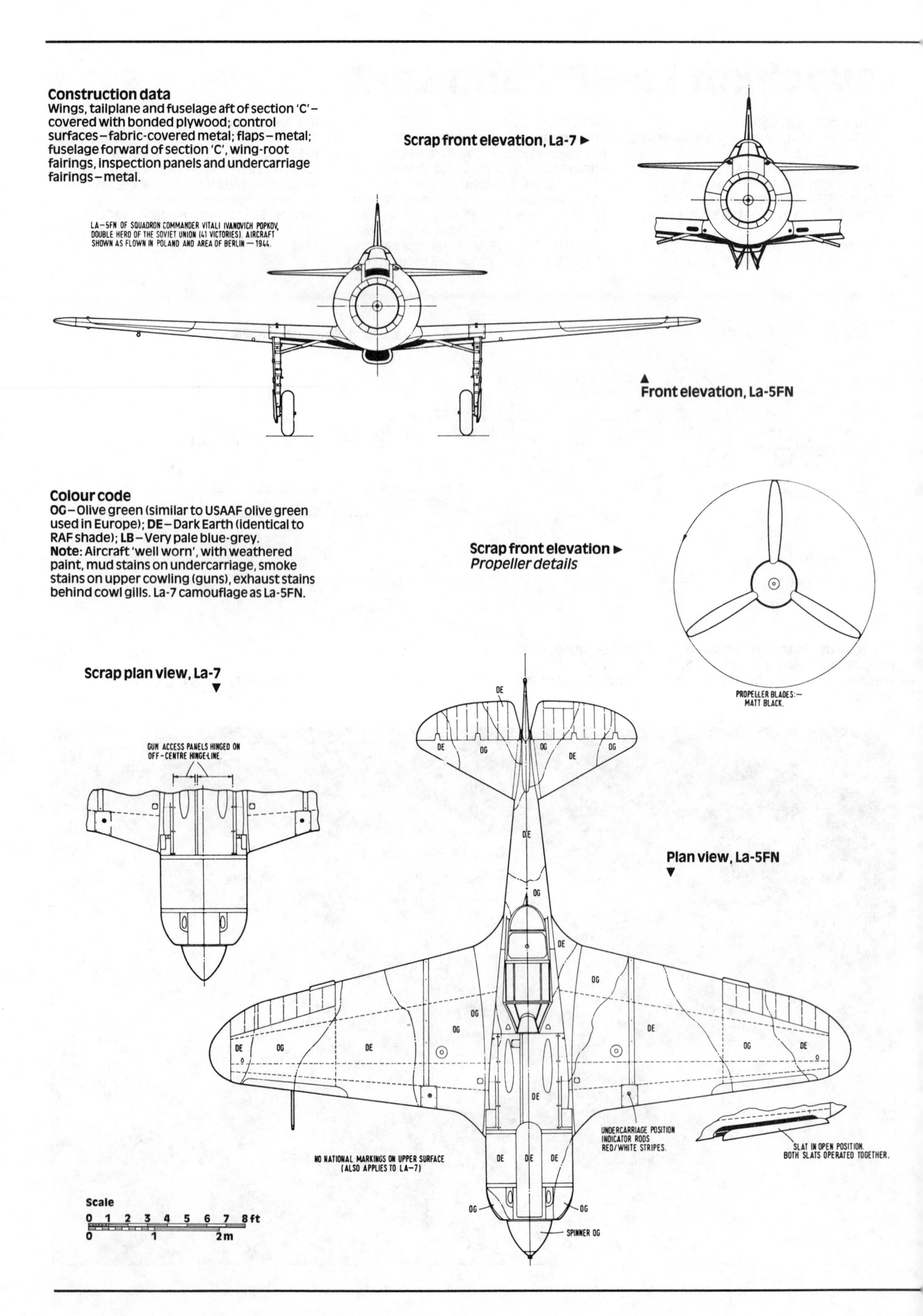

▲
Close-in view of the Prague La-7. The -7 differed from the -5FN in its new engine, revised inboard wing leading edge, revised main gear doors and relocated air intakes.

Port elevation, La-5FN
As flown by Sqn Cdr Popkov, 1944
▼

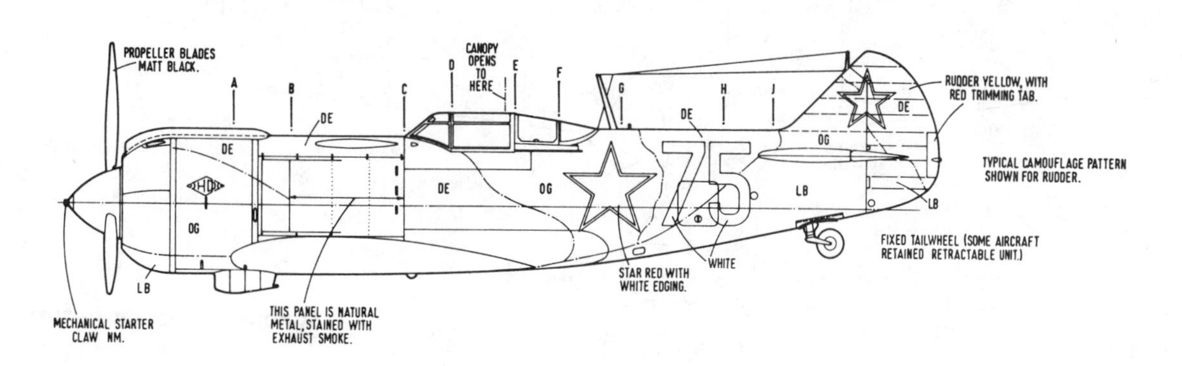

Fuselage cross-sections
▼

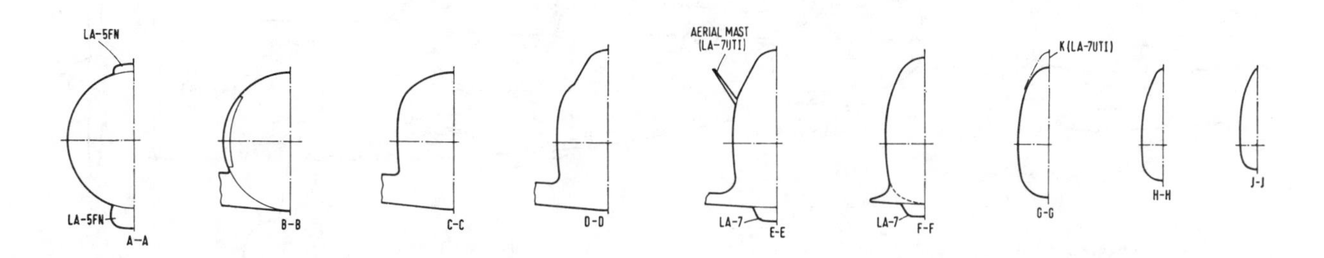

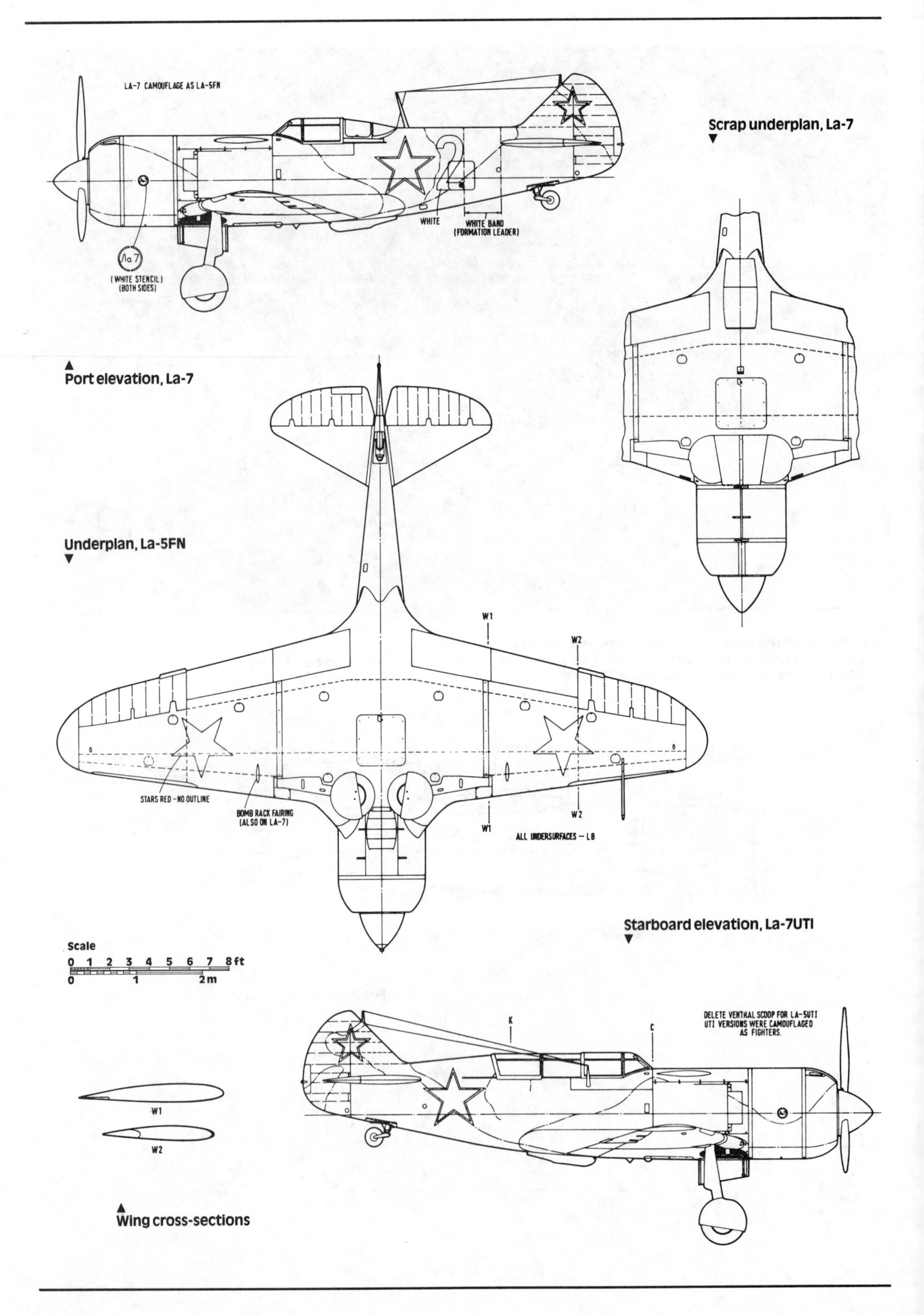

Port elevation, La-7

Scrap underplan, La-7

Underplan, La-5FN

Starboard elevation, La-7UTI

Wing cross-sections

Supermarine Spitfire Mks XII, XIV, XVIII and XIX

Country of origin: Great Britain.
Type: Single-seat, land-based fighter, (Mks XIV, XVIII) fighter or fighter reconnaissance aircraft and (Mk XIX) photographic reconnaissance aircraft.
Dimensions: Wing span (Mk XII) 32ft 7in *9.93m*, (FR Mk XIVE) 36ft 10in *11.23m*; length (Mk XII) 31ft 10in *9.70m*, (FR Mk XIVE) 32ft 8in *9.96m*; height (Mk XII, maximum) 11ft 0in *3.35m*, (FR Mk XIVE, maximum) 12ft 8½in *3.87m*; wing area (Mk XII) 231 sq ft *21.46m²*, (FR Mk XIVE) 242 sq ft *22.48m²*.
Weights: Empty (Mk XII) 5600lb *2541kg*, (FR Mk XIVE) 6600lb *2995kg*; maximum (Mk XII) 7400lb *3358kg*, (FR Mk XIVE) 8500lb *3857kg*.
Powerplant: (Mk XII) One Rolls-Royce Griffon III or IV V12, liquid-cooled piston engine rated at 1735hp, (FR Mk XIVE) Griffon 65 rated at 2050hp.
Performance: Maximum speed (Mk XII) 393mph *633kph* at 18,000ft *5485m*, (FR Mk XIVE) 448mph *721kph* at 26,000ft *7925m*; time to 20,000ft *6095m*, (Mk XII) 6.7min, (FR Mk XIVE) 7min; service ceiling (Mk XII) 40,000ft *12,190m*, (FR Mk XIVE) 44,500ft *13,565m*; range (Mk XII, clean) 329 miles *530km*, (FR Mk XIVE, clean) 460 miles *740km*..
Armament: (Mk XII) Two fixed 20mm Hispano cannon and four fixed 0.303in Browning machine guns plus (optional) one 500lb *227kg* bomb; (FR Mk XIVE) two fixed 20mm Hispano cannon and two fixed 0.5in Browning machine guns, plus (optional) one 500lb and two 250lb *113kg* bombs; (Mk XIX) none.
Service: Service entry (Mk XII) spring 1943, (Mk XIV) 1 January 1944, (Mk XIX) spring 1945.

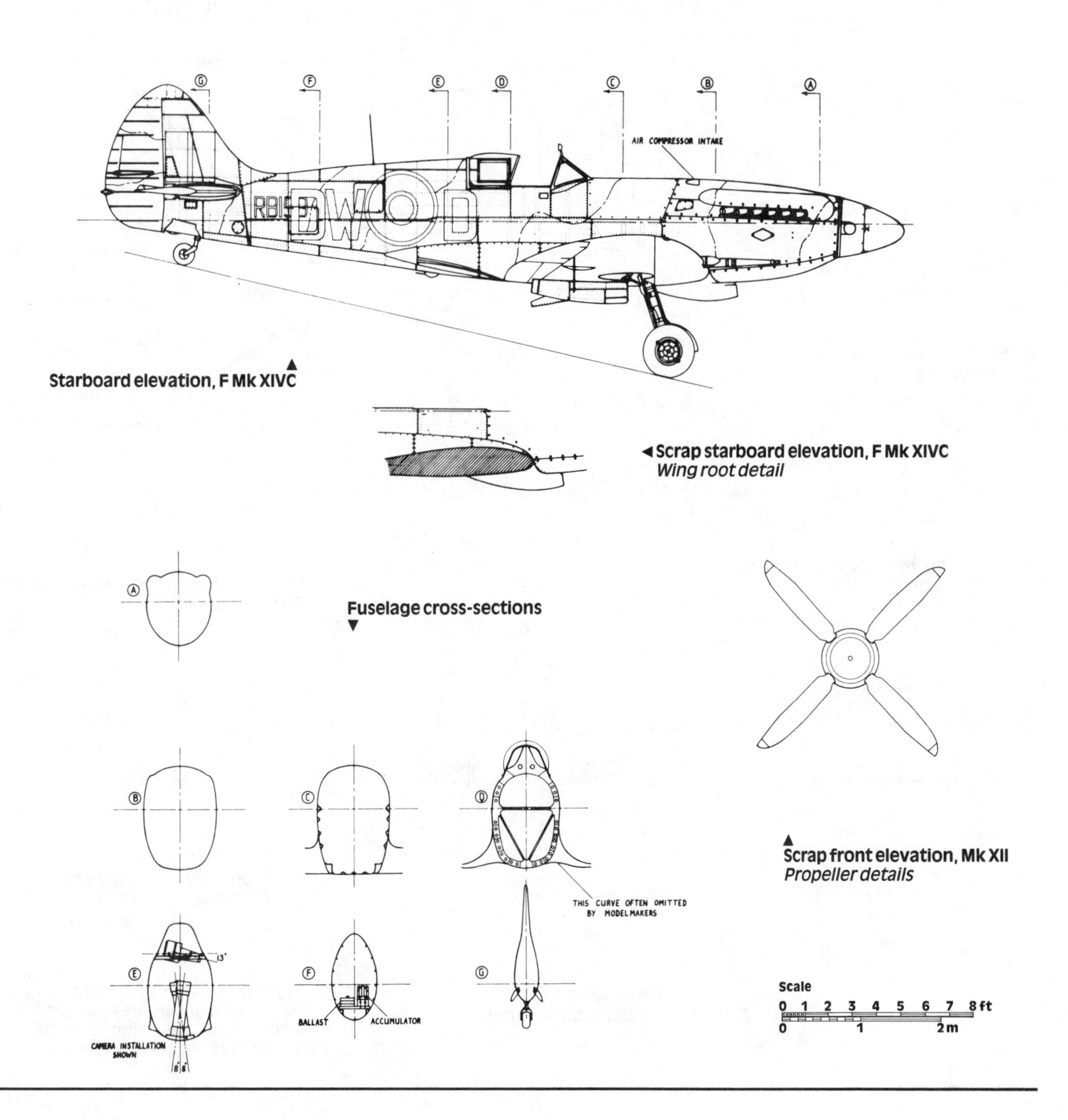

▲ Starboard elevation, F Mk XIVC

◄ **Scrap starboard elevation, F Mk XIVC**
Wing root detail

Fuselage cross-sections ▼

▲ **Scrap front elevation, Mk XII**
Propeller details

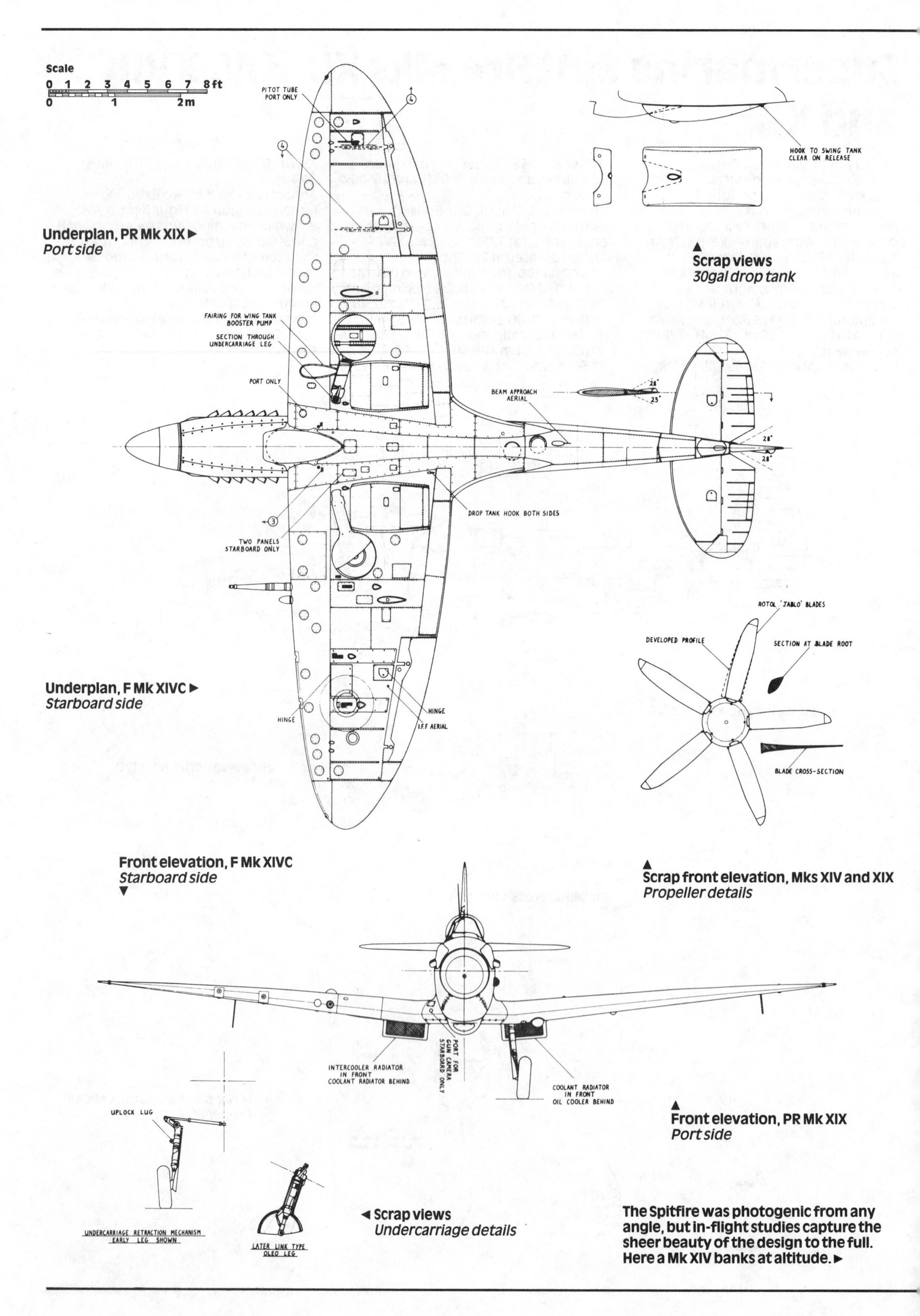

Underplan, PR Mk XIX ▶
Port side

▲ Scrap views
30gal drop tank

Underplan, F Mk XIVC ▶
Starboard side

▲ Scrap front elevation, Mks XIV and XIX
Propeller details

Front elevation, F Mk XIVC
Starboard side
▼

▲ Front elevation, PR Mk XIX
Port side

◀ Scrap views
Undercarriage details

The Spitfire was photogenic from any angle, but in-flight studies capture the sheer beauty of the design to the full. Here a Mk XIV banks at altitude. ▶

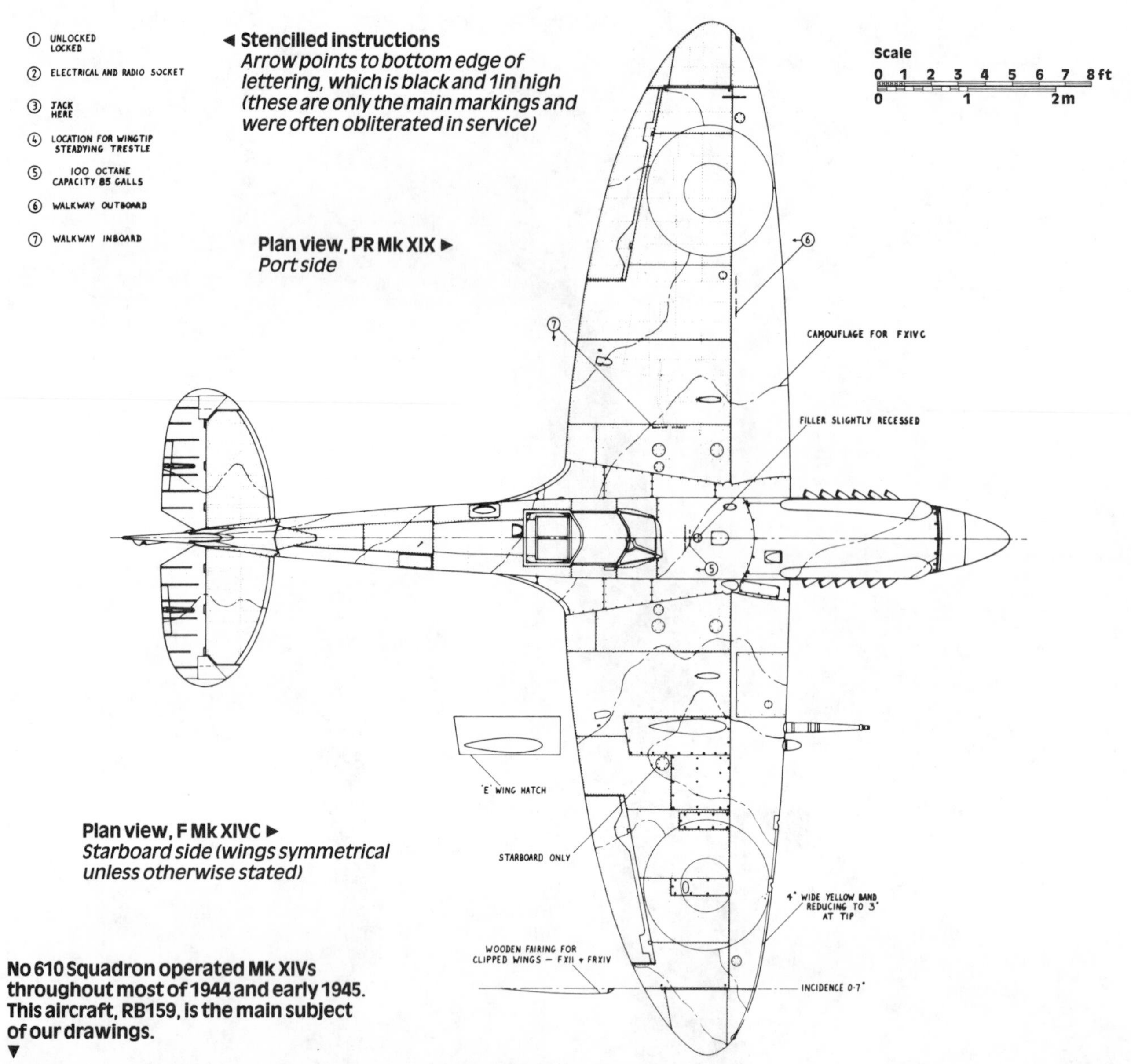

◄ **Stencilled instructions**
Arrow points to bottom edge of lettering, which is black and 1in high (these are only the main markings and were often obliterated in service)

Plan view, PR Mk XIX ►
Port side

Plan view, F Mk XIVC ►
Starboard side (wings symmetrical unless otherwise stated)

No 610 Squadron operated Mk XIVs throughout most of 1944 and early 1945. This aircraft, RB159, is the main subject of our drawings.
▼

▲
RB140 shows standard late-war camouflage and markings styles but as yet lacks squadron code letters. Note yellow leading edge to wing outboard of cannon.

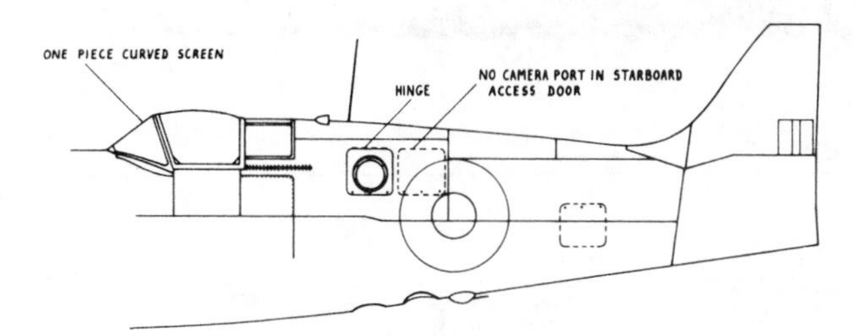

▲
Scrap port elevation, PR Mk XIX
Detail shown only where different from F Mk XIV

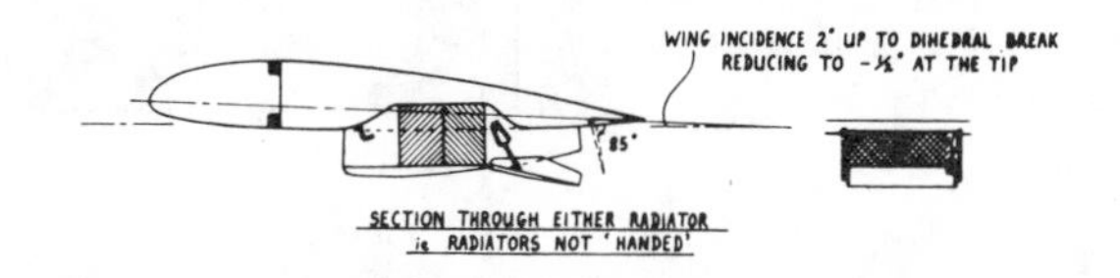

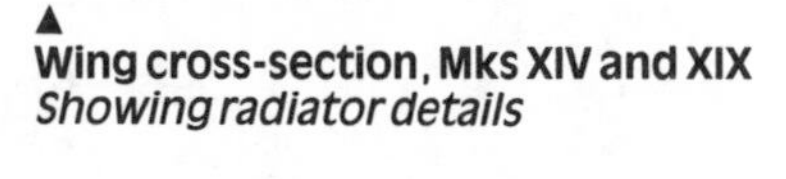

▲
Wing cross-section, Mks XIV and XIX
Showing radiator details

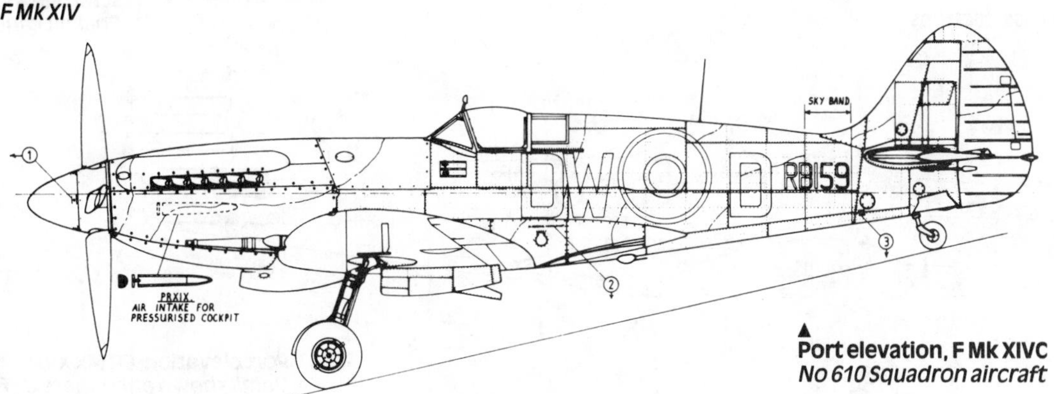

▲
Port elevation, F Mk XIVC
No 610 Squadron aircraft

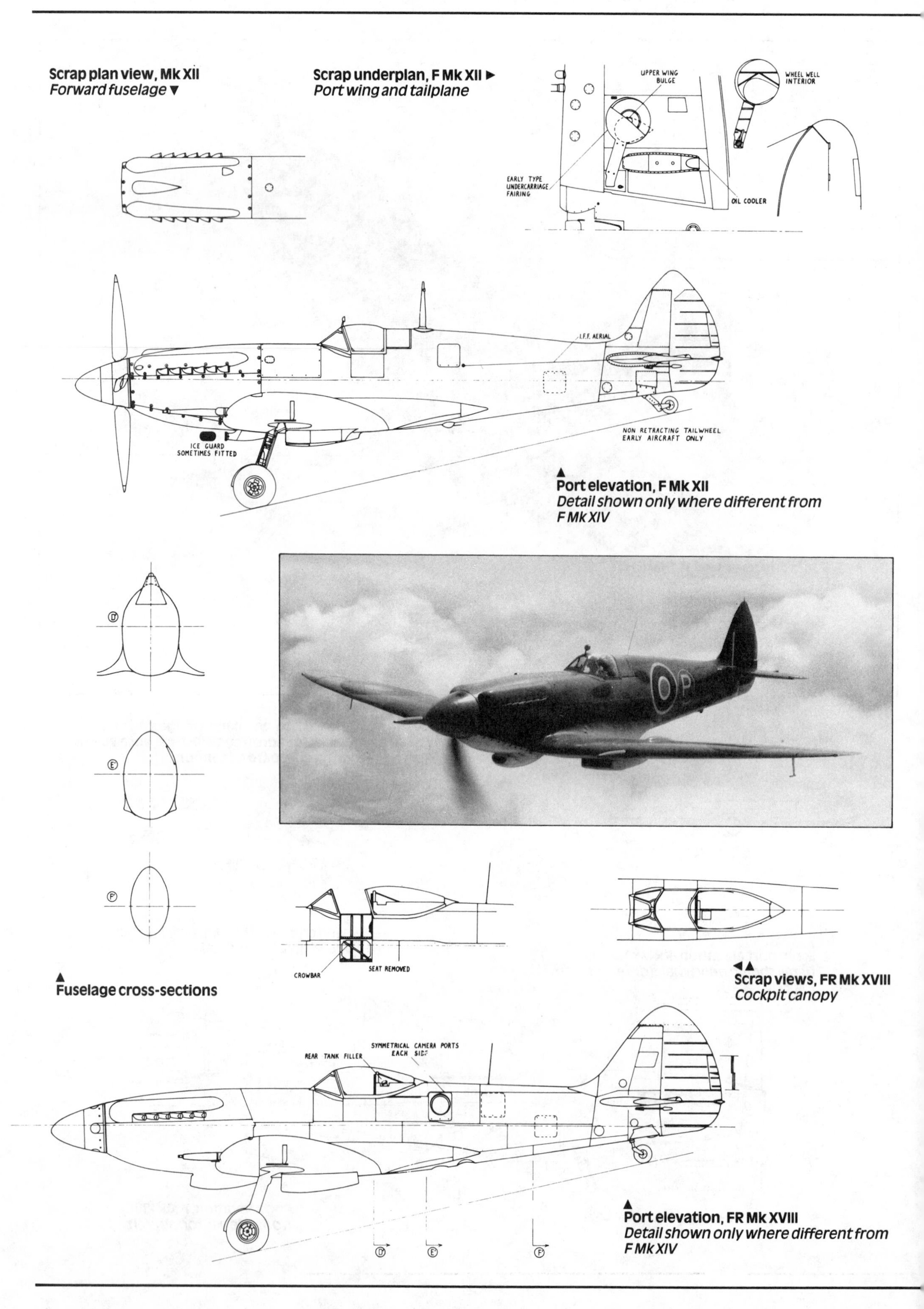

Scrap plan view, Mk XII
Forward fuselage ▼

Scrap underplan, F Mk XII ►
Port wing and tailplane

▲
Port elevation, F Mk XII
Detail shown only where different from F Mk XIV

▲
Fuselage cross-sections

◄▲
Scrap views, FR Mk XVIII
Cockpit canopy

▲
Port elevation, FR Mk XVIII
Detail shown only where different from F Mk XIV

Inboard plan view, Mks XIV and XIX

DRAWN BY P B COOKE

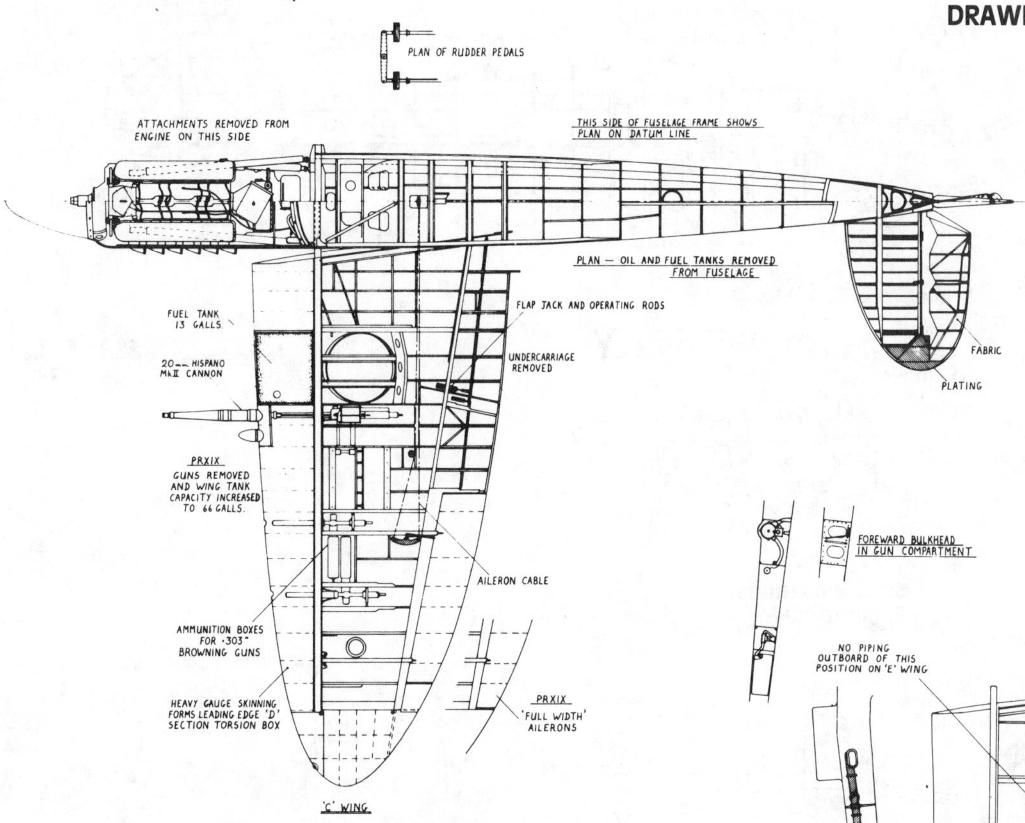

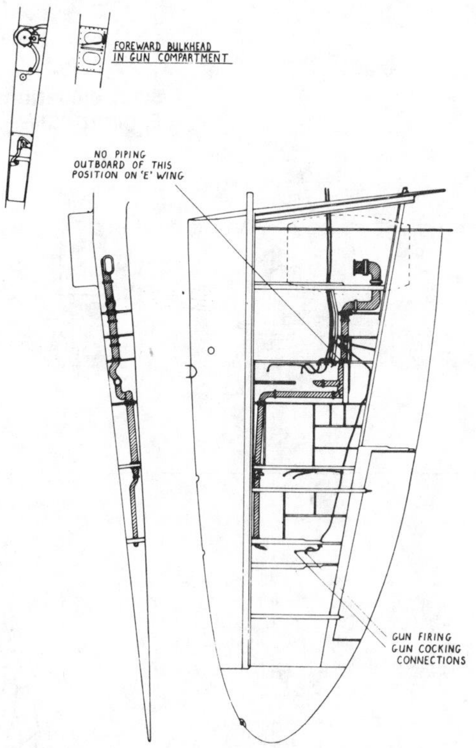

PLAN OF RUDDER PEDALS
ATTACHMENTS REMOVED FROM ENGINE ON THIS SIDE
THIS SIDE OF FUSELAGE FRAME SHOWS PLAN ON DATUM LINE
PLAN — OIL AND FUEL TANKS REMOVED FROM FUSELAGE
FLAP JACK AND OPERATING RODS
FUEL TANK 13 GALLS.
20mm HISPANO MkII CANNON
UNDERCARRIAGE REMOVED
FABRIC
PLATING
PRXIX
GUNS REMOVED AND WING TANK CAPACITY INCREASED TO 66 GALLS.
AILERON CABLE
AMMUNITION BOXES FOR ·303" BROWNING GUNS
HEAVY GAUGE SKINNING FORMS LEADING EDGE 'D' SECTION TORSION BOX
PRXIX
'FULL WIDTH' AILERONS
'C' WING
FOREWARD BULKHEAD IN GUN COMPARTMENT
NO PIPING OUTBOARD OF THIS POSITION ON 'E' WING

◄ **Seafire Mk XV was the first Griffon-engined shipboard variant, closely similar to the early Griffon Spitfires.**

Scrap views, Mk XIV
'E' wing armament

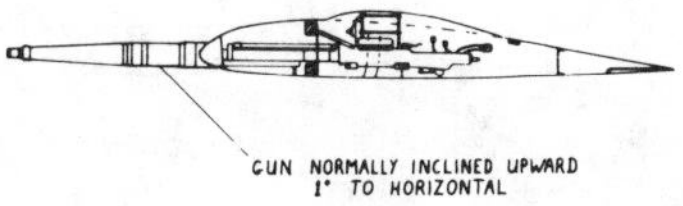

GUN NORMALLY INCLINED UPWARD 1° TO HORIZONTAL
GUN FIRING
GUN COCKING CONNECTIONS
NORMALLY CANNONS POINT INWARDS ½° TO CONVERGE AT APPROX 250 YARDS
INNER BROWNING GUN
24°
18°
FRISE TYPE AILERON

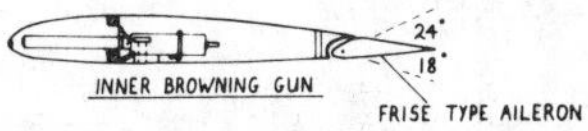

▲ **Inboard views, Mk XIV**
Gun control hoses and heating pipes

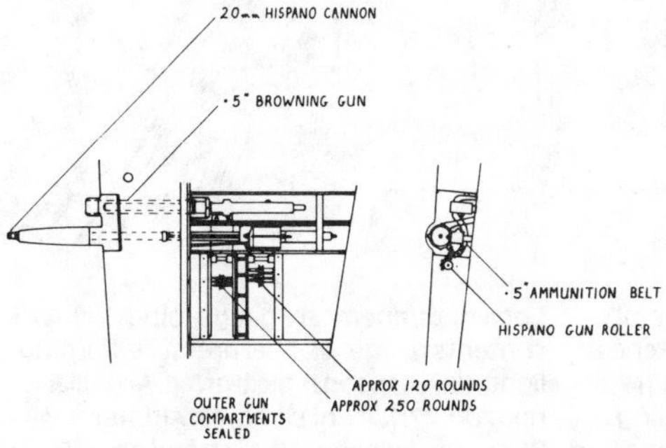

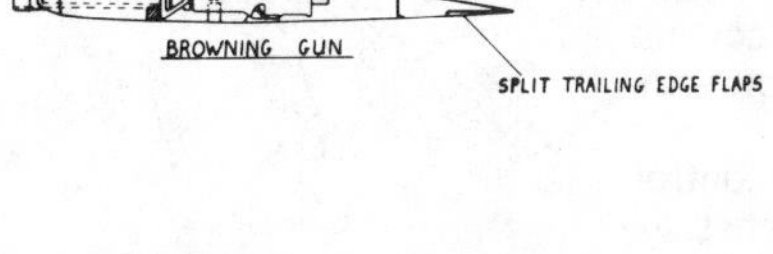

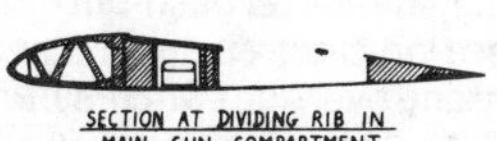

20mm HISPANO CANNON
·5" BROWNING GUN
BROWNING GUN
SPLIT TRAILING EDGE FLAPS
·5" AMMUNITION BELT
HISPANO GUN ROLLER
APPROX 120 ROUNDS
APPROX 250 ROUNDS
OUTER GUN COMPARTMENTS SEALED
SECTION AT DIVIDING RIB IN MAIN GUN COMPARTMENT

Scale
0 1 2 3 4 5 6 7 8 ft
0 1 2m

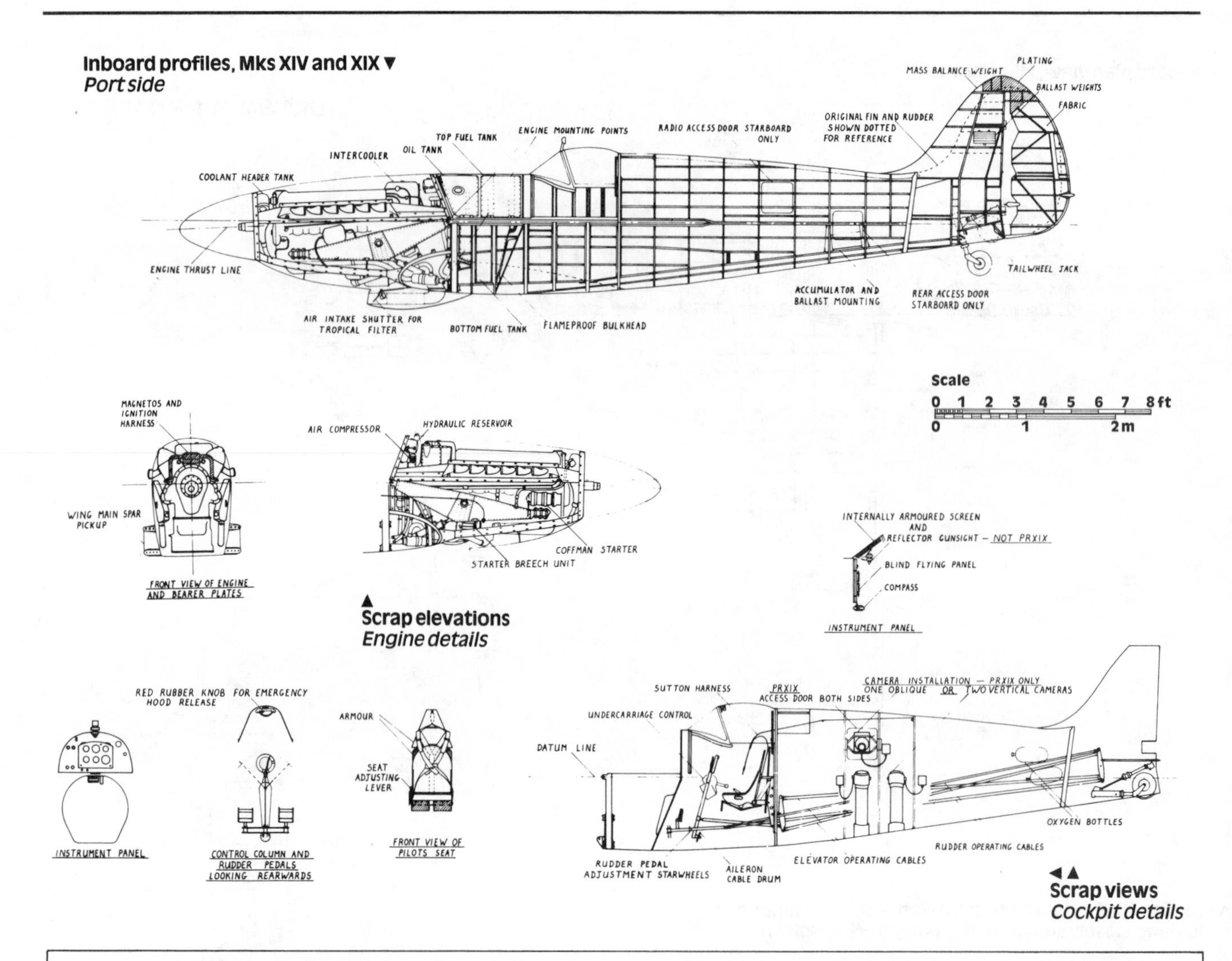

Inboard profiles, Mks XIV and XIX ▼
Port side

▲ Scrap elevations
Engine details

◄▲ Scrap views
Cockpit details

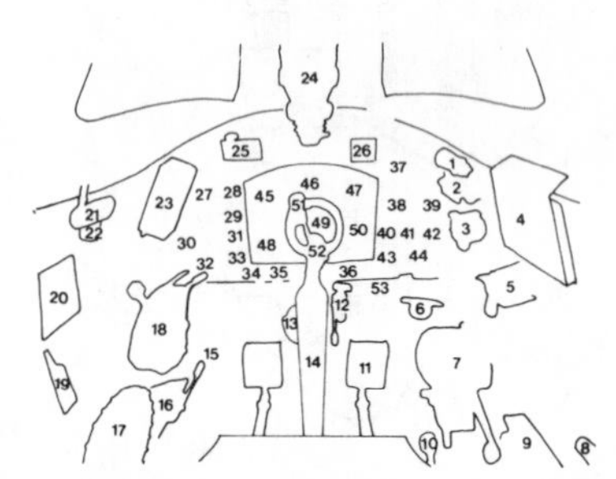

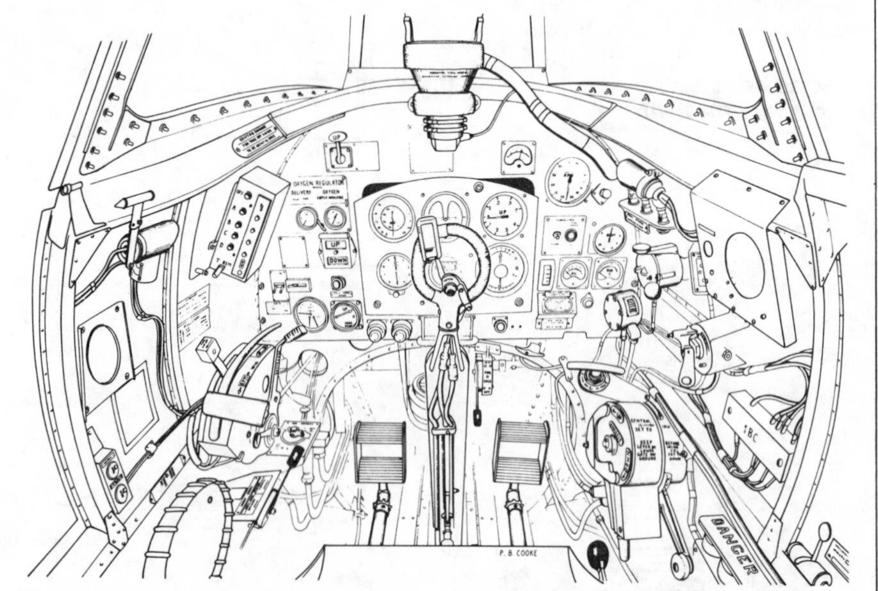

Key to cockpit drawing

1. Floodlight. 2. Reflector light spare bulbs. 3. Signalling switchbox. 4. Remote contactor mounting plate. 5. Cylinder priming selector cock. 6. Cylinder priming pump. 7. Undercarriage control lever. 8. Sutton harness release control. 9. IFF controls. 10. Fuel drop tank cock control. 11. Rudder pedal. 12. Fuel cock control. 13. Compass. 14. Control column. 15. Fuel transfer selector cock. 16. Carburettor air intake control. 17. Elevator trim tab handwheel. 18. Throttle and propeller control unit. 19. Bomb fusing and master switches. 20. Wedge plate for camera gun footage indicator. 21. Floodlight. 22. Socket for footage indicator plug. 23. Radio push-button controller. 24. Gun reflector sight. 25. Flap control (chrome lever). 26. Voltmeter. 27, 28. Oxygen supply gauges. 29. Undercarriage indicator. 30. Ignition switches. 31. Tailwheel indicator. 32. Pneumatic pressure gauge. 33. Elevator tab indicator. 34, 35. Cockpit floodlight switches. 36. Engine starter push-button. 37. Engine speed indicator. 38. Supercharger warning light and override switch. 39. Boost gauge (red rim). 40. Oil pressure gauge (yellow case). 41. Oil temperature gauge (yellow rim). 42. Coolant temperature gauge (blue rim). 43. Fuel contents gauge. 44. Fuel pressure warning light. 45. Air speed indicator. 46. Artificial horizon. 47. Rate of climb. 48. Altimeter. 49. Direction indicator. 50. Turn and bank. 51. Gun firing push-button. 52. Camera gun push-button. 53. Cartridge starter reloading control.

Dornier Do 335

Country of origin: Germany.
Type: Single-seat, land-based fighter-bomber and (A-6) night fighter.
Dimensions: (A-1) Wing span 45ft 3¼in *13.80m*; length 45ft 5¼in *13.85m*; height 16ft 5in *5.00m*; wing area 414.4 sq ft *38.5m²*.
Weights: Empty equipped (A-1) 16,000lb *7260kg*; normal loaded (A-1) 21,160lb *9600kg*, (A-6) 22,227lb *10,085kg*.
Powerplant: Two Daimler-Benz DB 603 E-1 twelve-cylinder, liquid-cooled piston engines each rated at 1800hp.
Performance: Maximum speed (A-1) 474mph *763kph* at 21,325ft *6500m*, (A-6) 428mph *689kph* at 17,390ft *5300m*; time to 3280ft *1000m*, 55sec; service ceiling (A-1) 37,400ft *11,400m*, (A-6) 34,120ft *10,400m*; range (A-1, clean, maximum) 1280 miles *2060km*, (A-6, clean, maximum) 1305 miles *2100km*.
Armament: One fixed 30mm MK 103 cannon and two fixed 15mm MG 151 cannon, plus (optional, A-1) 1102lb *500kg* of bombs internally and two 551lb *250kg* bombs externally.
Service: First flight (Do 335V-1) autumn 1943; service entry (A-1) January 1945.

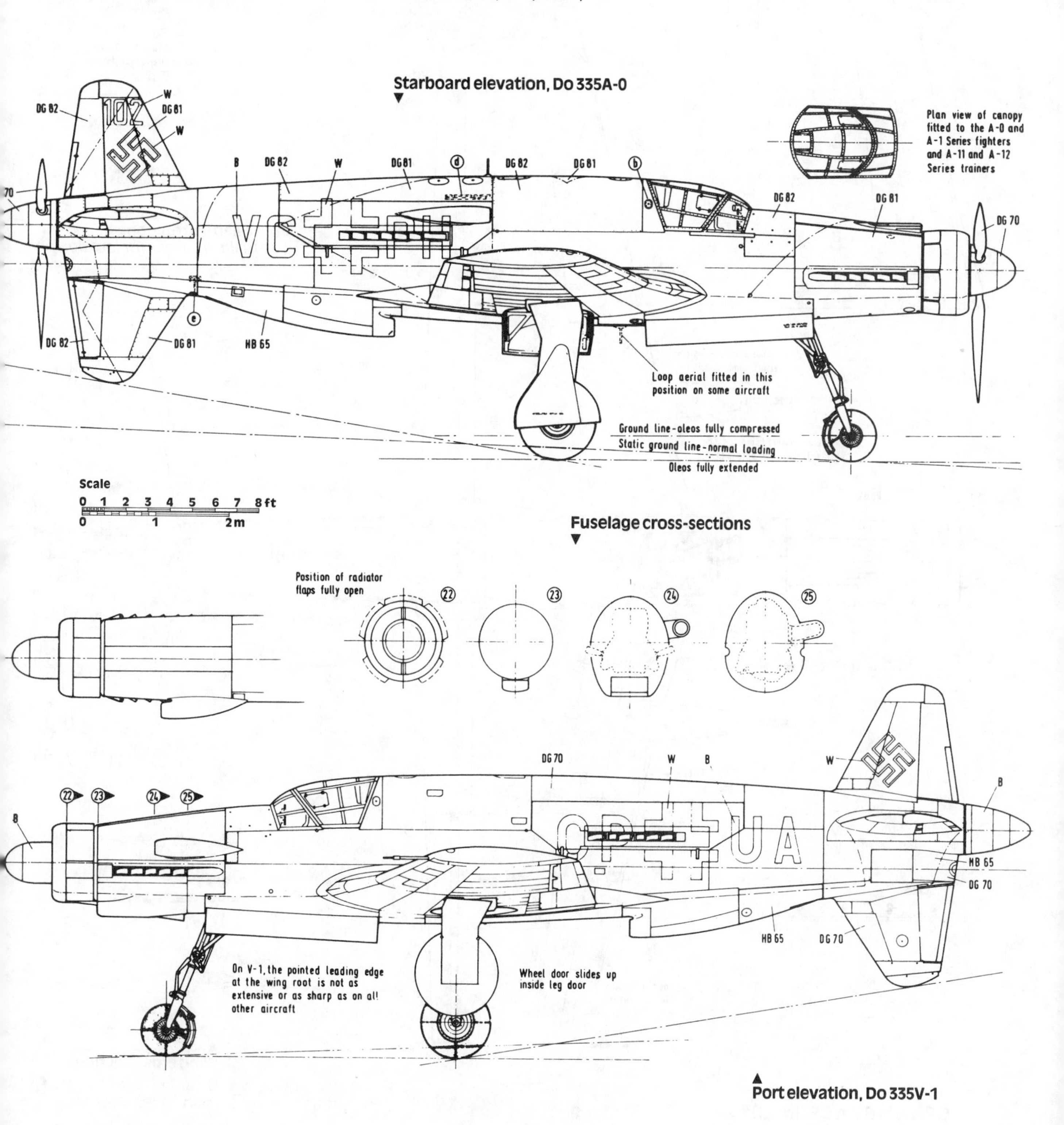

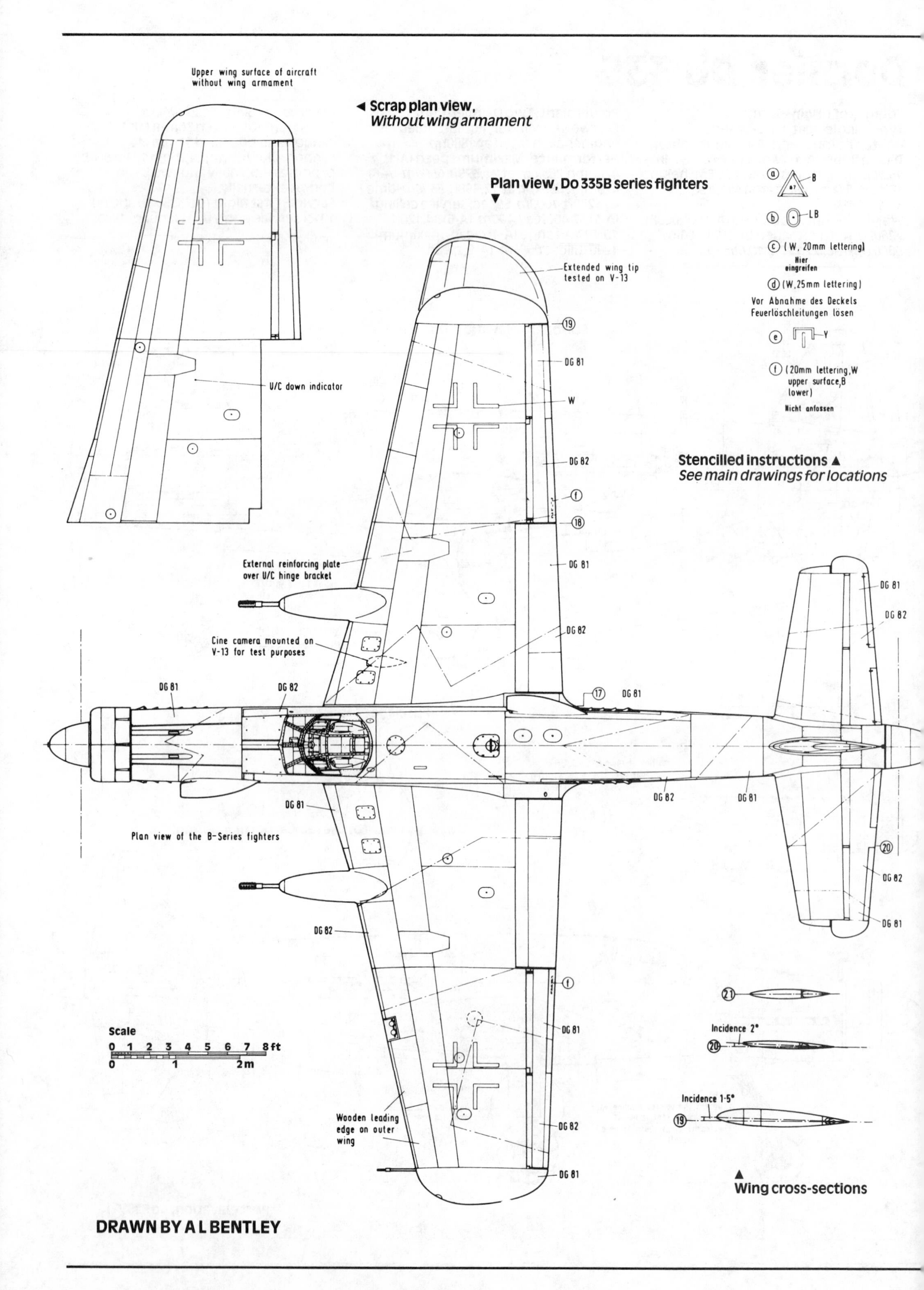

DRAWN BY A L BENTLEY

Port elevation, Do 335V-13

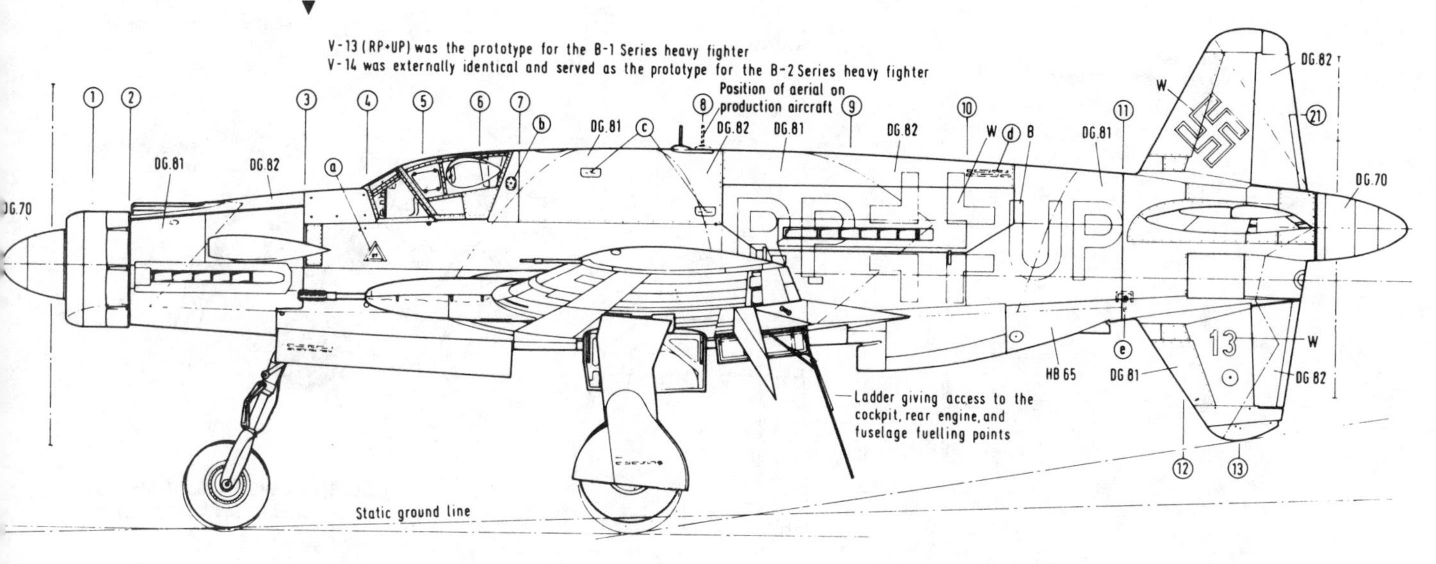

Wing cross-sections

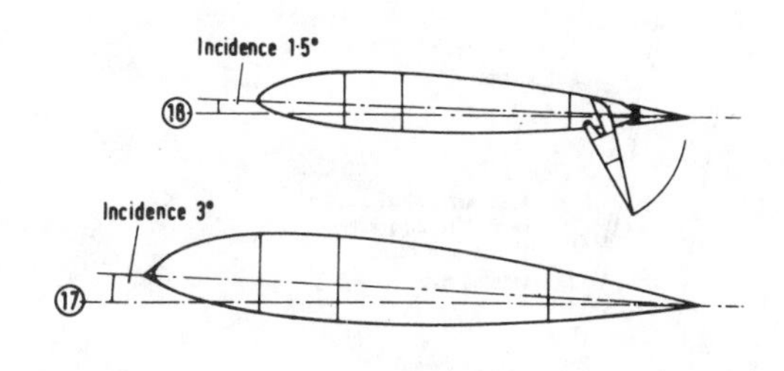

Scrap port elevation, Do 335V-13
Wing root fairings

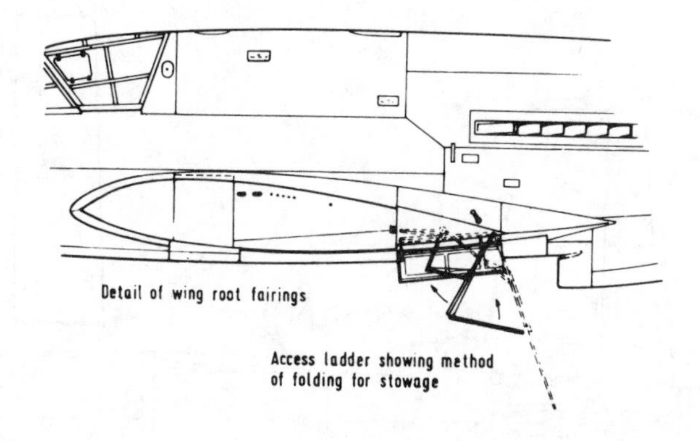

Colour code
DG 70 – *Dunkelgrün 70* (dark green); **DG 81** – *Dunkelgrün 81* (dark green); **DG 82** – *Dunkelgrün 82* (dark green); **HB 65** – *Hellblau 65* (light blue); **RLM.02** – *RLM Grau 02* (light slate grey); **W** – White; **B** – Black; **Y** – Yellow; **LB** – Light brown.

Do 335V-11, prototype for the A-10 two-seater, a proposed training version of the radical Dornier design.

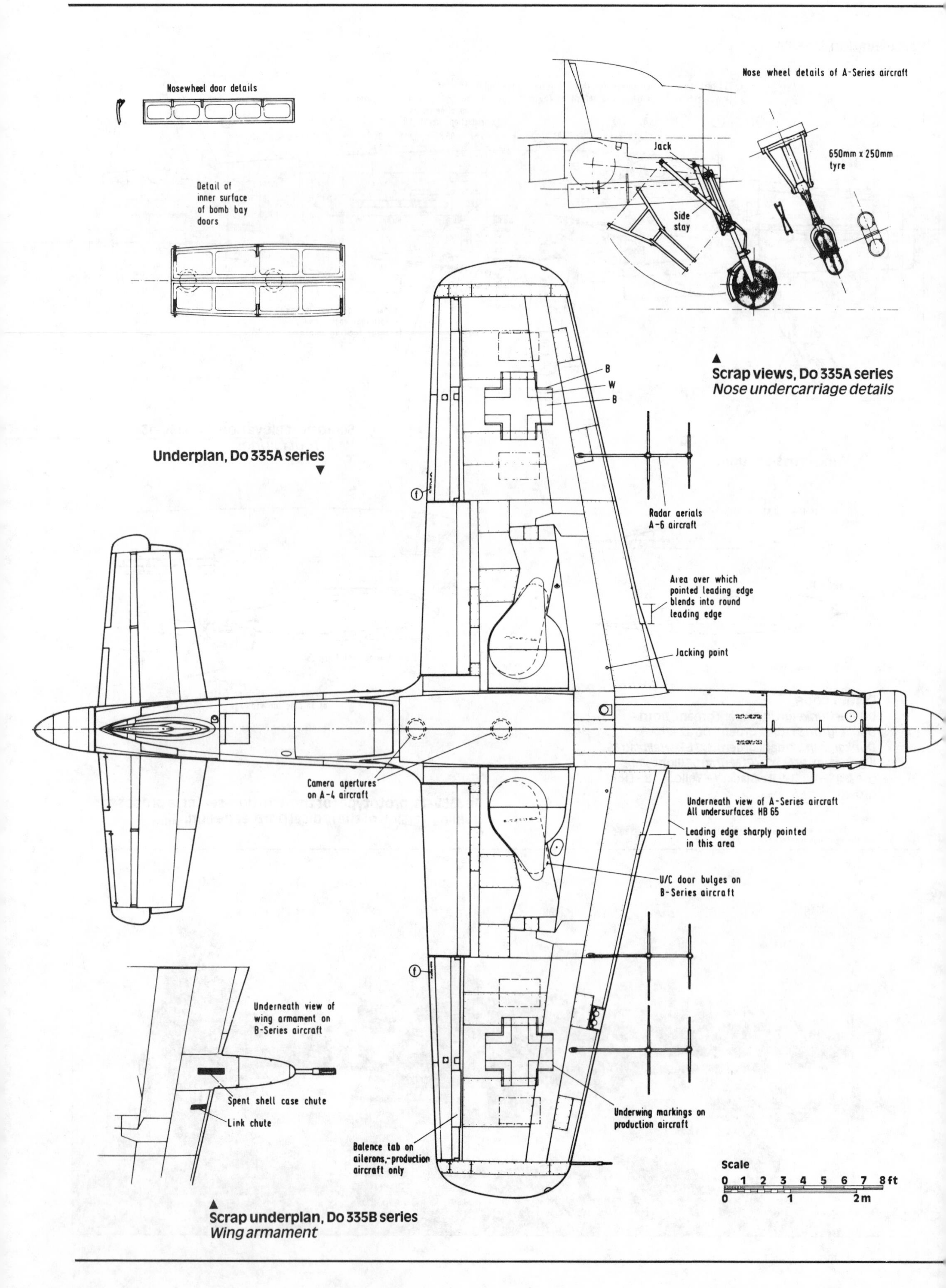

Scrap views, Do 335A series
Nose undercarriage details

Underplan, Do 335A series

Scrap underplan, Do 335B series
Wing armament

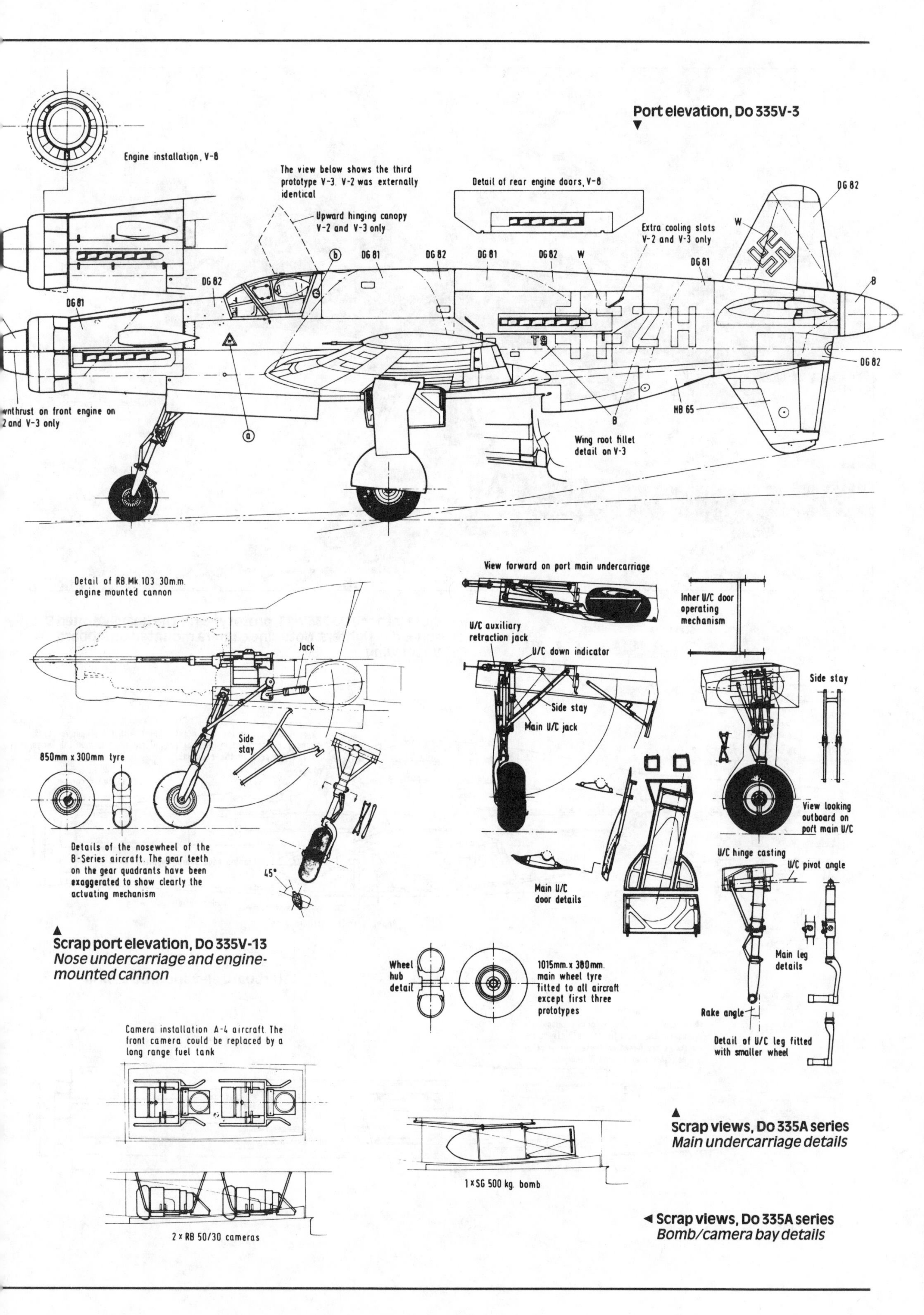

Port elevation, Do 335V-3 ▼

▲ **Scrap port elevation, Do 335V-13**
Nose undercarriage and engine-mounted cannon

▲ **Scrap views, Do 335A series**
Main undercarriage details

◄ **Scrap views, Do 335A series**
Bomb/camera bay details

▲
Close into the Do 335V-13, prototype for the heavily armed B-1 series day fighters. Note cine camera mounted on inboard upper wing.

Scale
0 1 2 3 4 5 6 7 8 ft
0 1 2 m

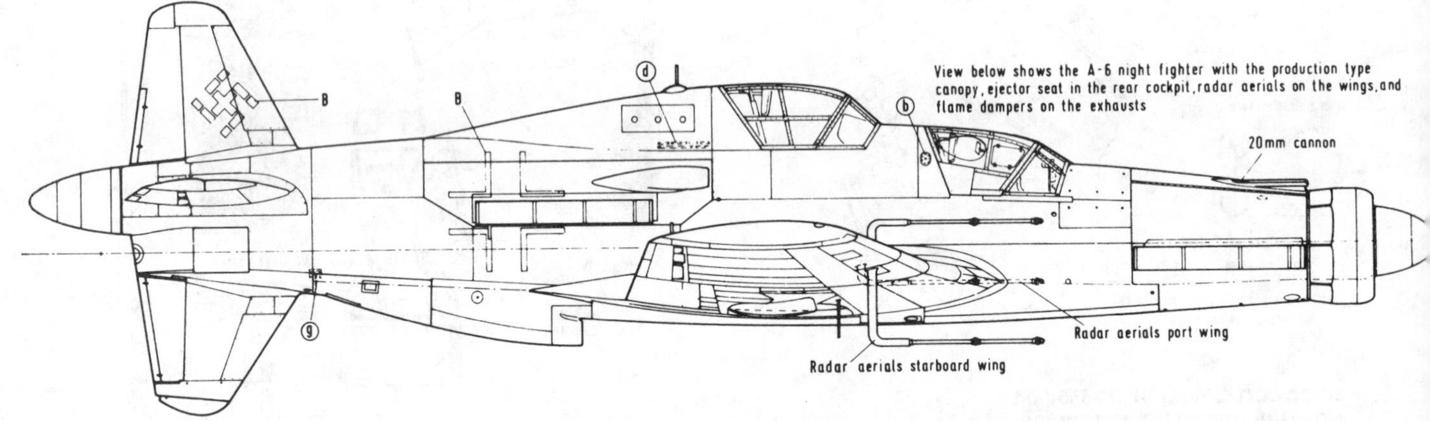

Starboard elevation, Do 335A-6
▼

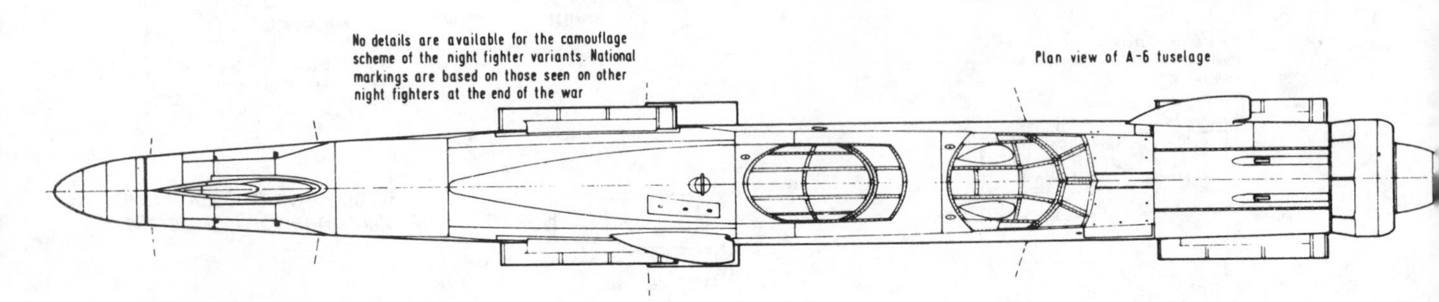

▲
Scrap plan view, Do 335A-6

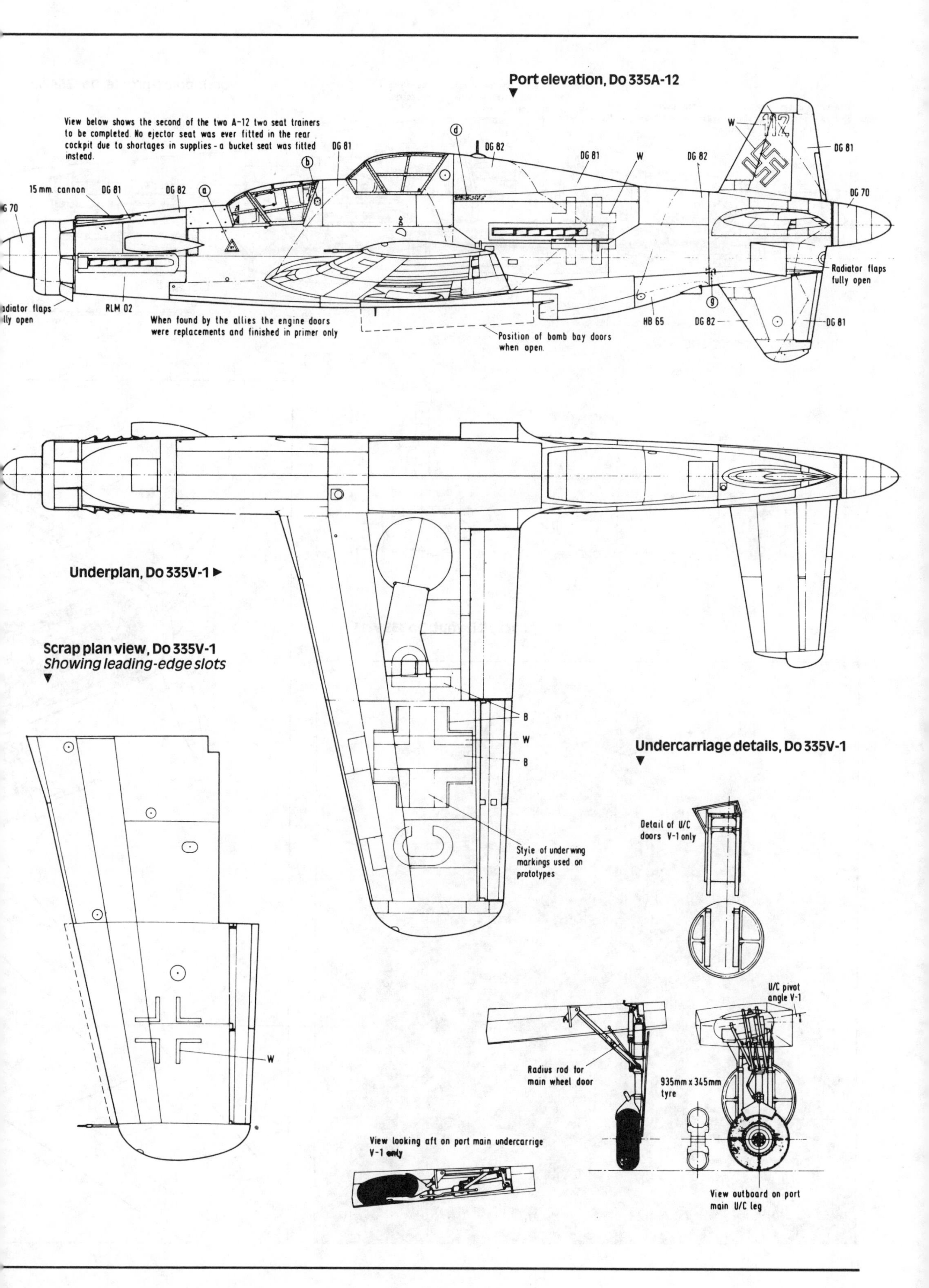
Port elevation, Do 335A-12
View below shows the second of the two A-12 two seat trainers to be completed. No ejector seat was ever fitted in the rear cockpit due to shortages in supplies - a bucket seat was fitted instead.
15 mm. cannon
DG 81
DG 82
DG 70
RLM 02
W
HB 65
Radiator flaps fully open
When found by the allies the engine doors were replacements and finished in primer only
Position of bomb bay doors when open.
Underplan, Do 335V-1
Scrap plan view, Do 335V-1
Showing leading-edge slots
B
W
Style of underwing markings used on prototypes
Undercarriage details, Do 335V-1
Detail of U/C doors V-1 only
U/C pivot angle V-1
Radius rod for main wheel door
935mm x 345mm tyre
View looking aft on port main undercarrige V-1 only
View outboard on port main U/C leg

Port inboard profile, Do 335A-12

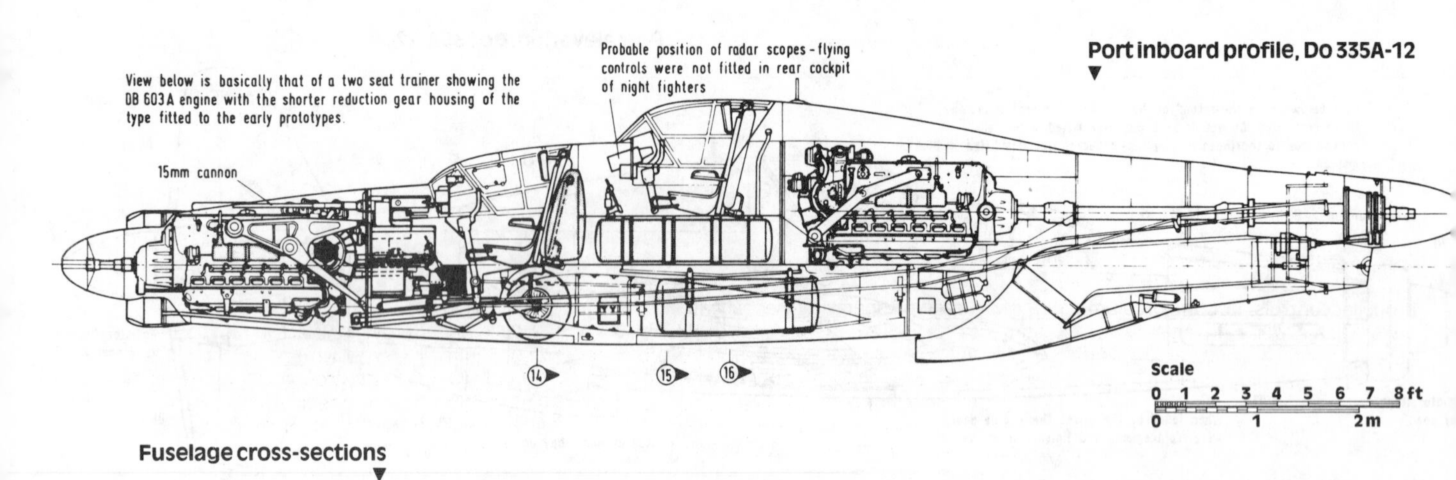

Fuselage cross-sections

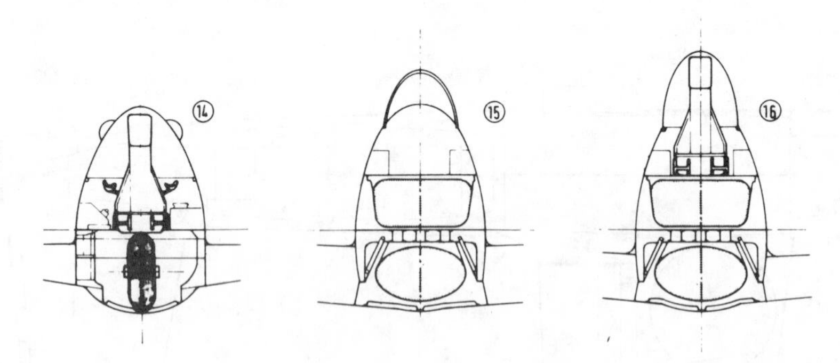

Cockpit layout, Do 335 V-13

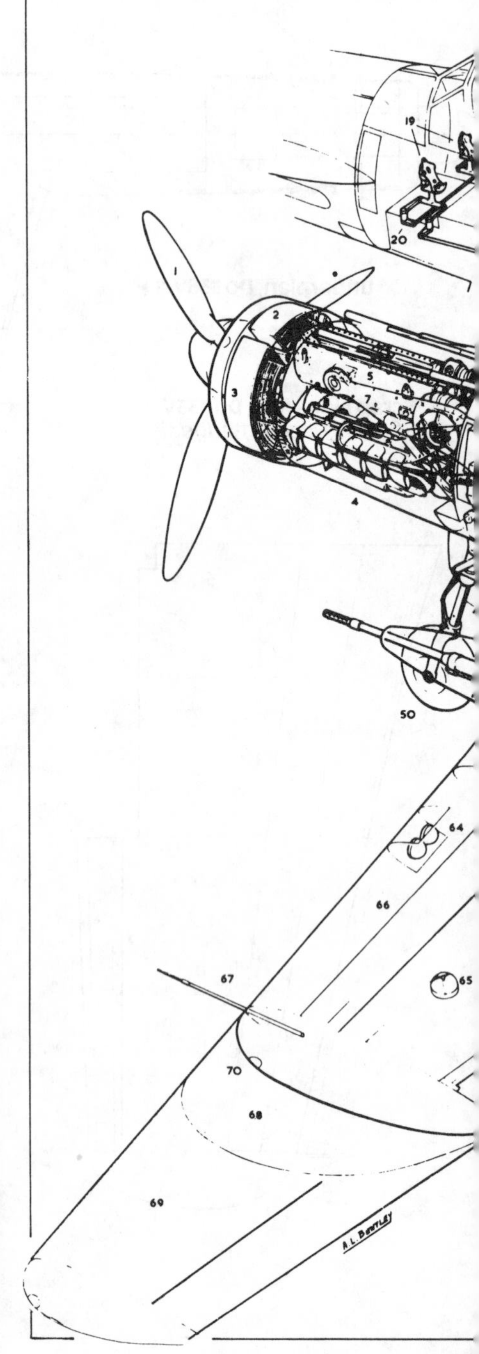

Key to cutaway

1. VDM propeller. **2.** Oil coolant radiator. **3.** Engine coolant radiator. **4.** Jack for radiator flap mechanism. **5.** DB 603E engine. **6.** Supercharger for DB 603E. **7.** Engine bearers. **8.** Port container of liquid coolant. **9.** Armoured V-windscreen. **10.** Sideways hinging canopy. **11.** Direct vision windows. **12.** Rear view mirrors. **13.** Canopy lock. **14.** Canopy retaining cord. **15.** Instrument panel. **16.** Side console radio equipment. **17.** Side console engine and propeller controls. **18.** Control column. **19.** Rudder pedals. **20.** Rudder pedal parallelogram linkage. **21.** Very pistol. **22.** Firing handle for ejection seat. **23.** Ejection seat. **24.** Compressed air bottle to eject seat. **25.** Oil tanks. **26.** Fuelling points for main fuselage tank. **27.** Main fuselage tank. **28.** Outer wing tanks (only fitted when wing armament displaced wing leading edge tanks). **29.** Bomb bay tank. **30.** Rear DB 603E engine. **31.** Rear engine mount. **32.** Port container for liquid coolant. **33.** MW-50 (water-methanol) tank. **34.** Extension shaft for rear propeller. **35.** Aft propeller gearbox. **36.** Rear VDM propeller. **37.** Rear engine coolant radiator. **38.** Rear engine oil cooler. **39.** Actuator for flap for oil cooler. **40.** Coolant air outlet flap for rear engine radiator. **41.** Actuator for rear engine radiator flap. **42.** Rudder and elevator control rods. **43.** Flying control mechanisms in centre fuselage. **44.** Aileron control linkages in wings. **45.** Throttle control rods. **46.** Nosewheel actuating jack. **47.** Gear type operating mechanism. **48.** Nosewheel side stay. **49.** Nosewheel leg (nosewheel turns to lie at 45° to datum when retracted). **50.** Nosewheel. **51.** Mainwheel. **52.** Mainwheel leg. **53.** Actuating jack for mainwheel. **54.** Auxiliary actuating jack for mainwheel. **55.** Mainwheel side stay. **56.** Mainwheel up-lock. **57.** Inner mainwheel door mechanism activated by mainwheel pressing against it. **58.** Bomb bay doors. **59.** Bomb bay door mechanism (omitted when not used as a weapons bay). **60.** Access ladder (stowed in wing root when not required). **61.** Oxygen bottles. **62.** Hydraulic reservoir. **63.** Flap jack. **64.** Landing light. **65.** Master compass. **66.** Main wing box spar. **67.** Pitot tube. **68.** Extended wing tips tested on V-13. **69.** Outer wing panels designed by Heinkel. **70.** Navigation and identification lights. **71.** Twin MG 151/20 20mm cannon. **72.** Ammunition feed chutes. **73.** Ammunition boxes 200rpg. **74.** Collector boxes for spent cartridges and links. **75.** Chute to drop spent cartridges into lower collector box. **76.** RB MK 103 30mm cannon firing through engine shaft. **77.** Ammunition box (70 rounds). **78.** Collector box for spent cartridges and links. **79.** Opening through which empties from MG 151/20 reach main collector box. **80.** Chute for unloading spent cartridges and links on ground. **81.** Battery. **82.** Wing-mounted RB MK 103 30mm cannon. **83.** Ammunition box. **84.** Armour for ammunition box. **85.** Chute for spent cartridges. **86.** Chute for used links. **87.** Compressed air bottle for cocking guns. **88.** Fug 125. **89.** Fug 25a. **90.** Fug 15. **91.** Fire extinguisher bottle. **92.** Tail bumper. **93.** Tail bumper shock absorber. **94.** Aerials.

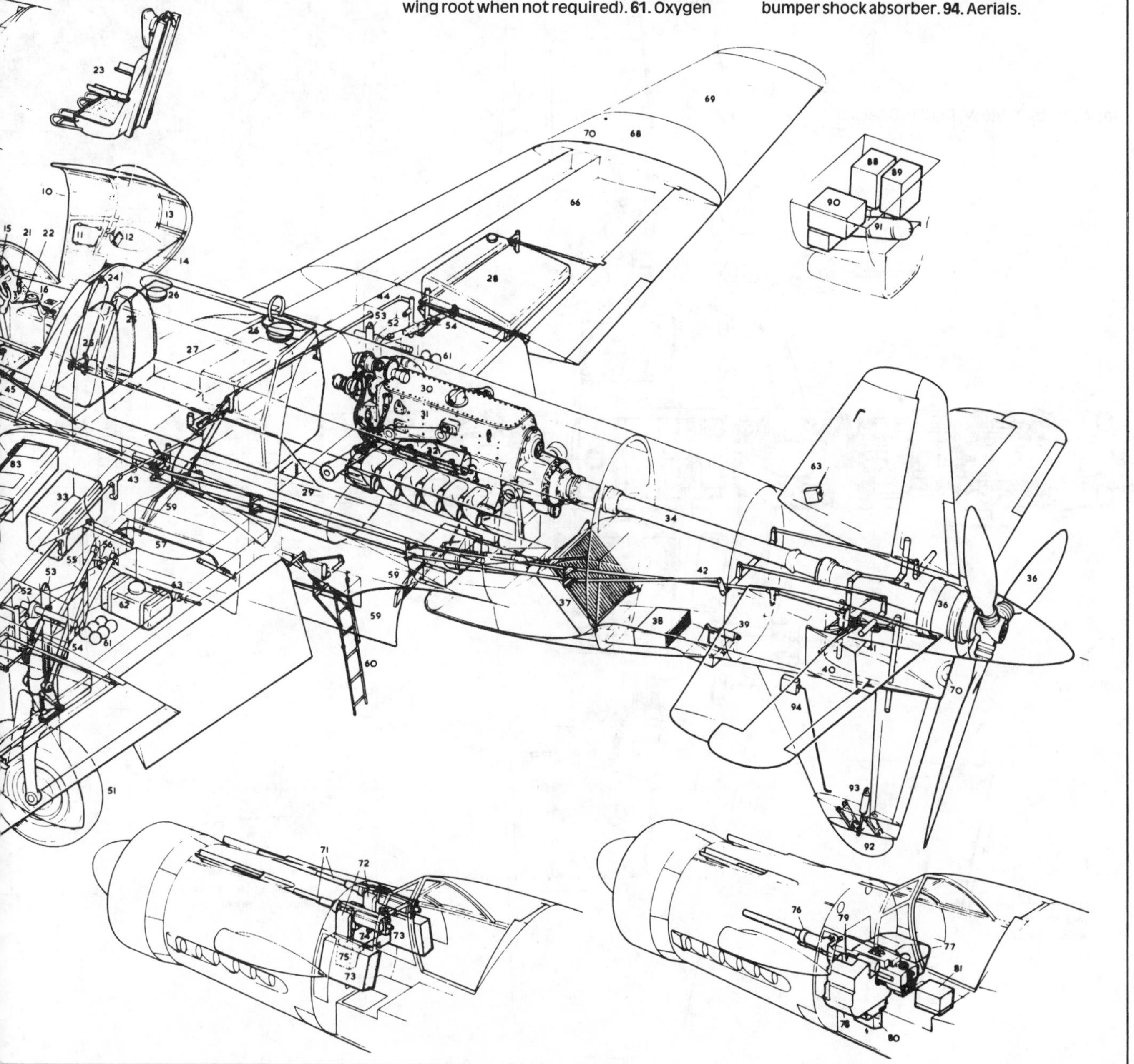

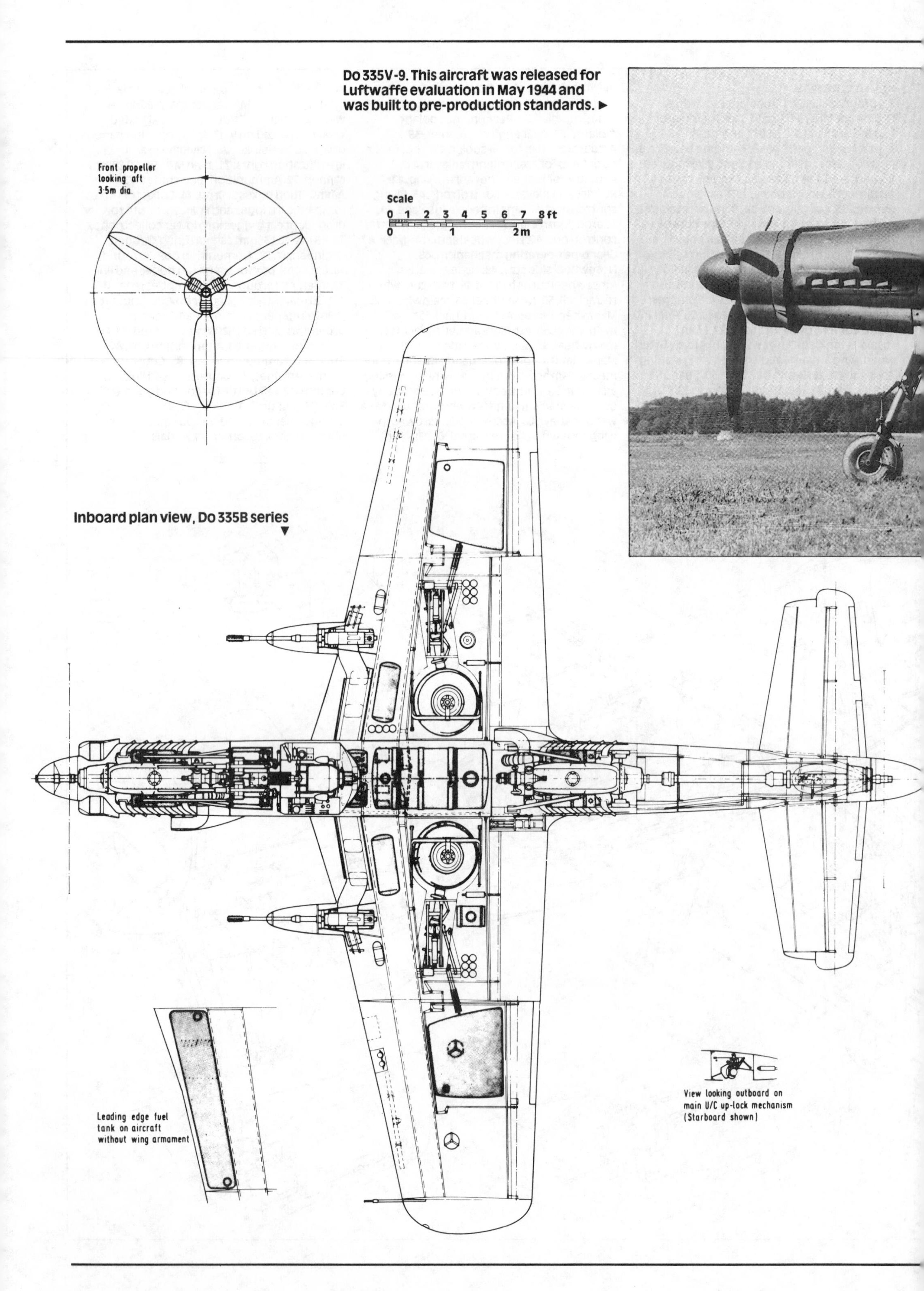

Do 335V-9. This aircraft was released for Luftwaffe evaluation in May 1944 and was built to pre-production standards. ►

Inboard plan view, Do 335B series ▼

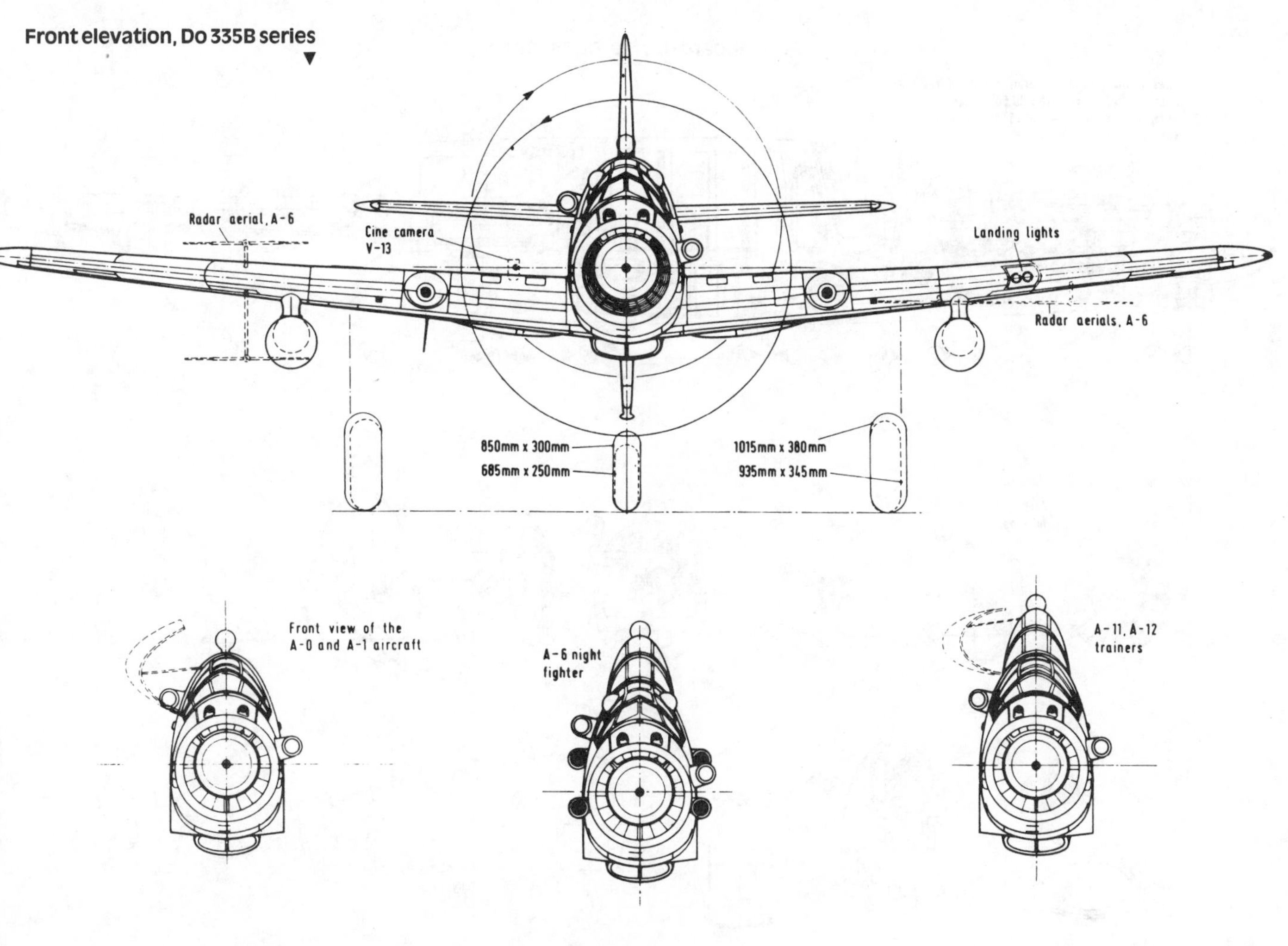

Front elevation, Do 335B series ▼

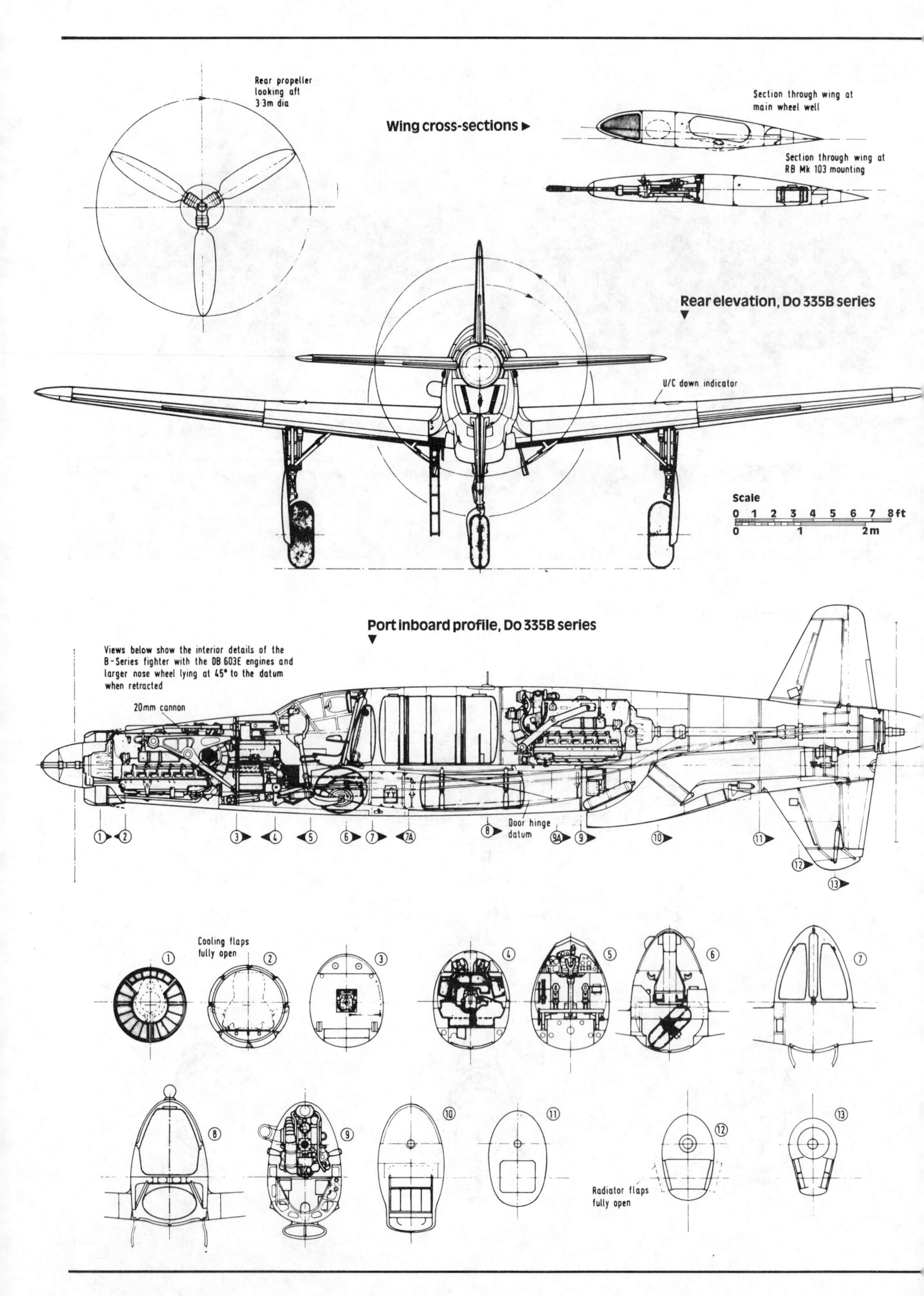
Rear propeller looking aft 3·3m dia
Wing cross-sections
Section through wing at main wheel well
Section through wing at RB Mk 103 mounting
Rear elevation, Do 335B series
U/C down indicator
Scale
0 1 2 3 4 5 6 7 8 ft
0 1 2 m
Port inboard profile, Do 335B series
Views below show the interior details of the B-Series fighter with the DB 603E engines and larger nose wheel lying at 45° to the datum when retracted
20mm cannon
Door hinge datum
Cooling flaps fully open
Radiator flaps fully open

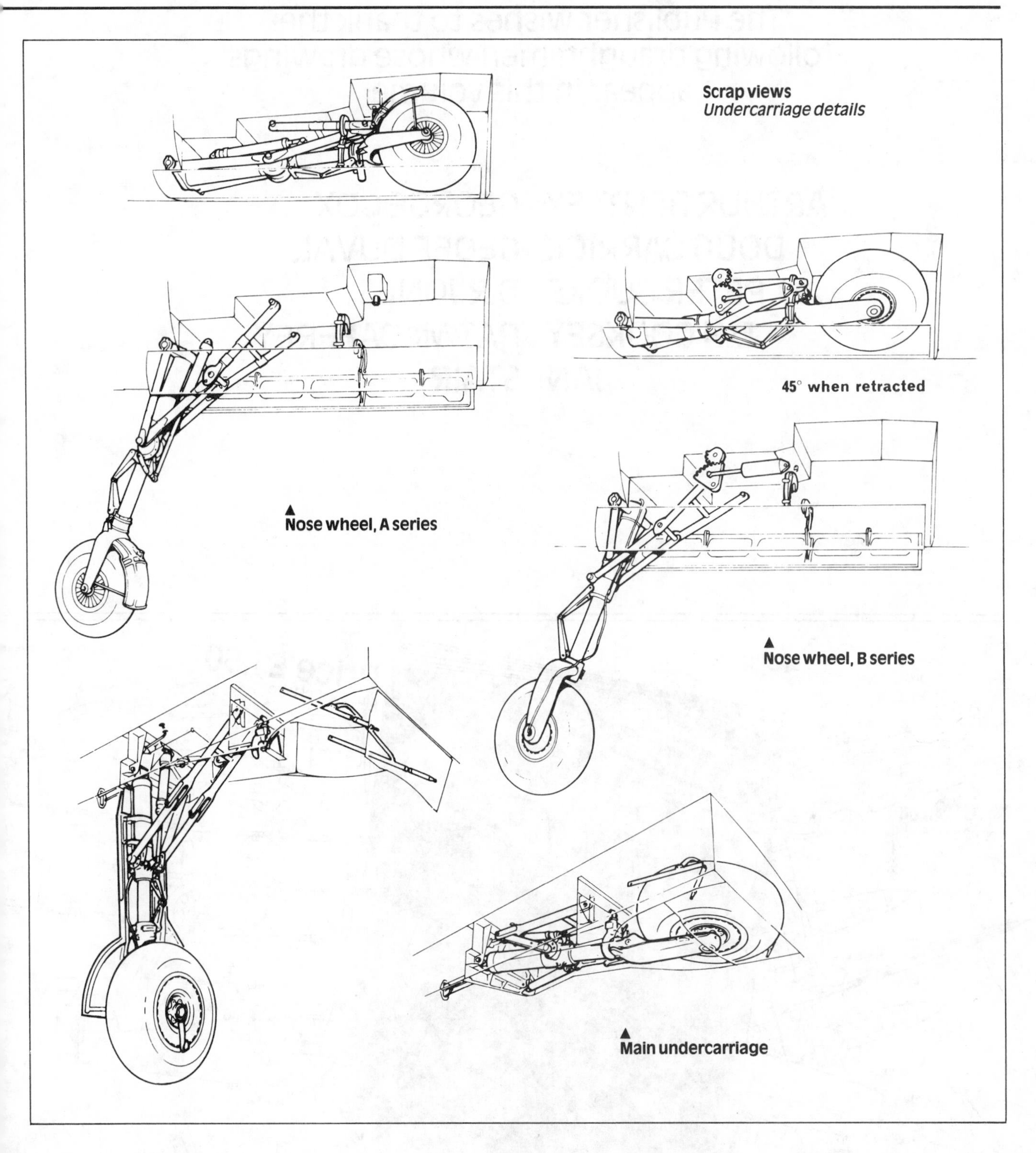
Scrap views
Undercarriage details
45° when retracted
Nose wheel, A series
Nose wheel, B series
Main undercarriage

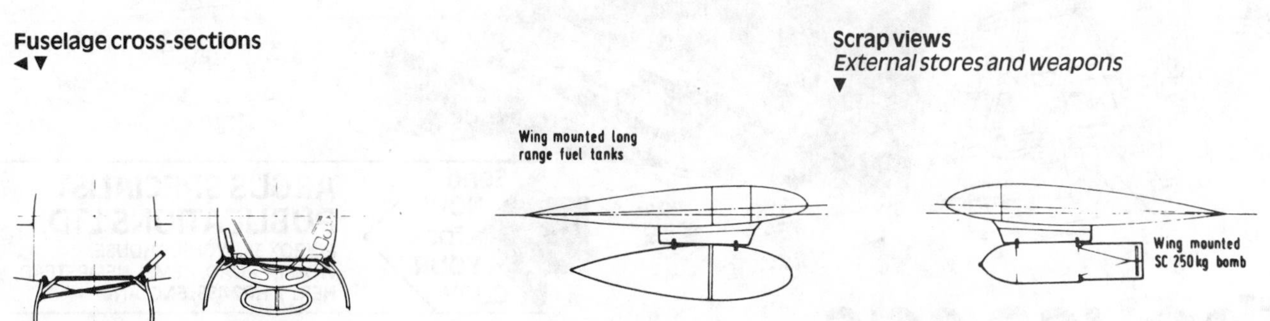
Fuselage cross-sections
Scrap views
External stores and weapons
Wing mounted long
range fuel tanks
Wing mounted
SC 250 kg bomb
7A
9A

The Publisher wishes to thank the following draughtsmen whose drawings appear in this volume

ARTHUR BENTLEY
DOUG CARRICK
PETER COOKE
D H COOKSEY
GEORGE COX
GEOFF DUVAL
D R JONES
PAT McCAFFREY
IAN STAIR